TRIUMPH
BOOKS

ONE TOUGH OUT

Fighting Off Life's Curveballs

ONE TOUGH OUT

Fighting Off Life's Curveballs

ROD CAREW with JAIME ARON

TRIUMPH
BOOKS

First Triumph Books paperback edition 2021

This book is available in quantity at special discounts for your group or organization. For further information, contact:

Triumph Books LLC
814 North Franklin Street
Chicago, Illinois 60610
(312) 337-0747
www.triumphbooks.com

Printed in U.S.A.
ISBN: 978-1-62937-878-7
Design by Nord Compo

"A life is not important except in the impact
it has on other lives."

—Jackie Robinson

CONTENTS

Part III

PROLOGUE

_____

September 20, 2015:
The Day My Heart Stopped

M Y TOES WERE TAPPING as I stood in the parking lot of Angel
Stadium. My buddy Manny Rodriguez and his Carlos
Santana cover band were wrapping up a great show when
Manny caught my eye. He smiled and pointed to a spot on
the stage. He wanted me to join him.

He'd never made such a ridiculous request. He knows
I'm not comfortable being the center of attention—and I'm
certainly no singer. But something about this performance, on
this night, in this setting, inspired me to samba toward him.
Along the way, someone handed me a pair of black maracas.
I shook them and the crowd whooped and hollered. Once
Manny got to the chorus, I leaned into the microphone and
sang the only words I knew.

Oye como va!

Loosely translated, the line means, "Hey, how's it going?" Had someone asked me that question at that moment— around 8:00 PM on Saturday, September 19, 2015—I would've smiled and shaken those maracas in celebration of how great my life was going.

Thirty years since my last at-bat, I remain strongly connected to the game. I go to spring training every March as an alumni coach for the Twins and to Cooperstown every summer for the annual reunion of us Hall of Famers. I have other duties with the Twins and with the Angels, keeping me involved with both teams I played for during my 19 years in the majors. With only a few weeks left in this season, both of my teams were in the thick of the playoff race. Regardless of who won the World Series, October would be memorable for my wife, Rhonda, and me. We were headed to Italy with two dear friends. Takeoff was set for a few weeks after my 70th birthday. Best of all, I didn't look or feel 70.

I weighed 190 pounds, only a few more than my final season in the majors. I remained in shape the old-fashioned way, by keeping active and eating plenty of fruits and vegetables. I didn't smoke and rarely drank alcohol. My only vices had been chewing tobacco and devouring deep bowls of ice cream. Five months earlier, a physical confirmed my good health. Well, there was one red flag. My cholesterol was a little high. The doctor prescribed Lipitor. I took it for a few months and didn't feel any different. I stopped taking the pills and still couldn't tell a difference.

My joy also came from the reason we were at the ballpark. This was the after-party for the Light The Night Walk, the annual fundraiser for the Leukemia & Lymphoma

Society. It's one of several groups I've supported since my daughter Michelle died of leukemia in 1996 at the tender age of 18. As event co-chairman, I was thrilled by the turnout and by how much fun everyone was having. I also was still riding high from the success of another event near and dear to my heart, the Rod Carew Children's Cancer Golf Classic. The 20th annual tournament was held three weeks earlier. We pushed the all-time amount of money raised for the Pediatric Cancer Research Foundation to almost $4 million.

After my turn on stage with Manny and the boys, Rhonda and I headed home. I decided to get up at 6:00 AM on Sunday and head to Cresta Verde Golf Course in Corona. It's about a 45-minute drive but worth the trek because, at that hour, I'd pretty much have the place to myself. I could drop two or three balls per hole if I wanted and still be done in time for a late breakfast with Rhonda.

The college kid working the front desk of the pro shop didn't think twice when I signed in as my pal Jim Duran. I like using aliases to avoid anyone seeing my name on the sheet and catching up to me so they can tell their friends they played golf with Rod Carew. I rarely warm up at the driving range or putting green; I go straight to the first tee. So when the kid gave me a cart key, I hopped in and drove about 30 yards to the shade of a spruce tree overlooking the hole—a 500-yard par–5 that plays downhill to the right. I pulled out my driver and a fresh sleeve of balls from my golf tournament. I dropped two balls into my pocket, kept one in my hand, and headed to the tee box.

I'm right-handed in everything I do except for hitting baseballs and golf balls. I'm nowhere near as successful hitting golf balls as I was hitting baseballs, but I'm not bad, either. I usually start strong, and, sure enough, my opening tee shot was a beauty. It soared high and straight, right down the middle, coming to rest on a perfect spot in the fairway. Those other two balls could stay in my pocket.

Walking the few steps back to the cart, I felt a strange sensation in my chest. It was both tight and burning, like acid reflux with a grip. As I shoved my driver into my bag, I realized my hands were clammy. I instantly remembered a recent conversation with my buddy Chris Ferraro. He'd been playing craps in Las Vegas when his chest tightened and his hands turned clammy; he was having a heart attack. He only lived through it because he asked for help right away. He was telling everyone he could that if they felt anything weird in their chest, don't mess around—get help right away. So that's what I had to do. I threw the cart in reverse and rolled back uphill.

I staggered into the pro shop, dropped a hand on the desk, and told the kid to call 911. While he dialed, the gal at the snack bar, Gina Besheer, came to my side. She saw that my lips were white and my breathing was more like huffing and puffing. Gina called her husband, a paramedic. He told her to squeeze my fingertips and release, pushing out the blood and watching to see what happened next. If color returned quickly, that was a good thing. It meant blood was flowing properly. If the fingertips remained white, that meant blood wasn't circulating properly—that I was probably having a heart attack. My fingertips remained white.

Through coaching from her husband, Gina eased me out of the chair and placed me on my back on the floor. She propped up my feet on the seat I'd been sitting on. She also found a rag to sop up all the sweat on my forehead.

I asked Gina to call Rhonda. As Gina finished explaining where I was and what was happening, Rhonda heard the siren of a Corona Fire Department ambulance pulling into the parking lot.

My blood pressure was so low that paramedics knew I was in shock. The first heart exam they did showed an irregular heartbeat. Next came a more thorough electrocardiogram, or EKG, the machine that draws squiggly lines representing the heart's electric activity.

"Tombstones," one paramedic whispered to another. The term has a double meaning. First, it describes the pattern on the screen. The second interpretation is as ominous as it seems. I was having a massive heart attack, the kind so lethal it's dubbed "the widowmaker."

Blood wasn't getting to a large part of my heart. Time lost is heart muscle lost, and there was no telling how much healthy muscle I had left. It was like the wick of a candle burning down, only with no idea how much wick remained. As the paramedics loaded me into the ambulance, they feared I wouldn't survive the 14-mile drive to Riverside Community Hospital.

At Riverside, a team was waiting for us in the emergency room. They turned me over to another crew in the catheterization lab. Doctors put a tube in a vein near my groin and snaked it into my heart. When they began inserting the stents that would clear the blockages, there was a problem.

The percentage of blood leaving your heart with each pump is called ejection fraction. A good number is 50 percent or more. Anything less than 40 is trouble. Mine dipped into single digits and was still dropping. In addition to the heart attack, I was in cardiac arrest. The wick was about to burn out.

Out came the paddles to jolt my heart back into rhythm.

Soon, rhythm was restored and my arteries were clear. Blood was flowing. My heart was still weak, so doctors inserted a balloon pump to provide a boost for the next few days.

By the time I arrived in the recovery room, I had to be the luckiest guy there.

At some point during my ordeal—maybe in the pro shop or ambulance with the paramedics, maybe in the ER, maybe in the cath lab—something bizarre happened.

I heard someone screaming, "We're losing him, God damn it, we're losing him!" I managed to open my eyes enough to see the outline of a man looming over me. The color of his skin, hair, and eyes was a blur. Only one feature stood out: a golden, celestial glow all around him. Right away, I knew what this meant. He was my guardian angel. He was here to protect me.

I realize how this sounds to anyone who hasn't experienced it. I know because I nodded and smiled politely myself
the first time I heard it. It was the fall of 1995 and my daughter
Michelle was battling her wretched disease. She'd recently
overcome her heart having stopped for about a minute. In a
quiet moment, she told me that when her heart stopped, she
saw a man in the corner of the room surrounded by a glowing
light. He was her guardian angel. I considered it a hallucina-
tion, perhaps a side effect of one of her medications or an
indication the cancer in her blood was eroding her mind. I'd
given that no thought in the nearly 20 years since that night.
But as soon as I saw that glow around the man trying to save
my life, my mind connected those dots. I knew Michelle sent
me this guardian angel.

———————

When Rhonda arrived at Riverside Hospital, the woman
working the admissions desk said I wasn't there.

The ruse of me being Jim Duran had ended at the pro
shop. Although the folks at the golf course told paramedics
that was my name, one of them recognized me. He asked if
I was Rod Carew, and I said yes. The lead paramedic told
the ER doctor who I was, but—perhaps realizing my desire
for privacy—the hospital kept my name out of circulation.

Rhonda knew I was at Riverside because a woman from
the hospital had called to say I was on the way. (I'd been
conscious enough to give Rhonda's phone number to the
paramedics.) Her drive from our house took about an hour.
While she was obviously alarmed, Rhonda kept her emotions

in check because the caller from the hospital had been so reassuring. One of the paramedics called soon after and he too inspired confidence. With only those conversations to go on, Rhonda figured things were playing out as smoothly for me as they had for my buddy Chris. None of our family or close friends had suffered a heart attack, so he was our only frame of reference. Since he got a few stents and bounced back quickly, Rhonda expected the same for me.

Darker thoughts tried buzzing into her mind during the drive, but she shooed them away with the tool she always relies on: faith. We're strong believers that God gives you only what you can handle. We know things are out of our control anyway. She reminded herself that remaining calm was the best way to handle whatever she would encounter at the hospital. And, right away, she faced the challenge of the receptionist saying they had no patient named Rod Carew.

Someone from the ER eventually acknowledged she was in the right place. A nurse brought her to a waiting room downstairs near the cath lab.

Finally, a doctor arrived to say the stent procedure was done and he felt good about my prognosis.

———————

There's a gap in my memory. It leaves off with me on the ground at the pro shop. It picks up with the sedation wearing off.

My mouth was dry. My throat hurt; a tube in it was helping me breathe. Someone squeezed my right hand. The touch was warm and familiar. Wherever I was, Rhonda was there too.

"Honey," I rasped.

She leaned across the tubes and wires and kissed my forehead. Tears filled my eyes.

"I think I dodged a bullet," I said. "God gave me another chance at life."

————————

By all accounts, I should have died on September 20, 2015.

Probably at the golf course. Maybe in the ambulance. And very nearly in the cath lab.

But I don't go down very easily. I didn't as a hitter or any other time life has thrown me a curveball—and I've seen some of the nastiest pitches that life can throw.

PART I

"Whenever I hear my favorite song, I know I'm going to get two hits that day. The song? The national anthem."
—Rod Carew

1

ROUGH START

WHENEVER MY LIFE STORY IS TOLD, it often starts at the very beginning—my birth on a train in Panama. The charming anecdote is that I was delivered by Dr. Rodney Cline and, in his honor, I was named Rodney Cline Carew.

The outline is correct. The details aren't.

My parents, Olga and Eric, already had two girls and a boy when they learned another baby was on the way. They lived in a small town in the Panama Canal Zone, a place so poor that it only had a dirty clinic more suited for dying than for delivering a baby. So when my mother went into labor the evening of October 1, 1945, my parents boarded a Panama Railroad car and headed to a U.S. Army hospital 40 miles away, praying for the wheels of the train to move faster than my mother's contractions.

At that time, Panama was as segregated as the Bible Belt, so trains were divided into a white section and a colored section. Riding among the coloreds, Olga screamed and moaned. The men looked away, trying to ignore her. Only Margaret Allen stepped forward to help.

Mrs. Allen grew up in Panama and became a nurse in New York. She was back in Panama on vacation. She comforted Olga and coached her through labor. My arrival into this world was into the strict, loving hands of Mrs. Allen. Once the wails of a newborn rang out, the conductor summoned a physician from the white section—Dr. Cline, of course.

While Dr. Cline became the inspiration for my name— and, over the years, treated me as my doctor—Mrs. Allen became my godmother. This was the first of many times she would have a profound impact on my life.

A map of the Americas shows the only natural way to connect the Atlantic and Pacific oceans comes from navigating around the tip of South America. It's such a long, difficult journey that within 50 years of Christopher Columbus coming over from Spain, visionaries were looking to carve a shortcut. The obvious target was Panama, a nation at the tip of Central America with a relatively thin land mass—50 miles from ocean shore to ocean shore. The challenge was engineering a way through. After years of trying by the French, the United States took over in 1904. A decade later, the great waterway known as the Panama Canal opened.

By the 1920s, many of the Americans who'd helped build and maintain it were ready to abandon Gatún, a town on the Atlantic end of the region known as the Panama Canal Zone.

Buildings that housed the workers were converted to wooden apartments for the locals. As with the train, everything in the Zone was segregated into sections for whites and coloreds. In the colored neighborhood, homes were small and simple. For families like mine that had come from Trinidad and other parts of the West Indies in hopes of finding work and building a better life, they were good enough.

In the 1940s, my mother spent weekdays in Panama City, living in the home of a white family while working as their housekeeper. She earned $1 per day. We needed every cent because my father was a terrible provider. He worked as a painter for the Panama Canal Company. Because the company was also our landlord, rent was deducted from his paycheck. He got to keep whatever was left. He usually spent it on himself, mainly on booze.

When I was eight, we moved a few miles south in the Canal Zone, to a town called Gamboa. It was slightly bigger, though equally poor. We settled in one of several new buildings in the black section. Nobody bothered naming the streets on our side of town. Still, our neighborhood became known as the Dust Bowl because of all the construction.

We lived only blocks from the water, close enough for the foghorns and screeching of the enormous vessels passing through to remain the soundtrack of our life. For fun, sometimes we'd go up in the hills and watch the ships navigate the locks—rising and lowering, their colorful flags flapping. I liked drawing sketches of these scenes. I became pretty good at it. I gained a reputation as an artist. Whenever friends or teachers needed a design for something, they always came to me. All those hours of watching the action in the canal also spawned a fascination with how the locks worked. While the Canal Zone wasn't a place where poor black kids usually dreamed big, I imagined a career in art or engineering taking me to the faraway places those big ships were headed.

By the time we moved to Gamboa, I was no longer the baby in my family. My mother had another girl. However, the number of people in our apartment remained the same for the strangest reason: my oldest sister moved in with my father's parents.

The four of us who remained with Eric and Olga (we called our parents by their first names) were jammed into one bedroom. I shared a bed with my brother, Eric Jr., who went by Dickie. My sisters Deanna, the oldest at home, and Dorine, the baby, shared another bed. Most of my clothes were hand-me-downs. Previous owners wore them for as long as they could. By the time I got them, there wasn't much left. At one point, my only pair of shoes had soles that flapped against the bottom of my feet when I walked. At school, I walked alongside a wall in hopes that no one would notice. I had to make do until my mother could find me a replacement.

I obviously didn't see how my mother cared for my older siblings when they were young. But something must've been different about the way she raised me, because everyone said I was her favorite. The term they used most was that I was her "pet." It was my identity in my formative years, and I wore it with pride.

The bond may have stemmed from the time we spent together in my first few years.

I kept getting sick—fevers, mostly—and my mother soothed me. When my friends were outside playing and I was too sick to leave the apartment, she found ways to keep my mind occupied. She also frequently told me I was special. It's something many mothers tell their kids, but the way she said it made me feel like it had to be true.

She encouraged me to think of a life beyond Gatún and Gamboa, beyond the Canal Zone, beyond our poor nation. Long before Earl Woods prophesized greatness for the boy he named Tiger, my mother was infusing me with the confidence that I would grow up to make a mark on the world.

Her love was never needed more than when I was 11 and suffered the worst of my childhood illnesses.

Rheumatic fever confined me to Gorgas Hospital, the place where I was supposed to have been born. I spent six months there, three in isolation. Extreme isolation. My mother visited as often as she could, but it was never often enough for a sick, scared child—especially a sick, scared Momma's boy.

I was usually alone when my fever soared, reaching such extreme temperatures that it triggered hallucinations. Monsters and airplanes zoomed toward me. Bullets whizzed by. Bombs exploded all around. How does a kid fight such horrors? I didn't. These scenes engaged my fight-or-flight instinct and I developed a knack for flight. Scared and sweating, I fled my room. More than once I made it out of the hospital. Nurses eventually learned to stay a step ahead. When my temperature began to rise, they buried me in ice in hopes of slowing or warding off the spike in fever that would unleash the fright show in my mind. They also restrained my hands and feet. Just to be safe, they put a net over my bed, too.

My father's father worked on a tugboat in the canal. Sometimes he brought Dickie and me along for joyrides. All my memories of Grandpa are of him being a sweet, serene man. Which is why it's so hard to understand what went wrong with his son, Eric. My father.

My theory is that it all traces to Grandma. She was the one with a mean streak.

My wicked grandmother snatched away my oldest sister, Sheridan, insisting that only she could raise the girl properly. Grandma didn't like my mother and didn't consider her capable of raising her oldest child.

How could my parents allow such a thing? Well, my mother shied from confronting my father, and he wasn't about to confront his mother. Eric feared Grandma, likely because she'd beaten him when he was a child.

Put it this way: someone taught Eric that it was okay to abuse your children, and it certainly wasn't Grandpa.

Eric stood six foot three. He was built lean and favored a thin mustache. His voice was high-pitched and he could let out a two-fingered whistle you could hear from blocks away.

This macho tough guy seemed angry at Olga for me not being a strong, healthy son. He also was disgusted by Olga's bond with me, his black sheep of a son. Of their five kids, why would she care so much about *that one*? It was as if life were a zero-sum game and any interest she showed in me meant less for him. From that warped perspective, he saw me as competition.

So what does a big, dumb bully do to control such a scene? He starts knocking us around.

In all their years together, he'd never hit my mother until after I was born. I don't know when it started, but I know that my earliest memory is of the police coming to our apartment following one of his blowups.

I was three or four years old, wearing only underpants, watching from a corner of the room as my father attacked my mother. I saw him smacking her over and over. Then I saw the officers come in. The replay in my mind ends with a neighbor carrying me out of our apartment to the safety of his place.

I later learned that neighbor was the person who'd called the cops. The fact it was bad enough to call for help indicates this was worse than usual or, perhaps, that it was a new thing.

Eric tore into Olga for years. Eventually, he came after me, too. Then, only me.

He saw a soft boy who needed toughening. Not only did he see me as sick and weak, he didn't think I liked girls enough for a boy my age—mind you, my age was roughly 10. To the stream of belittling nicknames he tabbed on me, "Sissy" became his favorite.

In his twisted mind, this was parenting.

Early on, he would shove me into a broom closet and keep me trapped inside for hours. His next step toward making a man out of me involved his fists. Nights when he drank heavily, his fists weren't enough. His arsenal grew to include a rope, a strip of wood, the knotted cord from an iron, and the wide leather belt around his waist.

These weren't isolated incidents. They were frequent enough that we developed a routine. I sat beside a little window in our kitchen that overlooked the route he took walking to our building. From five floors up, I could tell from his stride whether he was planning to unleash his frustrations against the world on my arms, legs, chest, back, and butt. When his stomping indicated it would be one of those nights, I met him inside the door of our apartment already holding his favorite weapons. *Here, pick one.*

To Eric, this signaled more weakness. So he developed another routine. He would sit on the sofa nursing a beer, the belt dangling over one thigh, the iron cord over the other thigh, the rope wrapped around the hand that wasn't holding a beer. Slowly deciding which tool he'd use this time was his idea of fun. Sometimes the sadist dipped the iron cord in water, making it heavier, harder—delivering more of a sting and deeper bruises.

Yet another violent tactic involved the shower. He would put me in and turn on the water as hot as possible. Trapped in a corner of this tiny box, I had nowhere to go. If I moved one way, I'd get scalded. If I moved the other way, I'd get swatted. Scalded, swatted; scalded, swatted. This vicious dance perpetrated by a grown man against his own son. And no one could—or would—stop him.

My mother, bless her heart, tried. She would get between him and me, absorbing the blows herself, or cause enough of a distraction that he would channel his rage toward her.

This was a very strong woman.

Every time Eric attacked Olga, she would stare at him and sing "Amazing Grace" or "Nearer, My God, to Thee." She refused to give him the satisfaction of seeing her suffer.

Eric was a wanderer, too. He could be gone from the apartment for days, sometimes more than a week. Oh, how I loved those breaks. Another vacation, of sorts, came when my mother took us to spend a night, or even several nights, with her mother, another wonderful woman.

There were times I ran away from home, sometimes seeking shelter at the home of my friend Carlos Long or at the field at our school. I had a favorite tree I liked to climb, a place where I could hide and feel invisible to the world. My mother had bought me a bike and some days my fear powered me to pedal as far as Panama City, nearly two hours away. One such escape was foiled when I was passed by a bus that happened to be carrying my father. He leaned out the window and spoke the awful truth, the grim reality that always made me regret having bolted at all: "You have to come home eventually." I'm sure he spent the rest of the ride plotting a new level of cruelty. If only he'd been as industrious as he was devious, maybe we could have afforded a better lifestyle, one that wouldn't have left him so angry.

How could he get away with it? How did people not notice my welts and bruises or my mother's fat lip? How come the cops weren't called more often?

Those are questions we ask today. The 1950s in the poor section of the Panama Canal Zone was a different time and place. People certainly knew. Aside from the neighbor calling the cops one time—which might've been the very first time it happened—nobody tried to help.

The person who came closest to intervening was Joseph French, a coach at my elementary school and my uncle; he was married to my mother's sister. From family gatherings, he likely knew that Eric was trouble. If he didn't, seeing me change into my gym clothes gave it away.

Mr. French confronted Eric about my injuries. My father told him to mind his own business. Mr. French dropped the issue between them. But he began paying extra attention to me. If he couldn't stop the beatings, he could at least provide some of the fathering I wasn't getting at home.

Mr. French made sure I was at school every day and that I was doing my homework. If my tattered clothes failed to cover the scars on my back or legs, he found a shirt or pants to help me maintain some dignity. On days when boys went shirtless in gym, Mr. French allowed me to keep my shirt on to hide my welts. This only traded one issue for another; now I was the only boy wearing a shirt. Still, I gladly drew looks for that rather than endure the shame and embarrassment that would come from revealing my bruises. There would be more mentoring by Mr. French, but these were the sad circumstances that brought us closer.

My friend Carlos also knew how Eric treated me. We walked to and from school together, swam together, explored together the jungle near our neighborhood, clearing paths with our machetes and plucking fresh mangoes off the trees.

Carlos knew me so well that most mornings he brought me something to fill my empty stomach. But Carlos couldn't relate to the violence. His father was a wonderful man. He was a mechanic and he enjoyed letting Carlos and me crawl under cars to see what he was doing. He patiently pointed out the name of each part, what it did, and how they all worked together to make the car move. Carlos enjoyed being with his father—talking to him, learning from him. I did, too. The only thing I didn't like was walking back home and going from one extreme to the other. The car story I have with Eric is a good example.

He'd just bought a new car and, boy, was he proud of it. He had me wash it and keep it clean. I was happy to do it, thinking this might bring us closer. Maybe this would be our thing. Nope. Eric never allowed me to ride in that car. He took my brothers and sisters, but not me. Unlikely as this may seem, I wanted to ride in it so desperately that I would've remembered going even a single block. Same with the pastries Eric baked every Christmas. They looked and smelled delicious. My siblings told me they were.

Can you imagine all this? I'll bet it makes you angry. That's what it did to me. I was angry at Eric, of course, and pretty much the entire world. Cuts and bruises heal. The ability to love and trust doesn't return easily, not after being punched, smacked, and shattered by someone supposed to unconditionally be in your corner.

I encased my thoughts and feelings in a hard outer shell. I resolved that nobody would ever take advantage of me. I'd rather push away potentially meaningful relationships than risk anyone making me feel the way Eric did.

Time helped. Not because Eric mellowed, but because I grew.

The poundings became less frequent, especially when Dickie was around. While he wasn't about to stand up to our old man on my behalf, Dickie was big enough and strong enough to protect Olga from Eric.

Dickie wasn't around, though, one night when Eric came home drunk. He started smacking her around again, then went into his bedroom. He passed out on the bed.

I knew this was my chance. I went into my room and got my machete. I was 12 years old and ready to murder my father.

My mother saw me emerge with the blade and head toward Eric.

"NOOO!" she screamed.

Her objection had nothing to do with right versus wrong or protecting her husband. She was looking out for *me*. This was not the mark on the world she felt I was destined to make. No matter how much physical and emotional damage I'd endured, this would be a trauma—and a stigma—I could never overcome.

I did as she said.

Of all the gifts she gave me, this was among the finest. As were the words that followed.

"You can't live with this bitterness," she said. "You must trust God."

One of the two foundational elements of my childhood obviously was suffering at the hands of my father.

The other was developing a beautiful relationship with my Father.

"God is there for you," my mother told me every day, sometimes several times a day. "He's always going to be there. He's going to take care of you."

She believed, so I believed.

She talked to God every day, so I talked to God every day.

Why didn't God protect us from Eric? She didn't ask those kinds of questions, so I didn't, either. Knowing that God was always going to take care of me was enough. Surely He had an explanation for our suffering. Maybe once I was older it would be revealed. I took solace in knowing that for all that was wrong now, eventually everything would be made right. How did I know this? Because my mother preached it and I nodded along.

"Father, I know it's not your fault that Eric beats me," I would say. "I know you're going to take care of me."

Proof that He was looking out for me came when I was 13.

When my friends and I wanted to swim, we had little choice but to use the canal.

The local pool was for whites only. We sometimes snuck in at night, but I was always scared of getting caught.

Swimming in the canal offered many challenges, starting with the choppy waves riled up by ships passing through. There also was an alligator always perched in a particular area.

We took turns playing the role of lookout man, keeping an eye on the alligator and hollering when he went into motion. You'd never seen kids move as fast as we did getting out of the water when the alligator moved in.

One day, the alligator remained on his perch while a bunch of us swam out pretty far. We decided to race back. I was churning along when a cramp stopped me. Next thing I knew, I was going under. I came up for air and went under again. On my way up the third time, I felt arms pulling me. Something was lifting me out of the water, keeping me safe. Dickie eventually came to my aid, but his arms weren't the ones that rescued me. Once I made it back to dry land, I understood that God had pulled me to safety. Like my mother repeatedly said, He was guiding me, protecting me.

Even before then, I often accompanied my mother to church. It was the rare place where I felt comfortable. The construct was perfect: I got to be with my mother, I felt closer to God, and Eric was nowhere to be found.

While I read the New Testament, faith to me was never about memorizing Scripture. I followed my mother's lead and developed a one-on-one relationship with God, a connection only He and I could understand. Seeing my mother tolerate the animalistic behavior of her husband because she clung to the premise that there's a reason for it—that it was somehow part of a larger plan—made a huge impression on me. It also showed me that people of God are defined by their actions. Jesus showed us a path, and it's up to us to follow our own, in His image.

———————

Throughout my childhood, I exchanged letters with my god-mother, Mrs. Allen. I trusted her enough to share some details of my father beating me and my mother.

When Mrs. Allen visited from New York, she asked our neighbors whether I was an imaginative boy who told tall tales. They realized what she was really asking. I hope they were too embarrassed to look her in the eye when they confirmed my stories were true.

Mrs. Allen began urging my mother to flee with her children and start over in the United States. Mrs. Allen herself fled Panama for greater opportunities, and she wanted us to do the same. She returned to New York intent on finding a way to get us far away from it all—the poverty, the dead-end future, and, most of all, Eric.

She called my mother one day with good news: she'd secured the necessary papers. If Olga could pay a $300 fee required of all immigrants and another couple hundred dollars for a plane ticket, she could move to New York.

The money ended up coming from Olga's brother, Clyde Scott. He was in the Air Force, stationed in Hawaii. Coincidentally, he was soon headed to New York, too. Eager to share the experience with her, he helped pay her way there. But there wasn't enough money for any of us kids to join them. The plan was for Olga to earn enough to pry us away.

In Manhattan, my mother earned $32 a week working in a purse factory. She saved enough that, months later, she was ready to bring one of her children. Picking a single one was a decision no mother should have to make.

Mrs. Allen eased the burden. She would pay for me. The woman whose hands brought me into the world would now provide me a new life, a rebirth into a world of endless possibilities.

My mother put the other three names and a hat and drew one. The lucky winner was Dickie.

––––––––––––

Wearing a suit for the first time, riding an airplane for the first time, I could hardly believe what I was seeing. As the plane descended into Idlewild Airport, the lights were so bright and they extended so far.

Exiting the jet, I put a little extra gusto into the final step. I made it. Thousands of miles from my father, I was free.

The date was June 30, 1961, smack dab in the middle of the summer that Mickey Mantle and Roger Maris chased each other in pursuit of Babe Ruth's single-season home run record. As a 15-year-old baseball fan, I should've been swept away by that, especially since it was playing out at Yankee Stadium, just a few miles from my new apartment in Washington Heights. Instead, I was swept away by sensory overload.

New York was unlike anything I expected. The TV shows and movies I'd watched in Panama glorified the city: Rockefeller Center, Madison Square Garden, the Empire State Building. They didn't show the reality I was facing: streets and sidewalks jammed with cars, trash, and people. Drunks everywhere. Rats, too. Mischief and mayhem were easy to find, if one were so inclined. Fortunately, I wasn't inclined. Mrs. Allen and Uncle Clyde made sure of it.

On one of our first nights in the city, Uncle Clyde took Dickie and me on a long walk. Clyde was in his late twenties, but seemed much older. He knew we lacked a father figure, so he tried to cram in as much fatherly advice as he could. It all boiled down to making good choices.

Mrs. Allen lived about two blocks from us, close enough that I was required to visit her each day after school.

Never had anyone been as strict with me as she was. Never had I been as grateful to anyone, so I wasn't about to cross any of the lines she set. I also knew those boundaries were created out of love. And she explained the purpose behind each.

The first bit of assimilation was to stop calling my mother "Olga." Now, she was "Mom."

Next came my language skills.

Like her, I'd learned broken, accented English growing up in Panama. She knew it was good enough to get by. She also knew I could get around our Spanish-speaking neighborhood without ever speaking English. But she wasn't about to let me fall into those traps. For instance, I often put the emphasis on the wrong syllables. She taught me correct pronunciations. She knew speaking crisp English would help me in school and work.

School was George Washington High, the alma mater of Harry Belafonte, Henry Kissinger, and other notables. New immigrants were generally set back a grade. Instead of beginning as a junior, I repeated my sophomore year. I soon discovered why: processing lessons in a new language took time. I essentially had to reprogram my brain to think in English first. I had to resist the urge to translate every sentence into Spanish.

Work was in the stockroom of a grocery store. I later delivered medications for a doctor who was friends with Mrs. Allen. To her, the value of a part-time job went beyond making money. Having someplace to be, and putting in long, tiring hours, meant less opportunity to run the streets.

Mrs. Allen, Uncle Clyde, and my mom hardly had to worry. Rule-breaking was not my thing. Back in Panama, sneaking into the pool at night had been too risky for my taste. There was no way I was going to get into the kind of trouble the streets of New York offered. I didn't want to do anything that might tempt anyone to send me back to Panama.

Trouble wasn't the only thing I avoided. I kept my distance from other people.

The scars my father beat into my psyche remained. I refused to trust new people. I just wanted to be left alone. I felt safe behind my hard outer shell.

Soon enough, everything fell into place. Including the one missing piece.

Baseball.

2

THE ONE THING THAT CAME EASY: HITTING

O NE AFTERNOON WHEN I WAS ABOUT FIVE, I was bouncing a rubber ball on the front stoop of our apartment building when a truck full of U.S. soldiers drove down our street. American military always had a presence in the Canal Zone, so trucks frequently rolled by on the way to or from a ship.

This time, something came flying off the truck, right toward me. I heard it whiz by my head, smack into the side of the building, and fall to the ground. I picked it up and ran inside screaming.

"I got a baseball! I got a baseball!"

It was the first I ever owned.

One of the best things about living in Panama was the mild
weather: temperatures between 72 and 90 degrees every day.

We took advantage by playing outside year-round. Every
day, everyone I knew was at the fields playing pickup games
of soccer, volleyball, basketball, and, of course, baseball. The
one thing we black kids didn't do was play football; that was
only for the kids at the white schools.

Thin and fast, I could run all day without getting tired.
What I enjoyed most, though, was hitting a ball with a bat.

Hitting came easy to me from the start. I could always
swing a stick of wood in the right place at the right time to
connect with a ball speeding and spinning toward me. I loved
the feeling of impact; I couldn't get enough of it. I never felt
more confident than when standing with a bat in my hands.
Regardless of whether I hit the last pitch over an outfielder's
head or missed entirely, I knew I'd crush the next one.

Early on, my friends and I hit bottle caps with broomsticks—
the coolest broomsticks you'd ever seen. Everyone customized
theirs. I slathered mine in black paint and added yellow trim.
In orange, I wrote 42, the jersey number of my favorite player,
the player everyone in our neighborhood idolized most: Jackie
Robinson. Under the 42, I painted 39 for another of Jackie's
black teammates, Roy Campanella. When we switched from
bottle caps to balls, they were taped-together concoctions. We'd
bind rags, newspaper, or sponge balls until forming something
roughly the size of a baseball and some approximation of round.
Tennis balls were terrific, too. Considering the caliber of our
bats and balls, we hardly needed gloves. But we wanted to look
and feel like the big kids, so we molded mitts out of paper bags,
cardboard, or swatches of canvas, weaving in string to create a

pocket. Just like I remember my first real baseball, I remember my first real glove. It originally belonged to the son in the family where my mother worked. He wasn't using it, so my mother asked if she could bring it to me. To make it truly my own, I dyed it black. I kept it oiled, polished, and brushed, guaranteeing that I always had the best-looking glove on the field.

You could find a game pretty much any time of any day. The closest park was Dust Bowl; I could see it from our fifth-floor window. Within 10 minutes of home, there were three more parks: Church Square, Front Street, and Parallel. Plus, there were two fields at Paraiso High School, a small one for the younger kids and a full-size one for the older kids. There was a church near that park. On Sundays, we sometimes got so loud that we drowned out the pastor's sermon. He always let us know it, too.

Sundays were great for us baseball fans because that was when Armed Forces Radio broadcast major league games. I always plopped down next to the radio and followed the action by keeping a scorecard, penciling in a double as 2B, a groundout to shortstop as 6–3, and so forth. The great thing about listening to a game on radio is that while the announcers give you a sense of what's happening, your mind colors in the details. I would imagine how each guy gripped and swung a bat…the look on a pitcher's face as he threw a fastball up and in…the way a runner tried a hook slide into a base to avoid being tagged out. Games became movies in my mind, and my filled-out scorecards let me replay them days and weeks later. I could picture many of the faces from their baseball cards. I'd get them at the grocery store and trade them with my friends. I became good at flipping cards, which boosted my collection. My goal was getting more Jackie Robinson cards.

By now, I'd seen the movie *The Jackie Robinson Story* and had a better appreciation of why he was so popular. If I fulfilled my dream of playing in the major leagues, it would mean traveling down a road he paved. I kept his cards in a prominent place by my bed, making his face the first I saw in the morning and the last I saw before I went to sleep. Like my friends, I also put cards in the spokes of my bicycle to make that flapping sound we all thought was so cool; of course, we now know we were ruining the cards. Regardless of their condition, I sure wish I'd held on to those cards for their sentimental value. The scorecards, too.

The Armed Forces Radio broadcast usually featured the best teams and biggest stars. We often heard Giants, Yankees, and Dodgers games—plenty of Willie, Mickey, and the Duke. I also grew quite fond of the Milwaukee Braves. I loved when it was Hank Aaron's turn to hit and the announcer said, "Here comes The Hammer." I had many favorites on that team: Eddie Mathews, of course, as well as Bill Bruton, Johnny Logan, Del Crandall, Warren Spahn, and Bob Buhl.

I listened to every World Series game, even if it meant cutting school. The broadcasts were easy to find. So many people tuned in while sitting on their porch, or with their windows open, that you could walk down the street and hear every pitch. The only ones you might miss were right after Jackie or Campy or another black player did something exciting and everyone was still cheering.

Hearing those games, I always noticed the roar of the crowd. It was so loud. During World Series games, announcers said there were more than 50,000 people in the stands. To a kid living in a town of 4,000, it was hard to fathom. Still, I told my mom that one day all those people would be watching me. Like all moms, she smiled and encouraged me to believe in myself.

Those broadcasts were all in English. Winter ball leagues from Latin America were the only games we heard in Spanish. The players I remember most from those games were Hector Lopez and Clarence Moore. Lopez made it all the way from Panama to the majors, while Moore came awfully close. We eventually heard major league games in Spanish on the "Cabalgata Deportiva Gillette" (Gillette Cavalcade of Sports), with the great Buck Canel calling the action.

Baseball was my father's favorite sport. He listened to all the games, too.

Having this in common hardly mattered.

I moved up from broomsticks to real baseball around age eight. The older kids let me fill in when they needed an extra player. I quickly realized I was as good as anyone.

By the time I was 12, Mr. French saw it, too.

"No more soccer," he said.

A decathlon champion in his youth, he knew the traits of a good athlete. He found them in the scared, scarred son of his wife's sister, the boy he was already keeping an eye on. In what became the first boost for my career, he signed me up for Little League.

My parents couldn't afford the fee, so Mr. French made a deal with me: I would have to work it off. As the gym teacher at Gamboa High School, he also was in charge of maintaining the field. I had to help him by removing rocks, painting fences, and such. The better I played, the more he let me treat my chores with the intensity of Tom Sawyer and the fence he was supposed to be painting.

Right away, I drew attention for hitting more frequently and more forcefully than anyone else, my age or older. Parents from other teams accused me of being older than 12. Mr. French taught me to treat this as a compliment.

I was named MVP, an honor that came with the prize of a Ted Williams model bat. I treasured it so much that I took it to bed with me. As with clothes, I made sure to extend the life of that bat as long as possible; when it broke, I nailed it back together. Now that I felt a connection to Ted, I started collecting more of his cards. I piled up his next to Jackie's in that place of honor next to my bed.

Once I was clearly the best player in Gamboa, Mr. French took me to other parks around the Canal Zone to see how I stacked up against other kids my age and older. Then we sought action throughout the interior of Panama.

The only time Eric came to a Little League game, I had three hits, two of them home runs. He showed no reaction to any of those. But after I made an error in the field, he was in the dugout waiting for me when the half-inning ended. He put his meaty hand around my throat and tried lifting me. Mr. French saw and screamed, "Take your hands off that boy!" He let go and I gagged, gasping for air.

Another mean trick Eric liked to pull was finding any reason to ground me. He knew that forcing me indoors stung me twice. Not only did it keep me from playing baseball, but he knew I would park myself in front of the window—the same window where I waited anxiously to read the demeanor of his walk—and suffer through watching my friends playing at Dust Bowl Park.

Once I was in the majors, I heard guys who were dealing with off-field issues say that games were their escape. I learned that as a child, I just didn't have the vocabulary to express it.

Growing up, the place where I felt most peace was on a baseball field—more specifically, in a batter's box. My ability as a hitter gave me an identity beyond being my mother's pet and my father's punching bag. I felt like I belonged. Like I was a king. I was safe and strong. Not only was I untouchable, I was going to inflict pain on others. You could even hypothesize that my anger toward my father was the reason I hit the ball so hard, my quick, strong wrists delivering blow after blow. This attitude extended to the base paths. Nobody wanted to get in my way. I came in fast, eager to slide hard. I didn't pitch often, but when I did, I threw my share of beanballs.

Funny thing is, at 14, I was still scrawny—five-foot-something and a little over 100 pounds. Unlike basketball, where you walk onto a court and know which guy you need to stop, people could look at my team in the dugout and say, "Which one is the kid we've been hearing about?"

And people were talking about me. As my reputation grew, I began getting recruited.

Like by the fire department squad in a fast-pitch softball league.

The one that included a team of canal workers.

Eric was on that team.

As a pitcher.

Here were my options: win the battle against my father and get whipped for showing him up or lose the battle and probably still get whipped for trying to show him up.

Damned if I do, damned if I don't.

Might as well do.

So I did.

I got a base hit in my first at-bat against him, unleashing all sorts of razzing from Eric's buddies. It was my biggest thrill yet on a baseball field, one that would take many years to top. I'm not usually vindictive and don't like it when others are. This, though, was different. I piled on by stealing second, which was rarely done. I ended up scoring. More hits off him followed, both that day and as the season went along.

This would've been a great time for Eric to let bygones be bygones, to take pride in his Sissy becoming a great hitter. He could've taken credit; "That's my boy!" Others would've clapped him on the back and praised him for having taught me so well, even though he knew he had nothing to do with it.

My only explanation is a phrase I used before about our relationship: he saw me as competition. Somehow, I was his rival in ways that went well beyond pitcher versus hitter.

―――――――

Okay, so my father wasn't my fan.

Omar Torrijos was.

As I was making a name for myself on the ballfield, Torrijos was making his way up the ranks of the Panamanian army, known as the National Guard. He became a captain in 1956 and a major in 1960. In 1968, he helped power a coup d'état that overthrew the president. General Torrijos, as he became known, vowed to look out for the little guys—farmers, workers, students—and not merely the elites. He established the Democratic Revolutionary Party and, in 1972, he reshaped the structure of the entire government, basically starting from scratch. He spent the next six years running the nation under the title "Maximum Leader of the Revolution." His crowning feat came in 1977, when he negotiated a treaty with President Jimmy Carter that gave Panama control of the canal in 2000.

Our paths crossed in 1960 or '61, before I left for New York. At a youth baseball ceremony, he told me that he expected me to be like Hector Lopez and go from Panama to the major leagues.

"You're going to be a star," he told me. "When you do, try and help these kids here."

Huh?! I'm a kid myself, and he's asking me to help kids? Wow, talk about a responsibility.

It was too much for a 15-year-old to comprehend. But I never forgot the conversation.

The first two years I lived in New York, I'm not sure I ever swung a bat.

In Panama, the weather was great, the fields were close by, and everyone wanted me on their team. I'd been playing almost every day for so long that it had been like breathing—I took it for granted. Living in Washington Heights, I struggled to fit the game into my new life. The rules set by Mrs. Allen limited my free time. I told few people that I even liked baseball.

I eventually discovered pickup games at various parks. I especially liked Macombs Dam Park. It was so close to Yankee Stadium that late-afternoon games were played in the shadow of the stadium's famous façade. That atmosphere alone made me dream big—though not big enough to go inside. I missed out on the fun of '61…and '62 and '63. Hector Lopez was on those Yankees teams, yet I never attended a game. I did make it once to the Polo Grounds. The Mets played their first two seasons there, and I happened to catch one of the games when Willie Mays returned to his old stomping grounds while with the San Francisco Giants. I can still hear the fans howling, "Say hey!"

My final semester at George Washington High, I finally tried out for the baseball team. The coach was a good man and knew enough about baseball that the Detroit Tigers paid him to tip them off to anyone with potential. He whiffed on me, though. He didn't even think I was good enough for the high school squad.

It's not as outrageous as it seems. Workouts began in February inside the gym. When we went outside in March, it was still windy with temperatures in the 40s. That's not baseball weather. I doubt I had ever even played in the 60s. There was no way my swing—already rusty from the long layoff—could come alive under these conditions.

"Coach, I'm going to get better," I told him.

By now, I did have one good friend, Ozzie Alvarez. He and another guy I knew played on the New York Cavaliers, a sandlot team in the Bronx Federation League. After I got cut from the high school team, they got me a tryout. Another kid I went to school with, Steve Katz, was trying out for the team, too. His father, Monroe Katz, was there watching.

Mr. Katz was a longtime baseball scout. Among the people he'd discovered was another George Washington alum, a guy who'd go on to more fame—and infamy—as a Dodgers executive: Al Campanis. Mr. Katz was now working for the Minnesota Twins. Well, that's a bit overstated. He was a "bird dog scout," an extra pair of eyes and ears in New York City. He made recommendations to the club. If they signed any of those players, he got a finder's fee.

Although Mr. Katz saw me botch some grounders and bounce some throws from shortstop, he liked what he saw. He recognized my instincts and figured I'd be better in warmer weather. He recommended the general manager give me a spot. The GM gave in. But my unimpressive fielding forced me to learn a new position: second base.

Our coach was a wonderful man named Sam Cummando. He became one of my first baseball mentors. He helped me adjust to second base, teaching me things like where to position myself in different situations. We talked a lot about thinking the game, imagining what might happen before each pitch so I'd be ready to react. After Sunday games, he invited the whole team to his place for dinner. His wife made delicious spaghetti and meatballs.

Mr. Katz saw me play practically every game that season. He even gave me a ride to the park for most of them. I appreciated his kindness, although I now understand there was more to it. He was earning my trust, while also continuing to watch my development and looking out to see whether other scouts had found me. (I wasn't the only future MLB All-Star in the Bronx Federation League this season. So was Ken Singleton, who went on to play for the Mets, Expos, and Orioles.)

Pretty soon, Mr. Katz recognized he was on to something big with me. He alerted his contact with the Twins, a full-time scout named Herb Stein, and he came out to take a look at me. Soon, Mr. Stein was at all my games, sometimes buying me lunch afterward. He began talking to me about pro baseball. He then brought in the head of the team's farm system, Hal Keller, to watch me play a doubleheader. By that point, scouts for several teams had discovered me.

In the games Keller watched, I went 8-for-9 with several doubles, a grand slam, and a bunch of stolen bases. Keller told me the Twins would be trying me out the next time they came to play the Yankees.

———————

On May 19, 1964, I made my first trip into the House That Ruth Built. I walked into the visiting clubhouse and was given a uniform—No. 6. Tony Oliva's. Tony was on his way to winning the Rookie of the Year Award and the batting title, but the Twins apparently figured he was unknown enough that they could get away with slipping in another left-handed-hitting, dark-skinned Latino, even if I was an inch shorter and much skinnier.

As I headed out for batting practice, it never dawned on me how far I'd come. Just three years after cowering under Eric's thumb in Panama, probably headed toward a dead-end job at the canal like most boys I grew up with, I was weeks from graduating from high school in New York. Immigrants have been coming to the Big Apple with big dreams for generations and now—two months after failing to make my high school team—I had the chance to make mine come true. And the potential launching pad of my career in pro baseball was the same batter's box that Babe Ruth and Lou Gehrig used to dig their cleats into. Come to think of it, it's a good thing I didn't let my mind wander like that.

Then again, I was always focused when it came to hitting. Back in Panama, I wasn't nervous stepping in against kids much older than me or in white neighborhoods or with Eric on the mound. So I wasn't about to be nervous now. Confidence is stoked by success, and I was batting well over .500 for the Cavaliers. I also was driving the ball with authority. That's right—I started out as a power hitter. Sam Cummando still tells the story of a ball I hit nearly 500 feet, flying out of Bronx Park and into a tree across the street.

Walking onto the field at Yankee Stadium, I heard a few fans call Tony's name. I looked around for him, too. Then I realized they thought I was him.

The temperature was around 80. Waiting for my turn to hit, I felt completely at ease, like it was any other day back in Panama on the fields I used to dominate.

"Hey, kid," someone called. "You're up."

Whap! Home run, right-center field.

Crack! Same spot.

I ripped a few more balls, then I was told to stop. Everyone got only five swings at a time.

The next round, I did it again. Two swings into my third round, Twins manager Sam Mele had seen enough. He came running over and said, "Get that kid out of there!" He sent me out to second base to field some grounders before the Yankees figured out what was going on.

This was a legitimate concern.

Under the rules of engagement, teams pursued amateurs in a Wild West–style free-for-all. Players could sign wherever they chose starting the day after graduating high school. (The amateur draft started the next year.) Rich teams like the Yankees blanketed the country scouts and armed them with deep pockets. They stocked their farm system with the cream of the crop. Teams like the Twins had to outsmart them or get lucky. If I kept showing off right there inside Yankee Stadium, the Twins risked losing me to their biggest competition.

I graduated from high school the night of June 24, 1964. Mr. Stein attended the ceremony. Afterward, he and Mr. Katz took my mother, Uncle Clyde, my older sister Deanna, and me to dinner at Stella D'oro, an Italian restaurant owned by the family that ran the famous bakery of the same name; their cookie factory was next door. This was the nicest place I'd ever eaten at, a fitting milestone to add to what was about to become the biggest moment of my life thus far.

Although several teams had shown interest, the Red Sox were the only other club that seemed serious. They'd offered around $2,000. Over dinner, Mr. Stein dragged out the conversation and negotiations. Finally, after midnight—making it the day after I graduated from high school—he got to his best offer: a $5,000 signing bonus and a $400 per month salary.

A week later, I was flying to Florida to start my career.

Three years before, the first flight of my life brought me from Panama to New York with the promise of a fresh start. Now, my second flight carried the same optimism. I could practically hear my mother telling me, "God is there for you. He's always going to be there. He's going to take care of you."

3

BREAKING IN

THE JOY OF BECOMING A PRO BALLPLAYER is followed by the harsh reality of playing pro baseball.

No more teeing off on amateur fastballs that aren't very fast or curveballs that barely curve. Every player at this level is here for a reason. Each was vetted by scouts, farm directors, and general managers. I'm guessing the process of starting over and re-establishing yourself at the entry level of baseball is something like freshman year at Harvard—classrooms full of kids who were valedictorians of their high school, or close to it, all with their grade point averages reset to 0.0, yet all expecting to finish near the top of the class.

For me, pro ball came with more challenges. It meant living on my own for the first time. Having more money than ever before. Playing in front of larger crowds. And, perhaps toughest of all, trying to fit in among my teammates.

The improved pitching didn't bother me. The tricky part was everything outside the batter's box.

———————

The Cocoa Rookie League was an experiment that lasted only this summer. It was set up for guys like me: recently signed players considered too raw to be thrown into the mix against higher-ranked prospects in established rookie leagues, like the Appalachian and Pioneer. We were a collection of wannabes from the Twins, Houston Colt .45s, New York Mets, and Detroit Tigers. Tug McGraw of the Mets, Jim Leyland of the Tigers, and I were among those getting our first chance to climb that steep ladder to the big leagues.

My first obstacle was getting into the lineup. I kept tripping over my glove.

As much as I loved the feel and smell of a well-oiled leather mitt, I'd never worked much on my fielding skills. My father certainly never hit me buckets of balls. Coaches rarely did, either. I spent my practice time in the batting cage. Then came years of not playing, followed by a position change—from shortstop to second base. My crash course in the Bronx helped, but I showed up to Cocoa as a novice on defense. I had hardly any muscle memory. I was still thinking instead of reacting and not always sure what to think. I wasn't even good at the basics of getting low and charging a ball, then watching it into the glove. At this level, fielders have to be willing to take the ball off their chest or face. I flinched. I was also gun shy as the pivot man on a double play—trying to take the toss from the shortstop or third baseman then

firing the ball to first base, all while avoiding a runner looking to take me out.

Uncle Clyde preached that guys in the majors weren't
simply the most gifted, they also were the hardest workers.
Having the gift and working hard to refine it—that's how
you build a great career. Buying into that was easy, especially
since I never considered long hours on a ballfield as being
hard work; what the guys I grew up with were now doing on
the canal, *that* was hard work.

I got into enough games to show that my bat belonged. I
hit .325 and had by far the most hits on the team, despite my
glove often keeping me out of the lineup. In our four-team
league, only one guy had a higher average.

I spent the next two summers in the minors, first for a team
based in Orlando, Florida, then in Wilson, North Carolina.
I hit around .300 in both places and slowly improved my
defense. I also got a taste of life in the Deep South.

Jim Crow laws were more of the same segregation we
had in Panama, so I understood that my skin color determined where I could and couldn't go. I wasn't looking for
any trouble, but trouble could easily find a dark-skinned,
Spanish-speaking teen in Florida and North Carolina in the
mid-1960s.

The Twins knew it, too, so they kept around older black
players, former prospects who could still hold their own but
whose best skill was keeping an eye on young hot shots. They
were, in a word, babysitters. We lived together, ate together,

went to and from the ballpark together. As a guy who struggled to make friends, having a full-time companion was a blessing in ways beyond what club officials intended.

In Orlando, my guy was a pitcher named Ollie Brantley. The son of sharecroppers, he began his journey in 1953, making it as high as Class AAA. He stuck around through 1969. Funny thing is, protecting people turned out to be his calling. After baseball, he became a sheriff in his hometown.

In Wilson, my babysitter was Chuck Weatherspoon, a catcher–first baseman with the claim to fame of having hit seven grand slams in a single season. It's still the most in the minors or majors. He'd been around since 1955. On his way up, he'd been teammates with Orlando Cepeda and Felipe Alou. Both credited him for helping them make it to the majors. Once Spoony's better days were behind him, he was a natural for this role. Like Ollie, it showed up in his post-baseball life, too: His daughter Teresa Weatherspoon grew up to become a star basketball player and a college coach.

Stories I heard from Ollie and Spoony gave me a deeper appreciation of what Jackie Robinson endured. My first real taste of it came in Leesburg, Florida, while playing with Ollie. Two white guys in the stands had a black dog they named "Nigger." Gee, weren't they clever—saying "Here, Nigger" when they were talking to their pet. Every time I came in and out of the dugout, they called me "coon." They did this every game we played in Leesburg. After our final game there, they were waiting for me in the parking lot. They wanted to shake hands, as if to acknowledge the battle was over. Whatever. I was moving up. They were stuck here in their small town with their small view of the world.

I know race relations remain a major problem. But at least things are somewhat better. For instance, when I went to spring training in 1967, *Baseball Digest* listed me as a "Panamanian Negro." That was just the way things were done back then.

Another sign of those times: a letter from the draft board. Like the one I got in 1964.

Although I've never become a United States citizen, I established permanent residency while living in New York. I received the letter after I joined the Twins. I showed it to Calvin Griffith, the team's owner and general manager. He recommended I get into a reserve unit. I went to each branch looking for an opening. That's how I became a Marine.

Joining the reserves meant committing to six months now, then two weeks and a few weekends every year through 1970. This would cut into my playing time, of course, but it seemed better to fulfill my obligation this way than to risk getting shipped to Vietnam.

Up to this point of my life, Mrs. Allen had given me the most tough love. I was introduced to a much higher standard when I reported to boot camp in Parris Island, South Carolina. I became a combat engineer. My duties included learning how to build and defuse land mines. It gave me a window into a whole new world. While pro baseball requires toughness, dedication, and physical strength, we have it easy compared with those serving in the military. To this day, I deeply admire everyone who puts on a uniform to represent their country. There's no such thing as an ex-Marine, either. I'm a Marine for life.

———————

Around the start of my senior year in high school, Eric started sending letters asking to join us.

He promised to be nice to my mother, Dickie, and me. She asked my opinion and I said it was a terrible idea. I hoped to never see him again. But he was her husband. I told her that if she wanted that surly SOB back, my opinion shouldn't matter.

Deanna and Dorine came with him. At the airport, I coldly shook his hand. There was nothing else worth saying. He moved into our apartment and Mrs. Allen got him a job. Things were fine—for all of a few weeks. Soon enough, he was cussing and screaming at everyone. His wandering continued, keeping him out on the streets late into the night. Some nights he didn't come home at all. My guess is he found all the places that Mrs. Allen and Uncle Clyde insisted I avoid. I never cared enough to find out. While he was up to all his old tricks, his biggest mistake was expecting we'd all snap into old roles, too.

The inevitable confrontation was sparked by something he said. For the first time in my life, I shouted back. I told him things were different now. Now he was in our home, crashing the life we'd built without him. He came at me with fists cocked and I stood my ground. *Bring it on.*

The balance of power had shifted. I stood six feet tall, more solid than scrawny. Dickie was six foot five, two inches taller than Eric. When Eric charged me, Dickie got between us. Dickie and I forced Eric into a back bedroom and delivered a message: "You put your hands on our mother one time, we're going to break both your arms and throw you out on the street." I ignored Eric the rest of my time in New York. He wasn't welcome at my graduation or the dinner at Stella D'oro with Mr. Stein and Mr. Katz.

Leaving New York to play baseball helped me escape. Still, this black cloud again hovered over my life.

At the end of my first season in the minors, the Twins invited me to Minnesota for 10 days.

While I wasn't on the roster, I got to do everything but play in games. Players and coaches all treated me like one of the guys. Second baseman Jerry Kindall even offered fielding advice.

I slept at the same hotel as visiting teams. The Yankees were one of the visitors. Fellow Panamanian Hector Lopez was still with them. When I introduced myself, he said he'd heard all about me. What a thrill that was.

I figured this taste of the big leagues put me on the fast track. So when I got sent to a Class A team in Orlando the next year, I was pissed.

My Orlando teammates razzed me for my sneak peek at life with the Twins. Just like I was once called my mother's "pet," now I was being referred to as "Calvin's bobo." Was this good-natured teasing or mean-spirited taunting? You can guess how it was interpreted by the angry young man I was back then.

So the kindling for an explosion was in place: I thought I was too good for Orlando and my teammates knew I thought it.

The match was lit one afternoon when I was out of the lineup because of a minor injury. I heard some of the white guys in the dugout accusing me of everything from being a lazy nigger to protecting my batting average. That did it. My fight-or-flight response was activated.

Rather than confront them, I reverted to acting like the scared boy in Gorgas Hospital hallucinating in the throes of rheumatic fever. I went into the clubhouse, packed my bags, and told general manager Bob Willis that I was leaving. I was quitting baseball. No way, he said—not on his watch.

He knew Calvin was fond of me. He wasn't about to be the one to call Minnesota and say I left. Bob also reminded me why Calvin was fond of me: I had major league talent. My skills just needed time to ripen.

In February 1966, I showed off my ripening skills at major league spring training.

Even though the Twins were coming off a trip to the World Series, I expected to make the team. Nope. Not only that, they sent me to Wilson—another Class A team. I stomped out of the clubhouse, sat on a big tree behind the field, and began sulking. Then company arrived. Calvin.

"I know you're saying that you've had better years the last two years than most of the guys that are getting promoted, and you're not getting promoted," he said. "But next year you're going to be my second baseman."

At the end of that season in Wilson, I played in the Florida Instructional League. Calvin was there, too, showering me with more praise. So when I arrived for spring training in 1967, I was both cautious and optimistic.

In my room, I kept a roster of everyone in camp. The list started with about 50 players. Only 28 would go north for the start of the season; after a month, three more would be cut. Each night, I put check marks next to the names of the 27 guys I thought would be joining me on the Opening Day roster.

Sam Mele—the manager who'd alertly gotten me out of the batter's box during my tryout at Yankee Stadium—was still in charge. Although he'd overseen a rise from 79 wins the season of my tryout (1964) to AL champions the next year, the Twins were coming off a second-place finish. There was speculation that at the first sign of trouble, Calvin would replace Sam with Billy Martin.

Billy had been a hard-nosed second baseman on some great Yankees teams. He was feisty on and off the field, and stars like Mickey Mantle and Whitey Ford loved him for it. His temper ultimately got the best of him, forcing him out of New York. His final several seasons as a player were for the Twins, then Calvin made him a scout. He found a pitcher for Calvin to sign. The kid wanted $50,000. Calvin refused. That's how the Orioles ended up landing Jim Palmer.

Calvin added Billy to Sam's staff in '65. Billy's insight and personality were a surge of electricity that helped turn a mediocre team into a great one. The Twins won 102 games, the most in franchise history, and reached the World Series for the first time since 1933, when they were the Washington Senators. Billy's specialties were coaching infielders and base runners. Shortstop Zoilo Versalles improved so much under Billy's tutelage that he won American League MVP. It's easy to see why everyone thought Calvin was grooming Billy to become manager.

Knowing his job might be on the line, Sam wasn't sure about trusting second base to a rookie. Then again, he knew bucking Calvin could be his last straw. The smart move was coaxing the best out of me.

At some point in the spring, Sam began standing behind me during practice, offering praise and encouragement. He also worked to bring me out of my shell, at least on the diamond. I don't know whether he knew about my blowup that nearly caused me to leave Orlando—or a similar, smaller episode in Wilson—but it also didn't take much to notice that I was a reluctant teammate.

"I want to hear you say something," Sam said. "Pull for the guy on the mound."

As spring went on, Sam's patience with me was tested by—of all things—my hitting.

Word got around that I could hit any fastball, no matter how fast or how well located. So pitchers gave me a steady diet of major league–caliber breaking balls. I whiffed 22 times in 23 games. I was so befuddled by the movement that most of the time I watched strike three float by.

At the time of final cuts, Sam wanted to send me down. I later learned that my name was sewn onto a jersey for the Class AAA Denver Bears. Although this was an era when managers had most of the say in determining the rosters, Calvin stepped in. He declared that I was ready. Billy brought me the good news—and the reminder that I was only guaranteed a month before the roster would be trimmed from 28 to 25.

As my emotions swirled, they included gratitude to Calvin. He backed up what he'd said to me under the tree the previous spring. Now I had to justify his support.

On April 11, 1967, the schedule had us in Baltimore for Opening Day against the reigning World Series champions. The Orioles won the title by sweeping the Dodgers, with Dave McNally throwing a four-hit shutout in the finale. Now McNally was on the mound again, facing us.

Sam told me the day before that I might be starting. Between nerves and excitement, I hardly slept. Sure enough, I was in the lineup, batting sixth.

In the bottom of the first, Frank Robinson hit a grounder up the middle, on my side of the bag. It would've taken a good backhanded snag to reach, and I wasn't up for the challenge. The hometown scorer gave him a hit, which was fine by me. I didn't want an error as the first mark of my career. That single helped start a four-run rally for the Orioles.

My first at-bat came in the top of the second, with two out and the bases empty. Sailing through the top of the lineup, pitching with a lead, facing a rookie susceptible to breaking balls, McNally threw a slider that probably wasn't his sharpest. I read it all the way and slapped it into center field for a clean single. Standing on first base, I watched the ball get thrown into the dugout for safekeeping.

At the end of my first week in the majors, I hit my first home run, a two-run shot in Detroit.

By the end of my second week, I'd earned a promotion to hitting second in the lineup.

In my 20th game, I went 5-for-5. That started a stretch of reaching base in 11 straight plate appearances. Someone else would lose a roster spot on the final cut. If they hadn't already unstitched my name from that jersey in Denver, it was time to do so.

In July, I batted second in the All-Star Game at Angel Stadium. I shared the same locker room as Mickey Mantle, Frank Robinson, and Brooks Robinson. I was on the same field with Hank Aaron, Willie Mays, and Roberto Clemente, practically the patron saint of Latino ballplayers.

As for the Twins, we were right at .500 in June when Calvin decided it was time to make a change. He fired Sam, as expected. But he didn't hand the reins to Billy. He went with another coach, Cal Ermer. It worked, too. We arrived in Boston for the final two games of the regular season holding a one-game lead over the Red Sox.

These were the days before division play. The World Series was still the only round of the postseason. So we went into this series needing one win to be crowned American League champions and to advance straight to the World Series.

In the first inning of the opener, I sliced a ball down the third-base line for a sure double. Except third baseman Jerry Adair snared it. We lost 6–4, leaving the teams tied for first place.

The next day, the winner-take-all finale, was my 22nd birthday. I made outs my first three times up but had a chance to make up for it in the ninth inning. I came to the plate with none out and a man on first. We were trailing 5–3, so I represented the tying run.

I grounded into a double play. The next guy also grounded out, ending our season.

I finished the year batting .292 despite having battled stomach problems and hemorrhoids and having left for two weeks in August to fulfill my military obligation. I was named the American League Rookie of the Year, getting 19 of the 20 first-place votes.

All in all, it was a great way to start my career, validating both my confidence and Calvin's support. And, I figured, if we could get this close to the World Series my rookie season, it would only be a matter of time until we broke through.

Everyone warned me about a "sophomore slump." They said pitchers would have a better idea of what to throw me and I'd have to adjust. I'd have to prove myself all over again.

That season, 1968, also turned out to be the "Year of the Pitcher," when hurlers were so dominant that the league later lowered the mound to give us hitters more of a chance. Only one player in the entire American League batted over .300— Carl Yastrzemski, at .301.

I hit .273, which would go down as the worst of my entire career. One of the lowlights came in June. After putting in my two weeks with the Marines, I struggled in my first three games back. Cal decided I needed more time to get acclimated, so he kept me out of the lineup. I was about to start the All-Star Game again, and this guy wasn't letting me start for my own team? That activated my flight response.

We were in Cleveland, and I went to my hotel room and started packing. A reporter heard about this and a story went out saying I was ditching the club. But I never left. I calmed down in time to return to the clubhouse long before the first pitch. I apologized to Cal and my teammates. My words weren't enough for Cal, though.

I watched from the bench as we failed to score off Indians starter Luis Tiant. However, the Indians couldn't score off us, either. We went into the 10th inning in a scoreless tie. Cal had plenty of chances to let me pinch hit. He knew I'd done well against Tiant before. He refused. We lost 1–0. Reporters asked why he didn't use me. He called it my punishment. I think Cal punished the team. That kind of summed up our season. We slumped from the verge of the World Series to a losing record. Cal was fired. This time, Calvin turned to Billy.

Billy and I got along great from the day we met. I think he liked the challenge of settling my shaky glove and turning me into a more disciplined base runner. He knew I had the skills to be an all-around player; I just needed someone like him to refine them.

Billy believed in his way of doing things. If you didn't like it, well, he didn't give a damn. One of his rules was being account-able. If you messed up, say so. I learned this early on, when he was helping me smooth the kinks out of my fielding. Whining about a bad bounce wasn't going to fix anything. There were to be no alibis. I had to admit my specific mistake—playing the wrong bounce, not getting my glove down all the way, etc.—before he would tell me how to do it better. He had a great BS detector, too. If I tried to pull something over on him, he'd bite my head off. Thus, our relationship was built on trust.

In spring training 1969, with Billy now in charge, he challenged me to reshape my game. So what if I was a two-time All-Star?

Learning second base from him was like going to graduate school. He worked tirelessly to help me improve at turning the double play. He would throw me the ball in different spots and correct my footwork. We also talked through pretty much every situation; I'd tell him how I would handle it, and he would tell me if there was a better way. He also wanted to change my approaches to hitting and base running. While we were at it, he thought I could become a better teammate.

"Listen to me," he said. "You work hard and I really believe in you. You're going to be a great player. But you have to do something about your personality. Stop being a yo-yo—up and down, up and down."

Yes, the hotheaded Billy Martin thought *I* was a head case. I could only laugh.

I knew that Billy was right about needing to change my swing.

After hitting eight home runs as a rookie, I began thinking about muscling up more—you know, to be like the kid who hit bombs in a tryout at Yankee Stadium. How'd that work out for me? I hit zero homers in '68 and saw my average sink. Billy reminded me that on a team with Harmon Killebrew and Tony Oliva, my job wasn't to provide the thump. As the second hitter in the lineup, my job was to get on base so Harmon and Tony could drive me in. Billy wanted me to hit the ball where it was pitched, knocking it from foul line to foul line, aiming for gaps, not the stands. He also wanted me to become a better bunter. With my speed, there was no telling how many hits I could scratch out. Even the threat of bunting would help. Fielders on the corners would play in, giving me more room to shoot line drives and hard grounders past them.

Billy had one more trick in mind: stealing home.

Nobody in the majors had routinely done that since Jackie Robinson. But Billy had been plotting this since becoming Sam's third-base coach in 1965. He noticed that most pitchers ignored runners on third. Lefties already had a tough time paying attention because their back was to third base. While righties looked directly at the runner, many were so sure the guy was staying put that they went to a full windup. Pulling this off was simply a matter of picking the right time against the right pitchers.

Everything Billy said made sense. I was ready for all of it, especially daring dashes toward home. I thought about Jackie doing it in perhaps the most famous play of his career. In Game 1 of the 1955 World Series, he slid in under a pitch from Whitey Ford to Yogi Berra, prompting Yogi to jump up and down in disbelief that Jackie was called safe. You know who else howled about that call? The guy playing second base for the Yankees that day—Billy Martin.

Thinking about that play wasn't all that heightened my fondness for Jackie. Better still was meeting him.

It happened at an offseason event. I walked up, reached to shake his hand, and introduced myself as Rod Carew, second baseman for the Twins. Taking my hand, he looked me in the eye and said, "I know about you."

Hector Lopez saying that was pretty cool. Being selected for two All-Star Games was better still. Nothing, though, could top being acknowledged like that by the man whose face was on the baseball cards I had admired every night and every morning, the player who inspired me to paint 42 on my favorite broomstick bat, the man whose life story was so meaningful to me and every black athlete. To this day, thinking about him saying those words still gives me goose bumps.

"You made it so I could be here," I said. "I am from this little country, but you were always in my heart. I've always thought about you."

Surely he'd heard this countless times. Still, he flashed his warm, wonderful smile, and my heart swelled with pride.

4

COLLECTING
SILVER BATS

BEFORE BILLY BEGAN reshaping my swing, he gave me something: a new bat.

The first thing I noticed was the thick handle.

Then I lifted it. This bat was heavy.

"I don't like it," I said.

"Oh yeah?" Billy said with a sly smile. "Look at the name on it."

Jackie Robinson.

He got me. Now I had to at least give it a try.

Billy knew the heftier lumber would slow my swing. Instead of creating a big looping arc to the plate, I'd have to be shorter, more controlled.

Sure enough, the Jackie model bat broke me of my bad habits. I began consistently sending balls into the spaces between

fielders—only now, in 1969, I was doing it more often. I hit
.332 and won my first batting title.

However, my more memorable contribution to baseball
history this season was reviving the straight steal of home.

––––––––––––

Stealing home was once common enough that Lou Gehrig did
it 15 times and Babe Ruth did it 10 times. By the late 1960s,
it had become a lost art.

The risk-reward wasn't worth it. You've already made
it three-fourths of the way to a run; why take a chance with
those final 90 feet? It had become so forgotten that batters
hardly knew what to do when a teammate came barreling
down the line. That was among my biggest worries. I didn't
want to run into anyone's legs or, worse, the friendly fire of
their swing. So we came up with a system. If I was stealing
home, I touched my belt. The hitter would acknowledge that
he knew I was coming by touching his helmet.

We talked about this so much that we could hardly wait to
try it. My first attempt came in the second game of the season.

We were in Kansas City, facing Roger Nelson, a righty
whose long limbs earned him the nickname "Spider." The
game was tied at 2 in the top of the fifth inning. I led off
with a double and moved to third on a fly ball. Me at third
with one out and Harmon at the plate was normally a good
enough situation. A steal of home was the last thing Spider
Nelson expected.

In the clips I'd seen of Jackie, he took a big lead from third
then danced back and forth, as if warning the pitcher. Billy

recommended I take a slow, walking lead that built momentum in the right direction without drawing any attention. Then I had to time my break. If all went well, I would be a few strides down the line before the pitcher realized what I was doing. The longer it took him to notice, the easier it was to score. Against Spider, I made it easily.

A week later, we were at home against the Angels. With two out in the bottom of the seventh, I was again on third with Harmon at the plate. What made this such a great opportunity was the man on the mound: Hoyt Wilhelm, a 46-year-old knuckleballer. He'd been pitching in the majors since 1952. Of the hundreds, maybe thousands, of runners who'd reached third against him, I was probably one of a handful to take off for home against him. I scored again, tying the game. But there was more to this play.

Even though Harmon had tapped his helmet to indicate he knew I was coming, he immediately forgot. He probably remembered when he saw Wilhelm's reaction. Harmon got out of the way in time, but when he got to the dugout, he copped to his lapse. Our teammates weren't about to let it go. When I got to my locker the next day, someone left a cardboard cutout of a tombstone. It read, "Here lies the body of Rod Carew, lined to left by Killebrew." While Harmon laughed, he also spent the next three days telling me how sorry he was. Over the years, it grew into one of those memories we shared every time we were together.

My next steal of home came in Seattle against the Pilots, and it showed how brazen we'd become: the bases were loaded. When I scored, Tony went to third and Harmon swiped second—a triple steal. The stolen base for Harmon was especially notable: he had only one across the previous six seasons.

Now the season was 20 games old and I'd stolen home three times. It had gone from a fluke to a trend, something teams needed to fear whenever I got to third. I still felt like I had the advantage because of how I was picking my spots. The next choice was easy. I just followed Cesar Tovar. Facing Mickey Lolich in Detroit, Tovar was so itching to run that he flustered Lolich into a balk, then stole third. After I walked, Tovar broke for home and I took second. Lolich still wasn't holding me close, so I stole third. And on the very next pitch, home.

In June, we pulled off another triple steal, this time humiliating the Yankees. Against the Angels, Tony and I had fun with a pair of double steals, taking me to third and home. That was my sixth steal of home, matching what was thought to be Ty Cobb's American League record for an entire season. (Years later, researchers determined Cobb had eight in 1912. Their work also found that six came on the back end of a double steal. That means he didn't take off for home until the ball was thrown to second base. Mine were all straight steals of home.)

On July 16, at home against the White Sox, we were up 3–2 in the second inning with the bases loaded. No way we'd try this stunt again, right? That's what pitcher Jerry Nyman thought. He went into the full windup and I nabbed number seven, matching Pete Reiser of the 1946 Brooklyn Dodgers for what was thought to be the single-season record.

I didn't try going again until early September. We were in Chicago facing the White Sox. With the bases loaded and lefty

Tommy John on the mound, I dashed home to try breaking the tie with Reiser. I didn't make it.

My final attempt came in the last week of the season. We were in Seattle and a rookie right-hander named Skip Lockwood was making his third career start. Skip would go on to graduate from MIT, so he was a smart guy. But I caught him in a lapse of concentration. I had a great jump and beat the throw. The problem was, I went in with a hook slide that took out home-plate umpire Jim Honochick. He had no way of seeing what happened. Instead of asking another ump for help, Honochick declared that catcher Jerry McNertney kept me from touching home. I showed him a pattern in the dirt that proved my toes crossed the plate. He didn't care. Disgusted, I threw my helmet. That did it; Honochick threw me out of the game. It was the first ejection of my career. The next day, McNertney told me I was safe—not because of my foot, but because he never tagged me.

Here's the odd thing about my thefts in 1969. I stole a total of 19 bases that season. That means only 12 times did I snag the traditional bags, second and third.

I finished my career with 17 steals of home, two shy of Jackie's career total and nowhere near Cobb's record of 54. Now that's a record that will never be broken.

There was one more mad dash in 1969 that I'll never forget.

The buildup began when my sister Dorine called with word that Eric was causing problems for my mother again. I thought about how bad it must've been for Dorine to bring it to my attention in the middle of a season. Soon, I could hardly think of anything else. In the dugout, in the on-deck circle—even in the batter's box—I found myself thinking about what that jerk might be doing to my sweet mom. Finally, I couldn't take it anymore.

I grounded out, returned to the dugout, and kept going. I went into the clubhouse, took off my uniform, and got into the shower. I was in fight-*and*-flight mode, ready to bolt to New York and put that bully in his place.

Someone alerted Billy. He was in the clubhouse when I got out of the shower. We hotheads got into a screaming match. He rightly asked what the hell I was doing.

"Personal problem," I said. "Gotta go."

"Lock the door," Billy told a clubhouse attendant.

I refused to share any details. When Billy saw me shaking, he said I should go. I went to the hotel and called my mom. She insisted that I stay with the team. After a sleepless night, I returned to the clubhouse. I apologized to Billy and explained what was happening. He told me he understood. He also told me something I'd heard from many people I trusted: I needed to stop holding everything in; I needed to discuss what I was thinking and feeling with people who I knew cared about me. If I stopped treating everyone like the enemy, I might realize they could help.

I knew he was right, but I wasn't ready to let my guard down.

Something else good came from this ordeal. I began keeping closer tabs on my mother. When she told me that Eric moved into his own apartment, I breathed easier. I begged her to never let him move back in. It wasn't long until he tried. She refused. They never lived under the same roof again.

———————

Every button Billy pushed that season seemed to be the right one. Consider Harmon. His numbers were turbocharged: 49 homers and 140 RBIs, both the most in the majors. He even had eight steals, by far the most of his career. He was the runaway winner of the American League MVP award.

The best impact came in the standings. We won 97 games, which was 18 more than the previous year.

This was the first season of division play, and we were the runaway winners of the new American League West. The Orioles won a whopping 109 games to claim the East. Under the old format, they would've advanced to the World Series. Under this system, we had a best-of-five chance to take them down. But in the inaugural American League Championship Series, we hardly put up any resistance. Baltimore swept us. Still, had there been a Manager of the Year Award back then, Billy would've won it. That's why what happened next was so stunning. Calvin fired him.

Although Billy clearly could teach and inspire his players, and he came up with strategies that caught opponents flat-footed, he couldn't control his temper. And Calvin couldn't tolerate that. He hadn't let Billy replace Sam Mele in '67 as punishment for an incident the previous season. Billy punched out traveling secretary Howard Fox during a squabble involving a hotel room key. This time, Billy had to pay for punching out pitcher Dave Boswell outside a bar in

Detroit. It happened in August. Writers covered up things like that in those days, but the story eventually hit the papers. When it did, Calvin said he was fining Billy $600 and that was the end of it. If indeed Calvin had let that go, then the final straw might have been Billy starting reliever Bob Miller in Game 3 against Baltimore instead of Calvin's preference, Jim Kaat. Whatever the reason, the punishment didn't fit the crime.

I couldn't believe Calvin would do this to Billy—or to the rest of us. It reminded me of Cal Ermer refusing to let me pinch hit against Luis Tiant, a decision that punished the team that night. Only this was far worse. Fans were outraged, too. Many said they would never buy a ticket again.

———————

Heading into the 1970s, I'd already become an All-Star regular and was now a batting champion. I'd even gotten some votes for MVP. The steals of home raised my profile, too. At 24, I was being mentioned among the game's bright young stars, along with guys like Tom Seaver and Reggie Jackson.

About six weeks into the 1970 season, my bat was sizzling. I carried a .411 average into a game against the Royals. I opened with a single and followed with a solo home run. A double in my next at-bat left me a triple shy of the cycle. You hear that phrase all the time—"all he needs is a triple"— and it's like a joke because triples are so rare.

Tiant was my teammate now, and he told me, "You've got a chance to do this. Don't slow down. If you slow down, I'll kick your butt." Doing as El Tiante said, I got a triple. I'm well aware that a cycle is a quirky thing. Still, I was happy to add it to my career resume. I later learned that it was the first in Twins history, and the first by a Hispanic player; not even the great Roberto Clemente had done it.

A month later, we started a series in Milwaukee. I was hitting .376 when I stepped in for my first at-bat. The Brewers were well aware of my hot start because I was 10-for-20 against them this season. Catcher Phil Roof greeted me at home plate with congratulations for the roll I was on. He said he hoped I could stay healthy to keep it going.

In the bottom of the fourth, Mike Hegan was on first when Mike Hershberger hit a grounder to Harmon at third. Harmon fired to me at second to start the double play. Among my well-established woes as a fielder, my biggest weakness was turning the double play. But it wasn't my footwork that failed me this time. In fact, I threw the ball in time to get Hershberger out at first and got out of Hegan's way. Hegan, however, was more interested in sliding into me than the base. I later heard that Brewers manager Dave Bristol had urged his guys to go after me because I was wearing out their pitchers. This was Hegan's chance and he took it.

There's a difference between a hard slide and playing dirty. This crossed that line. He slid late and hard, spikes up. Those sharp metal teeth bit into my right knee. His foot twisted, shredding cartilage and ligaments. I fell onto my back, screaming. Umpire Jake O'Donnell took one look at the damage and vomited.

"Just stay there, Rod," Jake said. "You're going to be all right."

I tried to move and felt a crunching sensation. By the time we got to the clubhouse, my knee was so swollen that the trainer had to cut off my pants.

Sports medicine in 1970 was caveman-like compared with today. Nowadays, a player would be rushed into surgery by a team of elite surgeons at a nearby facility. My biggest accommodation was a first-class plane ticket so I'd have more room for my leg on the flight back to Minneapolis. Team doctor Harvey O'Phelan repaired what he could and removed what he couldn't.

I awoke fearing that my leg had been amputated. I was in enough pain to wish it had been. I caught an infection that revived some old bugaboos—hallucination-inducing fevers. Dr. O'Phelan said the damage was severe enough that my career could be over. I was coming to grips with all this when two things happened: I was again chosen to start the All-Star Game, and AL president Joe Cronin visited my hospital room to present me with the Silver Bat Award for having led the league in hitting in 1969. Can you imagine trying to celebrate your top on-field feat at the same time as wondering whether you'll ever get back on the field?

Hegan sent a note apologizing. Sort of. He said he was sorry I got hurt, but not sorry for trying to break up the play. His words meant as little as the handshake from the guys in Leesburg who called me "coon." While I'll give Hegan the benefit of the doubt that he didn't intend to gore me, he knew he was risking it by choosing to take a cheap shot.

Getting over this injury was quite a test. Would my knee hold up? If so, would I be confident enough to turn a double play again? In dark moments, I considered going to school for engineering. A fleeting thought in childhood seemed like a possible career path if I could no longer play baseball. Sometimes I turned the fear into fuel—I'd come too far to let this stop me. I also drew strength from my mother's words that continued to echo in my mind: "God is there for you. He's always going to be there. He's going to take care of you."

Even without me, the Twins were cruising to the playoffs again.

Bill Rigney was our manager, and he would guide us to 96 wins and another division title. Wanting to join the fun also spurred my rehab. I was proud to be back on the field three months to the day after the injury. I pinch hit, grounding out to third and hobbling up the base line. I clearly wasn't the same player and could only hope this was because my scars were still fresh.

Rigney limited me to four at-bats over the final week of the season. We again played the Orioles in the ALCS. They stomped us in all three games. With nothing to lose, Rigney let me pinch hit in two of the blowouts. I flied out and struck out.

Given a full offseason to heal, I showed up to spring training in 1971 eager to see how my knee would hold up. Sure enough, it was back to normal. Now I had to resolve things between my ears. Could I still be a competent pivot man turning the double play? In a league filled with guys more intimidating than Mike Hegan, would I stand my ground to make the play? We'd have to wait and see.

Once again turning conventional wisdom on its head, I started the season with more problems at the plate than in the field.

I turned a double play before I got a hit. In fact, I started the season by hitting into 14 straight outs. I told the guys that I would kiss the base when I finally earned my way on. The breakthrough was a double, so I gave second base at White Sox Park a little smooch. That cracked everyone up.

About a month later, I was still struggling at the plate when I botched an easy turn of a double play. Rigney—who played more than 200 games at second base during his big-league career—was waiting for me in the dugout. In a tirade that would've made Billy Martin proud, Rigney said I needed to make that play or he'd find someone else who would. Problem was, Rigney was no Billy Martin. When Billy barked, I knew it was because he cared about me. This guy? Please.

Surely Rigney had gotten spiked, or worse, when turning a double play. So he either should've been sympathetic or had some tips on how to endure it. But in all our time at spring training—when questions loomed about my readiness to turn the double play again—he never came out on the practice fields and worked with me. Sam Mele was never a second baseman, but at least he stepped onto the practice fields to try building my confidence when I needed it.

After this game, I went to Rigney's office to talk more. This was no longer about the play at second. Now it was about him belittling me in front of my teammates. I made it clear that it better not happen again.

In years past, a run-in like this would've prompted me to flee. Instead, our verbal sparring ended with a promise. I told Rigney that even though I was hitting in the .230s now, I'd finish the season in the top 10.

Rigney kept riding me hard. In June, he forced me to play two games at third base.

But you know what? I hiked my average to .307, finishing fifth in the league. And in the coming years, it would continue to climb.

———————

I led the league in hitting in 1972, '73, and '74. My average rose from .318 to .350 to .364. My batting title in '72 came with a statistical novelty: I was the first batting champion not to hit a single home run since Brooklyn's Zack Wheat way back in 1918. Nobody has done it since, and the way people crush the ball these days, I doubt anyone else will join a club that includes only "Wee" Willie Keeler of the New York Giants in 1897, Wheat, and me. (Not a bad crew, considering we're also all part of another exclusive club: Hall of Famers.)

I remained a regular starter in the All-Star Game and among the vote-getters for MVP. These were meaningful because the Twins were stuck in neutral.

We broke even in '72 and '73, then were a measly one game above .500 in '74. Rigney got dumped during the '72 season. He was replaced by Frank Quilici, who'd been my teammate the first several years of my career.

Meanwhile, the business of baseball was changing.

Cardinals outfielder Curt Flood filed a lawsuit that broke the "reserve clause," which bound players to their teams for as long as the club wanted. This proved to be the first step toward free agency. Other changes came from the growing strength of our players union. Under the leadership of Marvin Miller, we went on strike at the start of the '72 season. For the first time, a walkout by players forced games to be scrapped—more than a week's worth. We returned after getting a deal that included the option of salary arbitration. This meant that if we didn't like how much the team wanted to pay us, and the team didn't want to pay what we wanted, then an impartial third party would decide which figure was more appropriate. Players build a case based on their statistics and the salaries of players with comparable stats. Teams build a case around everything you're not doing. The two sides clash in a hearing that turns people who are supposed to be friends into enemies. I know how heated it gets because I went through arbitration after the 1974 season.

My salary was $95,000—a very comfortable figure for a guy who grew up sleeping four to a room, two to a bed, in a poor neighborhood of a poor country. But that wasn't the point. My contemporaries who were perennial All-Stars and consistently leading the league in key categories—guys like Tom Seaver and Reggie Jackson, and the player whose game most matched mine, Pete Rose—were making in the range of $140,000. So that's what I wanted. The Twins started at $100,000 and went to $120,000.

Calvin sent to the hearing his son Clark, a vice president for the team, and George Brophy, the head of the farm system. They told the arbitrator I deserved their figure because I didn't hit enough home runs or drive in enough runs. This was a major cheap shot. I was a No. 2 hitter who'd molded his game to become a contact hitter for the benefit of the team. I wanted to get on base so Tony and Harmon could drive me in. Now I had a collection of silver bats proving I was the most consistent hitter in the league. Yet they pointed at my power stats? They might as well have said I didn't throw enough complete games. Actually, they made a similarly ridiculous claim by blaming me for the club not having reached the World Series. I was sitting right there as all this played out, too. I knew better than to say what I was thinking.

I wasn't the kind of person to go around talking about the Man keeping me down. I appreciated how much Calvin had done for me. But fair is fair. I have a strong code of what's right and what's wrong, and I knew everything the Twins said was very wrong. The arbitrator, though, fell for it. He ruled in their favor.

I guess saving $20,000 was worth the lousy way they made me feel. Finally able to speak my mind, I told reporters, "Now I know what kind of organization the Twins are. They don't consider me a superstar. I'm just a number."

Coincidence or not, the next year I set career highs for homers and RBIs. I still hit a robust .359, leading the American League for the fourth straight year, a feat last accomplished by Ty Cobb. Was it still my fault that we sank to fourth place in the division, winning only 76 games?

––––––––––

The bitterness in that statement is the angry young man speaking out. Only I wasn't so young anymore. A few days after the 1975 season ended, I turned 30.

5

BECOMING A MAN
THE RIGHT WAY

———————

WHEN I ARRIVED IN THE BIG LEAGUES, I was hotheaded and arrogant and proud of it. Those were the masks I wore to hide my insecurity.

Not about hitting a baseball, of course. I knew I could hit. What I didn't know was how to be an adult.

Luckily, I found myself in a clubhouse with two incredible role models: Tony Oliva and Harmon Killebrew.

When I broke in, Tony already had won two batting titles and Harmon was a four-time home run champion. Their skills alone commanded respect. Yet I gravitated to them because of qualities I hadn't encountered in many grown men.

Tony has never met a stranger. The warmth he exudes could light a cigar from the lush tobacco fields he grew up surrounded by in Cuba. He taught me things like how to knot a tie and where to eat on the road. Any question I had, about baseball or life, he answered. Sometimes he provided advice before I even realized I needed it.

Harmon only saw goodness in people. Raised on a farm in Idaho, he was the ultimate gentleman. His nickname, "Killer," was as accurate as a bald guy answering to "Curly." I always called him "Charlie" and he called me "Junior." It started my second season, when he decided he could no longer call me "Rook." Those terms of affection endured, symbolizing our fondness for each other.

My relationships with Tony and Harmon were different from the other father-figure types because of the dynamics. Mr. French and Uncle Clyde were kin. Ollie and Spoony were paid babysitters. These guys were my peers, my teammates. We won and lost together. We cherished good managers and endured bad ones. We griped about trades and laughed about things you had to be there to understand.

From my first glimpses of them in 1964, I studied the way they carried themselves when nobody was looking and when everyone was watching. I saw them treat clubhouse attendants and fans with the same kindness and respect they gave the commissioner of baseball. They were warm and caring in every situation.

"Junior," Harmon would often tell me, "it doesn't cost anything to be nice."

———————

It seems like Tony and I were fated to be pals, starting from the day I was given his No. 6 jersey for my tryout at Yankee Stadium.

He looked out for me later that year when I spent 10 days with the club in Minnesota. While I was in big-league spring training in '65, he made me feel welcome by including me in card games and locker-room conversations. The warmth continued in the spring of '66. Our relationship really took off in the spring of '67.

I was rooming with two other guys who often brought home women. I'd leave the room and wind up sleeping in the hotel lobby. Around 7:00 AM, the trainer would see me and say, "What are you doing here?" After hearing enough of my lame excuses, the trainer decided I needed a new room. Although Tony was established enough not to have a roommate, he let me move in. He also had a car—a Cadillac—and that opened up the town to me. Pretty soon, wherever Tony went, I followed.

Tony was a gusher of joy because he appreciated how far he'd come.

He grew up on a farm in Cuba. His father, Pedro, harvested tobacco and was known throughout the region for his skill rolling cigars. He'd been quite the baseball player, too. Pedro passed along his skills and insight to his four sons and six daughters.

Pedro loved baseball so much that he cut a diamond into his farm—à la the movie *Field of Dreams*. Every Sunday, locals gathered at the Oliva farm for pickup games. Tony broke into the lineup around the age of seven. By 15, he played alongside his dad in an adult league. Pedro worked to nurture and refine his son's talent.

Back then, Cuba was wide open to Americans. The Twins even had a scout who spent a big chunk of time on the island. He signed hundreds of players from there, several going on to great careers. He thought Tony could be next in that line. Tony signed in February 1961 and headed for spring training in Florida. Two months later, the Bay of Pigs invasion isolated Cuba from the United States. While Tony got out in time to chase his dream, the first steps were rough. The Deep South difficulties that I faced were a bigger challenge for him. Racist limits on where he could eat and sleep were jarring to someone who'd never grown up with such restrictions. He also was trying to learn English. (He still has a thick Cuban accent.) Tony being Tony, he rose above it all. Any scars on his soul went undetected.

Once I understood the depth of his character, I opened up to him. I explained the source of my anger and mistrust. He became the first person since my childhood pal Carlos Long to know how savagely my father abused me. He told me simple truths like, "You're a big-leaguer now," meaning I should leave the past in the past. There was even wisdom behind his insisting I learn how to knot a tie instead of loosening and tightening the same knot, as I'd been doing for months. "You don't have to go to work on the farm. You should look clean," he said. To this day, he puts me in my place by rolling his eyes and saying, "Roomie, you crazy."

Tony maintained an infectious smile no matter the circumstances. People would launch into conversations with him and he'd engage as if they were old friends. "Damn, Roomie, you know everyone," I'd say. Truth was, he often didn't—he just pretended that he did to make folks happy. Like Maya Angelou observed, people will forget what you did and said, but they'll always remember the way you made them feel. In the Twin Cities, there's another saying: if you don't have Tony's autograph or a picture with him, then it means you haven't tried.

I told Tony I could never be as accommodating as him. I hardly wanted to say hello to strangers. Still, my time around Tony softened me. It made me think, "If he can be this way all the time, maybe I can be this way at least some of the time." I wasn't ready to set my default to Tony-level friendliness, but I could at least twist the knob in that direction.

Mr. Personality taught me something else: toughness.

Don't let the smile fool you. This man has a deep reserve of grit and determination. I saw it up close for many years.

Tony tore up his right knee diving for a ball in 1971. Dr. O'Phelan wasn't as successful putting it back together as he'd been with mine. Tony was a casualty of that primitive generation of sports medicine. What probably would be fixed with an arthroscope today began a rapid decline. Tony lasted only five more seasons.

The way Tony forced himself through about 130 games a year from 1973 to '75 amazed me because I knew the extent of his pain. He'd moan and groan as he turned over in his sleep. Some nights, he could move so little that he cried. It hurts to see anyone you love suffer like that. It's even more difficult when that guy is known for his happiness. The impressive part went beyond his grinding it out through nine innings. Tony also put in several hours of work on his body before and after every game. There were all sorts of exercises to strengthen the muscles around the knee. There were massages and long stays in the whirlpool to loosen the ligaments and tendons. The part that made me laugh was his willingness to try every homemade remedy sent by fans. He was such an optimist that he thought each one might do the trick. He also bought every gizmo and gadget hyped to have healing powers.

Tony retired with nothing left in his legs, but plenty left in that sweet swing. That sense of "what might've been" lingered in the mind of sportswriters when Tony became eligible for the Hall of Fame. Voters dwelled more on the compromised back end of his career than his amazing heyday. I know longevity is a valued component of a player's candidacy and I can understand that he was dinged for it. But it shouldn't have knocked him out. Tony was no shooting star. In his first eight full seasons (1964–71), he was an All-Star every time. He was top three in hitting seven times, winning three batting titles. (The one year he didn't finish top three? He was eighth.) He led the league in hits five times and had the most doubles four times. He won a Gold Glove, was named Rookie of the Year, and was twice the runner-up for MVP. He was the first rookie ever to win a batting title; it's only been done once since, by Ichiro, who'd already established himself as a premier pro ballplayer in Japan. Tony was part of team success, too. The Twins went to the World Series and made two trips to the ALCS over his first eight years. They didn't make it back to the playoffs again until 1987, when they won the World Series. Guess who was the hitting coach on that team? Yep, Tony Oliva. He was the bench coach in '91 when they won it all again. By the way, even in those years when he hobbled around the bases, Tony averaged .279. His career average over 15 seasons landed at a stellar .304.

I can't say this strongly enough: Tony belongs on a plaque in Cooperstown. He deserves bonus points for all he's given to the game as an ambassador and a coach. Who do you think molded Kirby Puckett into a Hall of Famer? Even more recent players like Torii Hunter and Joe Mauer will tell you how much

Tony shaped their game. Ask Dave Winfield and Paul Molitor what Tony meant to them while growing up in Minnesota, then again as they played out their Hall of Fame careers on the Twins.

In 2014, I had the privilege of being among eight Hall of Famers who were part of the 16-member Golden Era Committee, one of the veterans' committees empowered to correct the biggest oversights from our generation. It took 12 votes to get in; Tony got 11. The selection process has changed. Our era is now reviewed only every five years. Tony will get another chance in December 2020. If he doesn't make it then, it wouldn't happen until December 2025.

I would love nothing more than for Tony to become my teammate again, this time on baseball's greatest roster. Regardless, he'll always be my roomie, my brother, my friend. He and his wife, Gordette, mean the world to Rhonda and me.

During his playing days, despite the distance and the difficulties, Tony remained close to his family. He found ways to get boxes of supplies and gifts back onto the island. He eventually brought his parents to visit. I loved meeting them. It was easy to see how much he was a reflection of them. When his siblings visited, there was no denying that they were all cut from the same cloth.

Seeing how Tony loved and supported his family made me try salvaging my relationship with my family. I ended up learning the hard way that only my mother loved me unconditionally.

Once I started making good money, I became very generous with my siblings. Yet no matter what I gave them, it was never enough. One time, Dickie visited me in Minnesota and I bought him a car, in part to help drive around our mom. He took it back to New York and, within a week, he sold it so he could pocket the cash. Then he wanted another car—after all, our mother still needed a ride. Mom saw things like this play out time and again. She understood why I remained distant from my siblings. She even encouraged me to live year-round in Minneapolis rather than being closer to her—and them—in New York.

Harmon and I only had one difference of opinion. And, boy, was it fun to argue about.

The issue: which of us could eat more ice cream.

By the looks of us, you'd think he would have a big advantage. But I was sneaky good. While plenty of star ballplayers throw back cases of beer or something stiffer, Harmon and I raced to the bottom of bowls of butter pecan and rum raisin.

Trips to ice cream parlors came later, after our relationship went deeper than teammates. That came following an incident already mentioned: the night in 1969 when I wanted to flee the team because Eric was again causing my mother problems. Later that night, Harmon tapped me on the shoulder and asked if we could talk. Once I was in the right frame of mind, we did. He asked, "Junior, why are you so mad at the world?" I'd been around him enough by now to appreciate his sincerity. I knew this was a man I could trust. So I told him about my father and he told me about his dad.

Harmon Sr.—who went by Clay—played fullback in college and for the Wheeling (West Virginia) Steelers in the early days of pro football before settling down in Payette, Idaho. He shared his given name with the youngest of his five kids. Harmon grew up to become a natural athlete like his dad.

They were both short, stocky, powerful. The two were close. When Harmon was 16, Clay died of a heart attack.

Harmon was headed to the University of Oregon to play football and baseball when a U.S. Senator from Idaho talked up the teen prodigy to a buddy in Washington, D.C. The friend was Clark Griffith, Calvin's uncle. This was the 1950s and Clark owned the Washington Senators, the club that would move to Minnesota and become the Twins.

Clark sent a scout to Payette. He arrived in time to see Harmon crush a home run more than 400 feet. Smitten, the scout gave the teen a contract lucrative enough for him to be declared a "bonus baby." That meant Harmon had to spend two years on the big-league roster before he could go to the minors. He was only 18 and fresh from the farm when he played his first game in 1954. He needed seasoning, but the rules wouldn't let him get it. Once he did, it took so long for him to pick up where he'd left off that he was being labeled a bust. Then came May 1959. Harmon hit 11 home runs in 17 games. He went on to hit a league-leading 42 home runs with 105 RBIs that season. Two years later, the franchise moved to Minnesota and Harmon clubbed 46 homers and drove in 122 runs. He was even better the next year.

In my rookie season, he bashed a league-best 44 homers, including one of the longest blasts I've ever seen. It came at home—Metropolitan Stadium in Bloomington, Minnesota—off Lew Burdette of the Angels. I was on second base and knew from the crack of the bat that this connection was something special. They measured it at 522 feet. The chair it hit was painted red to commemorate the feat. In batting practice, we'd look out there and marvel at it. The stadium is long gone, but the seat is still on display in roughly the same place it used to be. That spot is now inside the Nickelodeon Universe area within the Mall of America. If you're ever there, look up over the Log Chute ride and you'll see it.

I can attest to the strength of Harmon's arms because of the time he used them on me.

It was 1971, the night when Rigney met me at the dugout steps to chew me out for failing to turn a double play. I probably would've punched him had it not been for Harmon's grip. I tried going after Rigney a few more times and Harmon always held me back. It got to a point where Harmon could see me take an angry step toward Rigney and stop me in my tracks with one harshly spoken word: "Junior!"

Harmon and I were both in awe of the way Tony connected with everyone. We were both introverts. But Harmon understood that interacting with fans and media was part of his job. Rather than remain uncomfortable, he figured he might as well make the most of it. He went so far as to become a broadcaster. Knowing how he felt about putting himself out there, this really left an impression on me. I asked him how he could flip being in the spotlight from painful to positive. He said, "Just think that those people had a bad day at their job and you can be the one to put a smile on their face."

So Harmon was a big-hearted guy with the strength of a superhero. It's the perfect formula for someone fans should worship. For many years, they did. But in his final three seasons with us, the paying customers forgot all the highlights. They booed him mercilessly. Yet it bothered me more than him. I asked how he could tune it out, and he said: "You take it as it goes. I have a job to do. I know I'm going to strike out some and I know I'm going to hit some home runs." That was it. On the days when my fielding brought boos, I tried to remember the grace he showed.

Harmon played his final season in Kansas City. The Twins tried cashing in on his first trip back by holding a Harmon Killebrew Day. Fans were still so unappreciative that only about 14,000 people turned out. The no-shows missed seeing him rise to the occasion by smacking a homer in the first inning. You're not supposed to cheer for your opponent, so I hope nobody saw me grinning as he rounded the bases.

He finished his career with 573 home runs, fifth most in baseball history at the time he retired. In 1984, he became the first Twins player inducted into the Hall of Fame. As with Tony and me, his number is retired and there's a statue of him outside Target Field.

Over the years, I kept in touch regularly with Tony. With Harmon, it was more sporadic. Still, we had the kind of relationship where we could always pick up where we left off, no matter how long we'd been apart. In May 2011, I knew our time together was running out. Esophageal cancer was getting the best of him. One day, Rhonda and I decided to drive to his house in Arizona. His son greeted us at the door and said Harmon wasn't doing well. We understood and said we'd go to a hotel and come back tomorrow. We were about to drive away when his son came running out to our car. When Harmon learned we were there, he said he wanted to see us.

I stood by him, holding his hands, as we shared memories and laughs. Once I noticed him nodding off, I said it was time to go. He sat up, gave me a hug and said, "I love you, Junior." I replied, "Charlie, I will always love you, too." I promised we'd come back in the morning. Around 6:00 AM, we got a call at our hotel. Harmon died overnight.

A few weeks later, the Twins held a memorial service at Target Field. His family asked me to speak. I told the crowd: "Harmon Killebrew had a big heart. He loved people, loved treating people the right way, and he respected everyone. I tried to model myself after Harmon Killebrew, that's how much he meant to me. That's how much he allowed me to grow up as a person, and that's why to this day, I always give a helping hand to people who are in need, because of Harmon's hard work and dedication to helping others."

It's easy to see why Tony and I clicked—two dark-skinned, Spanish-speaking, left-handed-hitting line-drive hitters who bore enough resemblance that I wore Tony's uniform for my tryout and who, to this day, are sometimes confused for each other by fans. But Harmon and me? I can only say I was blessed to have had him in my life.

———

At my second All-Star Game—1968, in Houston—Roberto Clemente was looking for me.

"Tony tells me you're going to be a great player," he said. "I want you to help the Latinos when they come to the big leagues."

The code among baseball players is to always look after the next generation. Someone helped you on the way up, so you need to do the same. But I was 22, still so combustible that I was barely able to help myself. I was a kid still in need of mentoring—and here was the great Clemente asking me to be a mentor.

"All the young Latin players that are going to be following us, when you get a chance, try and teach them," Roberto continued. "They're coming from different countries, with different customs. Take care of them. Take them for a meal. Always talk to them."

Those words, from that man, carried a great deal of weight. They also echoed what I had heard years before from General Torrijos.

If the most powerful man in Panama and the most respected Latino ballplayer both thought I had what it took to be a role model, then there must be something to it. They saw something in me that I didn't see in myself.

In October 1972, Jackie Robinson died from complications of diabetes. On New Year's Eve 1972, Roberto died in a plane crash while ferrying supplies from his native Puerto Rico to the survivors of an earthquake in Nicaragua. To his final breath, he was looking after Latinos in a different country.

This being the offseason, I had time to think about these men and what they meant, to the world and to me.

I realized it would take many people to fill the void they left behind. Now that I was 27 and established in the big leagues, maybe I could help. Maybe I could muster some of Tony's warmth and Harmon's strength and put myself out there more. Maybe I could make the world at least a little better place. *Junior, it doesn't cost anything to be nice.*

The Twins had been encouraging me to go to more events, and now I was willing, especially if I could spend time with the people who I could relate to most: kids who were sick in hospitals or who had been abused.

You've never seen kids light up like when when a big-leaguer pops into their room to say hi and play cards. I enjoyed it so much that sometimes on the road I would visit children's hospitals.

One day in Minneapolis, I went into the room of a boy who was about 11 and had been severely burned in a fire. He was crying in agony as nurses treated his wounds. Then he saw me. "I'm sorry that I'm crying, Mr. Carew, but it hurts. Don't be mad at me," he said. Can you believe that? He was worried about how his pain was affecting me. We spent about an hour together and he kept apologizing. The next time I visited him, I had better timing. "I'm happy today. I'm happy to see you and I'm not crying anymore!" he said. Another boy I visited several times was so sweet and so brave. He kept telling me, "I'm not afraid of dying, Mr. Carew. I'm going to be with God." When he went to be with God, his parents called me and said, "You know how much our son loved you," then asked if I was okay with them burying him in one of my jerseys. I told them I'd be honored.

In 1971, baseball began recognizing players for their contribution to society by creating the Commissioner's Award. Two years later, after the plane crash, it was renamed the Roberto Clemente Award. I won it in 1977, and it remains among my proudest accomplishments. The proof can be found in my living room. I have a single, small trophy case, and this award remains in a prominent spot because of who and what it represents.

Also on those shelves is a medal called the Order of Vasco Núñez de Balboa. The head of Panama gives it out for distinguished diplomatic services. In 1975, General Torrijos presented it to me.

There's a postscript to my relationship with General Torrijos.

In 2004, his son Martín was sworn in as president of Panama. President George W. Bush called and asked me to join Secretary of State Colin Powell as part of the U.S. delegation at the ceremony. Powell was beloved in my native country for having led the U.S. invasion of Panama, the 1989 attack that deposed dictator Manuel Noriega, who'd taken over two years after General Torrijos left power. When Martín saw me, he gave me a big hug and whispered in my ear, "My dad really loved you." I told him the feeling was mutual.

Moments like these made me take stock of my life.

I knew I was far from figuring out my place in the world. But I also knew that by following the lead of Roberto and Jackie, Tony and Harmon, I was getting closer.

My mother always told me I was special. Once I reached the majors and became Rookie of the Year, an All-Star, and a batting champion, I figured that's what she meant. Once I began stepping out of my comfort zone and connecting with people, I understood the larger truth of my mother's declaration. Being special didn't mean the ability to hit a ball with a stick. It was taking the platform created by my ability to hit a ball with a stick and using that to make a difference in the lives of others—that's the special part. That was God's plan for me.

I must admit, I also discovered some selfish pleasure from doing this—putting a smile on someone else's face could put a smile on mine, too. And it wasn't only the happy occasions.

Although I cried when those parents asked to bury their son in my jersey, and I felt terrible that they'd never get to see him play another game in his Little League jersey, I took solace in knowing that watching me play and then meeting me had provided him—and his parents—with a measure of joy when they needed it most. That happened again at the funeral. Everyone looking into the casket saw him wearing a No. 29 Twins jersey and smiled, knowing his final wish was fulfilled. I also believed he'd be wearing that jersey when, as he told me, he went to meet God.

I'm no Bible thumper or quoter of Scripture. But I am driven by my faith. I haven't brought up God much in discussing my career because it hasn't been appropriate quite yet. We've been talking about games where there are winners and losers. In that context, I think it's wrong to suggest that God has a preference.

Still, throughout my rise in baseball, I felt His presence, best expressed in the echoes of my mother's words: "God is there for you. He's always going to be there. He's going to take care of you."

I believe each of us is born in God's image and has a purpose to fulfill. Some find it, some don't. Some don't even look. I bring this up now to credit my role models for steering me to these answers.

———————

At this point of my life, in the 1970s—in my twenties and early thirties—I still felt most comfortable behind my hard outer shell. But it was softening and sometimes coming down.

I got married. Although we later divorced, I became the father of three beautiful daughters: Charryse, Stephanie, and

Michelle. Because my first wife was Jewish, we raised the girls in her faith.

As my father-in-law was dying, he gave me a Chai, a gold pendant featuring two Hebrew letters representing the word "life." It's widely considered a Jewish good-luck charm. I wore it around my neck for many years, including during ballgames. The combination of the jewelry and partaking in my family's Jewish rituals fanned the flames on the theory that I was Jewish.

This is a good time to set the record straight.

I never converted.

I embraced Judaism. I appreciated the heritage and traditions. I gladly attended seders, bar and bat mitzvahs, and other Jewish events. As a black man who grew up in segregated Panama and endured more racism in the Deep South, I understood the intolerance and persecution that Jews have suffered. I especially agreed with the Jewish community's emphasis on social justice—the belief that, as Jackie said, "A life is not important except in the impact it has on other lives." And even though I considered converting, I never did.

I also considered becoming a U.S. citizen and never did.

Different though these may seem, there are parallels.

Religious affiliation and nationality are more than labels. They're part of your identity, to yourself as much as to the rest of the world. When I looked in the mirror, I saw a Christian who was Panamanian. Still do.

Besides, why "switch teams," so to speak, when I had the best of both worlds?

As a permanent resident in the U.S., I had nearly all the benefits of citizenship. As the husband and father in a Jewish family, I was essentially a permanent resident in Judaism.

I believe a prayer to God is a prayer to God, regardless of whether it's said while wearing a yarmulke in a synagogue or bare-headed in a church, regardless of whether that conversation occurs while reading the Old Testament or the New Testament. To me, religion is my one-on-one relationship with God. I know He is there for me and He knows I believe in Him. That's all that matters.

The fact I never converted probably surprises and even disappoints many people.

It sure stunned Adam Sandler when I told him.

Sandler has been singing about me since the 1994 episode of *Saturday Night Live* when he introduced "The Chanukah Song." If you're not familiar with it, he humorously rhymes the names of famous people from all walks of life, connecting the dots between them and his faith.

O.J. Simpson? Not a Jew.
But guess who is?
Hall of Famer Rod Carew.
(pause)
He converted.

Many years after the song came out, I visited a Hollywood studio to see a friend who was producing a TV show. Sandler was filming something on a nearby set. He saw me and came over to say hello. We had a nice conversation. I thanked him for including me in the song and told him he got the details about me wrong. He laughed. It seemed like he believed me, but he didn't change the song.

I guess he didn't want to mess with a good shtick.

6

CHASING .400

———

IN 1975, a nagging hamstring injury was slowing me and worrying me. My brother-in-law recommended I see a friend of his, a hypnotist named Harvey Misel. He worked with athletes on the mind-body connection. Maybe he could help me, too.

Talking to Dr. Misel, I realized my brain was getting in the way of repairing my hamstring. My fear of making the injury worse was keeping me from doing the work to heal it. That is, I was doing rehab exercises, but dialing back the intensity whenever I felt any discomfort. I became proof of the saying "no pain, no gain." And the lack of gain, of course, left me still hobbling. It was a cycle of sustained frustration.

Under the spell cast by Dr. Misel, I broke that cycle. Once I returned to full strength, I asked if he could make it easier for me to fall asleep. I'd come home from games needing hours to unwind. I'd be up until 3:00 or 4:00 AM, reading, watching

movies I'd seen countless times—doing anything I could to
nod off. Sure enough, he showed me a shortcut to dreamland.

Hypnosis isn't for everyone. Research shows that some
people are predisposed to going under and some never will.
Another group can, but only if they allow it. I proved to be
highly susceptible. When I came out of one of Dr. Misel's
trances, I felt relaxed and refreshed, ready to take on the
world. With my hamstring and sleep issues resolved, it was
time to see what kind of magic he could work on my swing.

Soon my pregame ritual included both batting practice
and focusing practice. I would sit on the bench, facing the
outfield wall. I'd stare so intently on the distances marked in
the corners that the rest of the world blurred. People would
wave a hand in front of my face to try breaking my concentration. They couldn't. Once I was locked in deeply enough,
my eyes could play tricks with the numbers. I'd make each of
them move. Dance, if I wanted. I realize this sounds silly, but
I felt like I had this heightened state of awareness. In sports
parlance, it put me into a zone.

———————

With three weeks left in the 1975 season, the Twins tried an
experiment. I played first base.

Unlike Bill Rigney banishing me to third base when he
thought I was too squeamish to play second, this wasn't
punishment. Quite the opposite. It was intended to preserve
my body. Playing on the corner instead of up the middle
meant less room to cover and fewer collisions. It was time to
think about things like that since I'd be turning 30 in October.

Keeping me out of harm's way would help me get as many at-bats as possible for as many seasons as possible.

The next season, 1976, Gene Mauch took over as our manager. He liked the idea of me playing first base so much that he personally worked with me on it during spring training. We went over fundamentals such as snagging throws that came in low and the footwork required to hold a runner on base. I appreciated the way Gene handled this and told him so. From the start, we had a good, professional relationship. In fact, he began calling me "Pro." Gene was the kind of guy whose highest praise was, "He's a real pro."

Gene also changed my spot in the batting order. By late April, I was locked into the three hole.

The leadoff hitter is generally the fastest and/or most adept at getting on base. I liked batting second because it usually meant more fastballs. With a guy on base, pitchers are more apt to throw strikes to avoid a walk. By the time you get to the No. 3 spot, the job description shifts to more of a premium on driving in those runners.

The previous year was our first without Harmon anchoring the middle of the lineup. Roles were in flux all season. I bounced between the top three spots. Considering I won the batting title, it didn't affect me much. So it shouldn't have made much of a difference this season. Still, I struggled through April and May.

By the All-Star break—my 10th straight year getting invited—my average was up to .326. I basically held on from there. Going into the final weekend, I was hitting .325. That set up the wildest batting race of my career.

When I was a rookie, the schedule sent us to Boston for the final weekend and a head-to-head series with the Red Sox to decide the pennant. In another bit of fortuitous scheduling, the '76 season concluded with the Twins in Kansas City to face the Royals and their hot-hitting duo, Hal McRae and George Brett.

Hal came in hitting .333. George was right behind at .328. I may have been in third place, but I was the four-time reigning champ. Don King would've loved promoting a heavyweight matchup like this.

The Royals brought in an outside scorekeeper to guard against claims of favoritism if any borderline calls went in favor of their players or against me. I thought it was silly. I figured our bats would determine this, not the pencil of some guy in the press box.

"Pro," Gene said, "if you go 7-for-12 and our pitchers hold, you're going to win it."

I singled in my first at-bat, then George came up in the bottom of the inning and hit a ball to shortstop. Roy Smalley should've made the play but didn't. The imported scorer ruled it a hit. Instead of avoiding controversy, it was as if the Royals had invited it to dinner. This was just the appetizer.

In the finale, George hit a ball to right field that Danny Ford misjudged. It went over his head for a double. Hal followed with a single. Standing on first base, he gave me an earful over Danny failing to catch that ball. Hal was really worked up over it. I guess he realized George had a Hall of Fame career ahead of him and was likely to win more batting titles, while this was probably his best chance.

"Hey Mac," I said. "You want a silver bat? I'll give you one."

He didn't find that very funny. Nor was he amused by what happened in the ninth.

George hit a ball to left field that Steve Brye misjudged. He'd been set up too deep and when he ran in, the ball slammed into the plastic turf and, like a kid's bouncy ball, took a huge hop over his head. This being the final inning of the final game—one with no ramifications for the standings—Steve didn't even bother chasing it. George got an inside-the-park home run. Hal considered it further proof that we were trying to give the batting title to George. Worse, he accused Gene of being behind it. Hal claimed Gene was a racist who wanted the white guy to win. It was ridiculous. Regardless, there was no consoling Hal.

With those two hits in the finale, George finished at .333. Hal was a tick behind at .332 and I was another tick behind at .331. Funny thing is, I went 7-for-12 that weekend, just like Gene suggested.

When athletes talk about being in a zone, they're usually referring to a moment or a game, maybe even a great week or two. In 1977, I felt like I was in that zone the entire season.

This was my 11th year in the majors. I was 31 on Opening Day. So this should've been the tail end of my prime years. Instead, everything peaked: my physical skills intersecting with my knowledge of my swing, opposing pitchers, even various stadiums. The focusing drill from Dr. Misel helped, too. So did good news in my personal life: my wife got pregnant with Michelle during spring training.

As the season unfolded, there were many at-bats where "the zone" took over while a pitch was on the way. I don't know how else to explain it.

During previous hot streaks, it looked like pitches moved in slow motion, giving me more time to recognize what kind of pitch was coming and where it was headed. Yet many times during this season, I enjoyed a bonus: while a slow, recognizable pitch was on the way I could also detect an infielder moving a step or two to his left or right. I managed to process that in time to slap the ball a few inches beyond the fielder's reach back in the direction he'd just abandoned. Crazy as this may seem, many infielders from 1977 will tell you this happened to them.

Tony retired after the last season and was now our batting coach. It was great having my roomie formally in that role since he'd been my de facto batting coach all along. We marveled as my average rose from .356 at the end of April to .365 by the end of May.

Then I got hot.

A streak of 40 hits in 87 at-bats rocketed my average to .396, sparking talk of whether I could become the first hitter since Ted Williams in 1941 to hit at least .400.

Hitting was contagious, as our lineup was filled with guys on a roll. We were dubbed "The Lumber Company." We reached the summer battling the White Sox for first place. They came to Metropolitan Stadium the final weekend in June for a three-game series. We won Friday night to claim the top spot, then they reclaimed it on Saturday.

Sunday was a clear, warm afternoon, great for watching baseball, especially if you had a nice cold drink. The game drew a sellout crowd and most people enjoyed several nice cold drinks. They counted the crowd at 46,463—the biggest ever for a Twins regular season home game. Another reason for the huge turnout was the promotion: Rod Carew Jersey Day. The first 20,000 received a T-shirt with my name and number on the back.

I doubled in the first inning, lifting my average to .398.

I singled in the second inning, boosting me to .400. The Twins flashed that magical number on the scoreboard and the crowd stood and cheered. They kept standing and cheering. I felt goose bumps on my arms. I didn't know what to do. Finally, I took off my helmet and waved to show my appreciation.

I grounded out in the third inning, then singled again in the fourth. That sent my average to .401. Another standing ovation. More goose bumps. Another wave of the helmet.

I walked in the seventh, then came up again in the eighth. I homered. This put us ahead 17–10, but you would've thought we won the World Series. The fans gave me another raucous standing ovation—the loudest and longest yet—as the scoreboard flashed my updated batting average: .403. I didn't know what to do. Acknowledging the cheers from the base was one thing. But from inside the dugout?

"Go out there and tip your cap, Pro," Gene said.

So I climbed the steps, looked around, and again saluted them. My goose bumps were the size of golf balls.

The totals for that day: four hits, five runs scored, six RBIs, three standing ovations.

This was the best day of what became my best season. It resonates primarily because of the reaction from the fans. The kinship and camaraderie developed over our decade-plus together crystallized in this moment. Seeing such a tremendous crowd, so many wearing or waving my No. 29 jersey— that's what made the goose bumps rise. They're forming again as I write this paragraph and remember the roars. Whenever I'm asking my favorite or most memorable day in baseball, the answer is always June 26, 1977.

———————

My average kept climbing.

With hits in my first two at-bats on July 1, it peaked at .415.

For anyone to have an average that high, that late in the season was a big deal. For that person to be the winner of five of the last eight batting titles, there was reason to believe I could join Ted in the .400 Club. Speculation was strong by 1977 standards—meaning, pre-Internet, pre-ESPN. Strong enough that about this time, *Sports Illustrated* brought Ted and me together.

He was fishing in Canada. The magazine hired a private jet to escort him to Milwaukee, where we were playing the Brewers. He stayed for a few hours, long enough for us to talk hitting while a photographer snapped pictures.

Knowing I would have this time with Ted, I thought back to the bat bearing his signature on the barrel that I received for being Little League MVP and how winning it prompted me to put his baseball cards on my nightstand, next to Jackie's. I'd met Ted before—briefly, as with Jackie—but now we'd be talking shop. This was my chance to pick the brain of the man I considered the greatest living hitter.

At least, that's what I expected. It turned into more of a chance to match wits with him.

Ted had a singular vision of how to hit. His way powered his remarkable career. His book *The Science of Hitting* remains an incredible resource. To this day, plenty of big leaguers keep a dog-eared copy tucked into their travel bags. So, to his view, the things I did differently from him were being done wrong.

My swing plane, for instance. He was an uppercut guy. If I played half my games in Fenway Park—where the Pesky Pole was only 302 feet away down the right-field line—maybe I would've molded my swing that way, too. But I'd shaped my swing to knock the ball in all directions. To do so, I kept my bat flat as I whipped it through the hitting zone. Ted thought I was wasting my bat-on-ball talent by not sending more of them skyward. (A generation later, he said the same thing to Tony Gwynn.)

Pitch selection was another talking point. Ted insisted I lay off balls that are down and away. They're hard to hit, harder to drive, he said.

"They're out pitches," he declared.

He had proof. In his book, there's a fascinating graphic that became the template for modern "heat zones" for hitters. It shows a box representing his strike zone and it's filled with a series of baseballs. Each is marked with his batting average for balls thrown there. The higher the average—thus, the hotter he was—the redder the ball. (The diagram comes to life with colored baseballs in a great display at the Hall of Fame museum in Cooperstown.)

Ted's breakdown shows he hit between .270 and .240 on balls down and away. This area is practically marked as toxic on his chart, getting its own box within the box of the strike zone. Balls in that vicinity are gray, a dark, lifeless contrast to the pastel colors across the rest of his strike zone.

"They're not out pitches to me," I said. "I probably hit .500 on them."

Ask anyone to describe the quintessential Rod Carew hit and they'll likely say it's a ball dumped into left field, over the heads of the shortstop and third baseman and in front of the left fielder. Most of those came on pitches down and away. Despite my success, I kept seeing them because—as Ted illustrated—that spot is so famously a cold zone for lefties. The only downside to me reaching out to hit those pitches was that I often caught them near the tip of the bat, creating a chip or crack. The Hall of Fame owns the bats from my 1,000th, 2,000th, and 3,000th hits—and all three are busted in that spot.

To clarify, Ted and I didn't argue. This was a friendly debate of his way versus my way. For me, it was a master class. A better analogy to the world of higher education might be that I was presenting my doctoral thesis on hitting, forcing me to explain and defend to the greatest living hitter why I did what I did and the way I did it. I loved every minute.

We found one important mutual ground: the point of contact. Our hands were in the same position. We also shared a routine in our setup. Both of us twisted the handle so that, when looking down the barrel, we saw only the smooth, unadorned part of the bat—no label or autograph. Seeing all wood gave us the sensation of more hitting surface; the bat felt longer.

The cover photo on the July 18, 1977, edition of *Sports Illustrated* shows us both with big smiles. Ted is standing with his left hand on his hip. I'm sitting on a stool, holding three bats. The headline reads, TED WILLIAMS ANALYZES ROD CAREW. The subhead: THE LAST .400 HITTER, AND MAYBE THE NEXT. One of the rooms where media gather at Target Field is decorated with blown-up images of magazine covers featuring Twins. This one hangs in a prominent spot, visible to anyone walking by. I gladly take a peek every time I visit the stadium.

To understand the difficulty of keeping an average above .400, consider what happened the day I reached .415. I went 2-for-5...and my average dropped.

I maintained the joy of seeing a "4" at the start of my batting average until July 11. A 1-for-5 performance took me to .398. Then it was time for the All-Star Game, which just so happened to be held at Yankee Stadium and thus the neighborhood where I grew up. A nice coincidence for this magical season.

Considering my long run of All-Star starts, and the kind of season I was having, it was no surprise that fans again chose me as the AL starter at first base. The surprise was how many votes I got: 4,292,740. That shattered the record.

In the first two games after the break, I didn't get a hit.
That marked the first time all season I went consecutive starts
without a hit. I bounced back with a 15-game hitting streak,
my longest streak of the season. Yet my average dipped five
points along the way.

Every season wears you down. I always compensated by
switching to a lighter bat in the second half. This time, the
grind was catching up to me more than usual. All the at-bats,
plus the burden of aiming for .400, left my arms feeling tired.
Then I woke up one morning and felt different. Stronger.
When I did my pregame focusing drills, those numbers on
the outfield wall started sizzling more. I was back in the zone,
or deeper into it.

Around Labor Day, my average was .375. Considering
how many at-bats I'd already had, and how few were remaining, simple math showed it was unrealistic to get back to .400.
However, a strong finish could get me to .388. That was the
closest anyone in either league had come to .400 since Ted
in '41. (Who did it? Ted in '57.)

By going 3-for-4 on the final day, that's exactly how I
finished: .388. Before my last at-bat, fans gave me a huge
ovation and the organist played "Thanks for the Memory."

My 239 hits were the most in the league since 1930. Only
10 players ever had more. My sixth batting title put me in
even more exclusive company. The only people who'd won
that many: Ted and Ty Cobb in the American League; and
Rogers Hornsby, Stan Musial, and Honus Wagner in the
National League.

Another tidbit about this title is that I sort of lapped the
field. My teammate Lyman Bostock finished second, and he

was 52 percentage points behind. Pittsburgh's Dave Parker was tops in the NL, 50 behind.

In my last at-bat, I hit an RBI single. That was significant because it was the 100th run I drove in for the season. It was my first and only time in triple digits. It also was my third straight year of hiking my RBI total since the Twins made an issue of it at my arbitration hearing.

The big disappointment was that the fun start of The Lumber Company faded over the summer. We went from leading the division in mid-August to finishing in fourth place.

By this point in my life, the angry young man had become a moody man in his thirties. I was more open with and accepting of my teammates. While I would never be a vocal leader, I knew that I led by example and took pride in it. My status as a perennial All-Star required me to be the face of the team, especially when the star power of Harmon and Tony began to fade. I did the best I could. My interactions with fans were overwhelmingly pleasant. I think the events of June 26, 1977, underscore the strength of that relationship. My daily dealings with the media, however, remained frosty.

In the summer of '77, *The Sporting News* wanted to shoot a cover photo of me and Larry Hisle. It made sense. I was leading the league in hitting and Larry was leading the league in RBIs. (He finished that way, too.) I agreed to participate in the photo shoot. Then I thought about how many covers I'd already been on this summer, such as *Time* the same week as *Sports Illustrated*. I also found it strange that *The Sporting*

News was only now getting around to writing about me. I mean, if a mainstream publication like *Time* was declaring me on its cover as BASEBALL'S BEST HITTER, shouldn't the publication that's considered the Bible of Baseball have picked up on it sooner? Putting all those pieces together, I reconsidered the photo shoot. I thought Larry deserved to have the spotlight to himself.

"Why don't you just give it to Larry?" I told the guy from *The Sporting News.*

Lyman was near me. He heard exactly what I said and how I said it. Yet the story got twisted into "Rod Carew refuses to take a picture with Larry Hisle!" Larry was understandably upset. Luckily, Lyman explained what really happened.

Another example along those lines involved, of all things, fan mail. I received bags full of letters asking for autographs or pictures. I accommodated as many as I could. There was nothing I could do, though, with letters that came without a return address. I had to throw those out. Well, some TV guy in Chicago twisted that into "Rod Carew trashes bags of fan mail!" Incidents like those made me mistrust anyone wearing a press pass.

I realize now that I was part of the problem. By being standoffish with the beat guys who were around us every day, I cost myself the benefit of the doubt. When half-true stories made the rounds, no one ran interference or took my side. People who felt jerked around by me found it easy to believe that I jerked around others. It's probably a good thing the media bubble was smaller and less intense in Minneapolis in the 1970s than it is everywhere these days.

There were a few national writers I liked and respected. Locally, I only felt close to one guy: Sid Hartman, the dean of Twin Cities reporters. Sid recorded every interview—and never misquoted anyone. That's how you earn respect. (Quick side story: I once went to Sid's house to give his son, Chad, a batting lesson. Chad grew up to become a broadcaster, so we still see each other occasionally. Sid is still reporting well into his nineties. Whenever I see either of them, they always mention the batting lesson on their front lawn.)

I bring up my lousy reputation among reporters because they voted for MVP. Although I won it for the 1977 season, it wasn't by the landslide most fans expected. I was named first on only 12 of 28 ballots. And, two days later, I celebrated again: Michelle was born.

November 1977 also held great news for my buddies Larry and Lyman. Both became millionaires. Granted free agency, Larry hit the jackpot with the Brewers while Lyman cashed in with the Angels.

As for me, I had one season left on a three-year contract. The deal paid me $170,000 in my MVP season. *Sports Illustrated* called me the most underpaid player in baseball. I wasn't about to try any sort of power play to get a raise. I agreed to those terms and was going to honor them. But I also was looking forward to getting my market value, whatever that might be, on my next contract.

I didn't use an agent. A lawyer negotiated for me. A few days before the 1978 season opener, Calvin agreed to meet with my lawyer and me to start talking about that next contract. It was just the three of us in Calvin's office. Yet instead of reviewing our proposals, Calvin opened with a tirade about how his fellow owners were ruining the game by giving players huge contracts. Not him, he told us. He was holding a hard line. We walked out knowing this was the beginning of the end.

Two years before, Calvin shipped out our best pitcher, Bert Blyleven, who was only 24 and on his way to the Hall of Fame. After failing to keep Larry and Lyman, this rant made it clear that he wouldn't give me the raise I deserved.

Calvin understood that if he wasn't serious about signing me, then he should trade me. Better to get something, as he did for Bert, than nothing, as with Larry and Lyman. So we started talking about trade destinations. This wasn't out of the goodness of Calvin's heart. This was thanks to the union. Any player who'd been in the league for 10 years, the last five with the same team, could veto any trade. Thus, I had a say in my next destination. I gave Calvin five options: the New York Yankees, Boston Red Sox, Kansas City Royals, Texas Rangers, and California Angels. Then I waited to see what he could work out.

The trade deadline arrived June 15. On June 16, I was still with the Twins. I was fine with that. Actually, it was a big relief. A month later, I started another All-Star Game. I led off the game with a triple. In my next at-bat, I tripled again. Pete Rose was playing third base for the NL. As I slid in the second time, he screamed: "That's a record! Nobody's ever hit two triples in an All-Star Game!" Leave it to Pete to know something like that.

The Twins went into the All-Star break only a few games under .500. Then we opened the second half by losing nine straight. That turned the rest of the season into a lost cause. The only surprise was that the bottom didn't fall out sooner.

Subtract the reigning RBI champ (Larry) and the runner-up in the batting race (Lyman), and what do you get? A lineup that scores 201 fewer runs than the previous year. We lost 89 games, the most of my career so far.

Without Larry and Lyman to worry about, I didn't see many strikes. Teams were willing to put me on base and take their chances with everyone else.

I walked 78 times, the most in my career. That included 19 intentional walks, the most in the league. The Red Sox walked me three times in a single game. A week later, they upped it to four times.

As for my batting average, I picked up where I left off in '77—in late May, I was hitting .388. My average began dropping as the trade deadline approached. It dropped further as our games turned more meaningless. I finished the season hitting "only" .333. It was still good enough to claim another American League batting title. This was my seventh, breaking a tie with Ted on the all-time list. Only Cobb had more.

———————

The Thursday before the season ended, Calvin was in Waseca, Minnesota, to speak to the Lions Club. During the questions-and-answers session, he was asked why he moved the team from Washington, D.C., to the Twin Cities. He asked if there were any black people in the audience and looked around the room to make sure the answer was no. Then he said, "I'll tell you why we came to Minnesota. It was when I found out you only had 15,000 blacks here. Black people don't go to ballgames, but they'll fill up a rassling ring and put up such a chant it'll scare you to death. It's unbelievable. We came here because you've got good, hardworking white people here."

As for this particular black man, he called me "a damn fool" for agreeing to my current contract.

"He only gets $170,000 and we all know damn well that he's worth a lot more than that," Calvin said.

We know he said all this because a reporter from the *Minneapolis Tribune* was among the good, hardworking white people in the audience. He wasn't there as a reporter, though, merely as his father-in-law's guest. Still, he knew a good story when he heard it.

I saw the quotes on Saturday before a game against the Royals. My old flight instinct kicked in. I raced back to the clubhouse, threw my uniform on the ground, showered, and got ready to leave the stadium. I got talked into returning for that game. But that was it. Calvin's quotes hit the paper on Sunday, the final day of the season and my 33rd birthday. I didn't play in that game. I never again played for the Twins.

The animosity has long since run its course. But that Sunday, having had a full day to digest Calvin's comments, I said, "I will not come back and play for a bigot. I'm not going to be another nigger on his plantation." I spit on the clubhouse floor and said, "Spit on Calvin Griffith."

Calvin had meant a lot to me since I was a minor leaguer. During my MVP acceptance speech the year before, I mentioned my respect and appreciation for him. But the statements in Waseca made it clear that it was time for me to leave.

His wayward stewardship of the Twins started when he fired Billy after the '69 season. The business of baseball changed in the '70s and Calvin refused to keep up, yearning for a return to the good old days. Was it really the notion of black millionaires that set him off? Or was he just a tightwad who didn't want to give any player a seven-figure contract?

Regardless, the only question I needed to answer was, *Where do you want to play next?*

My 10-5 rights, as they're known, left me in control of the trade market. This time, I narrowed the field to the Yankees and Angels, and a new option: the San Francisco Giants. Then I visited each team.

The idea of joining the Yankees had a storybook feel. Like I escaped my father in Panama for a fresh start in New York, I would be escaping Calvin and the Twins to spend the second half of my career in New York. I'd be joining the team that won the last two World Series, giving me a terrific opportunity to finally play for a championship. On the way to work every day, I'd pass Macombs Dam Park, a humbling reminder of how my career started. At the introductory news conference, we'd all laugh about how many people George Steinbrenner would've fired if he'd owned the team back in '64 and a neighborhood kid slipped in for a tryout that he turned into Home Run Derby without anyone from the Yankees noticing. I would've looked good in pinstripes, too.

The reality, though, wasn't as enticing. The spotlight of New York could be tough, especially for someone with my personality. I wasn't worried about it affecting me on the field. I simply didn't want to deal with the rest of the "Bronx Zoo," as Sparky Lyle called it. Steinbrenner talked up all the money I could make in endorsements and other off-field opportunities. I didn't care about that. I knew my next contract would provide my family and me with all the money we'd need. I also wanted to avoid the personal homecoming. The fact my siblings and Eric lived in New York was why I had grown roots in Minnesota. All told, it wasn't worth it.

The Giants seemed like a good idea until I took a closer look. Players warned me, "We don't have a summer here." It was so cold and miserable that, a few years later, the club gave away buttons as badges of honor for any fan tough/crazy enough to make it through games that went extra innings. I knew enough about harsh weather from winters in Minneapolis. Why sign up for that? Plus, this was long before interleague play. The All-Star Game was the only time I faced National League pitchers like Steve Carlton and Tom Seaver. While I knew I could handle any pitcher and I could figure out every stadium, why choose to start from scratch? Put another way, why flush the dozen years of information I'd accumulated on AL pitchers and stadiums? Again, it didn't add up.

That left the Angels.

I liked team owner Gene Autry right away. I must admit, as a huge fan of movies, especially Westerns, I came into the meeting expecting to like the "Singing Cowboy." I also liked the idea of joining a lineup featuring Don Baylor and Bobby

Grich, and playing behind a rotation that included Nolan Ryan and Frank Tanana. Throw in the weather and scenery of Orange County, and what was there *not* to like?

On February 3, 1979, the front offices struck a deal. The Twins traded me to the Angels for Ken Landreaux, Dave Engle, Brad Havens, and Paul Hartzell. When the news broke, I was nowhere to be found.

It wasn't the old flight instinct kicking in. But it was a good reflection of why I didn't see myself fitting in on the Yankees.

All the chatter and speculation about the looming trade had gotten to me. At home, the phone kept ringing. Everywhere I went, people wanted to know where I would play next. Ironically, I escaped to New York. I hung out at the house my mother shared with Uncle Clyde. I arrived the morning of February 2 with one request: don't tell me anything about a trade.

The morning of February 4, it was time to fly home. I went to La Guardia Airport, bought a newspaper, and there it was: Carew traded to the Angels.

It's funny: a plane flight into New York on June 30, 1961, started a new era of my life. Now, a flight out of New York was starting another era.

In the air, I began wrapping my head around the fact I was part of a new team. I also thought about another element of the deal: a new contract that would pay me $4 million over five years. After making little more than $800,000 over my entire career, I would be making that much *every* year.

There used to be the saying that "home run hitters drive Cadillacs, singles hitters drive Fords." Well, this singles hitter was now the highest-paid player in baseball.

This kid from the Panama Canal Zone who used to wear shoes that flapped on the bottom because his family couldn't afford anything else was now the highest-paid player in baseball.

This "damn fool" for having taken his last contract was now the highest-paid player in baseball.

The money itself was wonderful, of course. But the pride I felt was more about what this status represented. It meant I was valued—treasured, even. From being called Sissy by my father and considered not good enough to make my high school team, I was headed to sunny Southern California because the Singing Cowboy gave up all those players and all that money for me to be the star of his team.

7

WELCOME
TO THE CLUB

THE FIRST TIME my girls visited Orange County, they asked if we could go to a drive-in movie. Between the sticky summers and frigid winters, we didn't do that much in Minneapolis.

The five of us piled into my truck and went to see whatever was popular in the spring of 1979.

Between bites of snacks, one of the girls suddenly realized something.

"Daddy!" she said. "No mosquitoes!"

"We want to stay in California!" another of the girls said.

We bought a house in Anaheim Hills. While it was being prepared, we lived in another neighborhood, Villa Park. Several of my teammates lived there. At first, we lived on the same block as Nolan Ryan and his family. Our houses were built by the same company. One day, we ran out of hot water. I figured the pilot light had blown out on our hot water heater. But I couldn't find the hot water heater. I asked Nolan for help. He came over and we went up into the attic so he could show me where it was and how to fix it.

"Be careful," I said, laughing, as Nolan lit a match. "Can you imagine what Gene would say if this blows up?"

———————

While I was living in a new city and playing on a new team, the results were the same. I went into June 1979 leading the American League with a .355 average.

Playing the Indians, I picked up a ground ball near the line and went to tag the runner. My right thumb got caught in his shirt and bent all the way back. I tore some ligaments, knocking me out for six weeks.

Here I am, the highest-paid player in baseball, and I can't contribute. Needing another way to support my new teammates, I did something way out of character. I turned into the class clown.

Wearing a cast from my knuckles to my elbow, I stood on the steps of the dugout, turned toward the crowd, and led the fans in singing "Take Me Out to the Ballgame."

Our team's rallying cry had become "Yes We Can," as in, yes, we can make the playoffs for the first time in the franchise's 19-year history. I joined fans in waving poster-sized cards bearing this slogan whenever we needed or deserved cheers.

Before a game against the Tigers, I told their manager, Sparky Anderson, that I would be holding up a K sign every time Nolan struck out one of his guys. I didn't want Sparky to think I was showing them up. He said he knew that wasn't my style. Still, it was a good thing I warned him. I waved the card 16 times that night. It was the most strikeouts Nolan had all season.

The goofing around helped offset worries about my right hand.

For a left-handed hitter, the right hand holds the bottom of the bat. This makes it the steering wheel of my swing. It guides the bat through the strike zone and controls the follow-through. The great touch I was known for stemmed from the feel of the bat in my hands. Now that was compromised.

Once I was healthy enough to play, I wasn't the same hitter. I finished the season at .318. It was my lowest since 1972. More importantly, "Yes We Can" turned into "Yes We Did." We won the division.

The heart and soul of our team was another of the finest men I ever met, Don Baylor. Or, as Frank Robinson dubbed him early in his career, "Groove."

Groove led the league in RBIs and runs. But his leadership stretched way beyond the box score. He set the tone in everything we did. He worked hard and played the game the right way. He made sure others did, too. Anyone who strayed knew they had to answer to him. He also flashed a big, warm smile.

For me, Groove filled the roles in my life that Tony Oliva and Harmon Killebrew filled during my early years with the Twins.

Like Tony, Groove became my closest friend on the club, my confidant. He knew how to calm me when I needed it. Better still, he knew how to prevent me from needing it.

Like Harmon, Groove was a mountain of a man with a heart of gold. But there was more of an edge to Groove than Harmon. With good reason.

Groove and his brother were among the first black students at their middle school, then again at their high school. The varsity football coach told Groove there weren't enough uniforms for him to have one. He found a way onto the squad anyway. That backbone served him well throughout life. He didn't go around with his fists up, but he didn't back down, either. It's summed up best by this fact: when Groove retired, he'd been hit by more pitches than any player in big-league history.

So now it's the postseason—the first for many of my teammates, but my third try. As luck would have it, my path to the World Series went through Baltimore for a third time.

We lost the opener in extra innings. A big, late rally in Game 2 fell one run shy when Brian Downing grounded out with the bases loaded. Although we were down 0–2 and facing elimination, Groove reminded everyone how close we were to being up 2–0. He said we could still pull this out. Back at home for Game 3, he led by example, hitting a home run that put us ahead 2–1.

In the bottom of the ninth, we were losing by a run with one out and the bases empty. The Orioles were poised to sweep me out of the playoffs again. Only now I had a chance to do something about it. I stepped in against Dennis Martinez and crushed a ball into the left-center gap for a double. I came around to score the tying run, then Larry Harlow drove in Downing for a walk-off win. It was the first postseason victory in Angels history, of course, and a first for me, too.

The celebration ended there. We got stomped the next day. Still, there was a lot to savor about this first season in California. I also was happy to have finally come through in a playoff series: 7-for-17 with three doubles.

――――――――――

Fans didn't scream "Yes We Can" in 1980. They screamed in frustration.

The mood turned in the offseason when the front office let Nolan leave. Despite all the thrills he'd given Angels fans, and how much life still seemed left in his arm, our general manager, Buzzie Bavasi, pointed to Nolan's 26–27 record over the past two years and said he wasn't worth the money he wanted: $567,000 for each of three years. The Astros gladly brought Nolan back home to the Houston area, giving him a contract that topped mine, making him the highest-paid player in baseball. Nolan's deal paid him $1 million per season, the first time any ballplayer reached seven digits. It proved to be a heck of an investment for the Astros because they won their first division title that season.

Every personnel move Buzzie made seemed to backfire. Same with the buttons pushed by our manager, Jim Fregosi.

He could never set on a regular batting order or fielding assignments. I was DH 32 times, my most ever, and I ping-ponged through the first, second, third, and fifth spots in the lineup. We won only 65 games. This would go down as the worst team I was ever part of, as a player or coach. My solace came from my thumb returning to full strength, and my average being closer to my standards. I hit .331, fifth best in the league. Meanwhile, I cheered from afar as George Brett got on a scorching hot streak in July and took a heck of a run at .400. He finished at .390.

Buzzie overhauled our roster for 1981. A slow start cost Jim his job. His replacement? A real pro—my old pal Gene, who'd been fired by Calvin. He settled on me playing first and batting leadoff. But from June 12 to August 10, nobody played. Our union went on strike.

Having benefited as much as anyone from the rights negotiated by Marvin Miller and the MLB Players Association, I supported this fight. Ultimately, though, I'm not sure if it was worth it. We didn't gain much and the long layoff alienated fans—especially now that we had a guy making a million dollars to play a game they'd play for free.

The strike cost me $230,000 in salary. It didn't have to, though. The lawyer who drew up my contract actually had protected me by wording my deal in a way that ensured I still got paid. But this didn't feel right to me. I respected Gene Autry too much to collect money I didn't earn. I told my attorney to return the paychecks I received while we weren't playing.

We were out for so long that the league decided to break the season into two halves. Given the chance to start over after a middling first half, we…wasted it. We flopped all the way to last place in the second half. I finished the season hitting .305, a down year for me even if it was still 11th best in the league.

The front office went to work again to reload our roster for 1982. The big addition: Reggie Jackson.

I knew Reggie quite well. We'd come up around the same time and spent our entire careers in the AL. We'd been All-Stars together many times. That included 1971 in Detroit, when he hit a home run that might've gone 600 feet if it hadn't hit a light tower on the roof of Tiger Stadium. Standing in the on-deck circle, I had a great view. The only blast I can compare it to was Harmon's ball in '67 that was commemorated with the chair painted red. In my mind's eye, both balls are still soaring.

But what kind of teammate would he be?

Everyone knew the stories of Reggie wanting to be "the straw that stirs the drink" in New York and that he had his own candy bar. We'd seen him live up to the hype and become Mr. October, but we'd also seen him clash with a guy I loved, Billy Martin.

Reggie proved to be a terrific addition to our clubhouse and our lineup.

Plugging him into a batting order that already featured Groove, Fred Lynn, and me gave us an impressive claim to fame: four former MVPs. Only the Big Red Machine ever had anything like it. Gene often penciled in a lineup that deployed all four of us in a row. How would you like to pitch against that?

In only our 10th game, we were playing the Twins. We hit one of their guys, so their pitcher, Darrell Jackson, retaliated. But he violated protocol by trying to hit Bobby Grich in the head. When he missed, he had the audacity to try again. He missed again. On the next pitch, Bobby hit a comebacker to Jackson. Bobby started toward first base, then turned left and charged at Jackson. Both benches emptied. Unlike the pushing and shoving you see nowadays, we had actual fights back then. I punched Jackson in the head. As bodies flew around, my right hand got stepped on. Between the punching and the stomping, my right hand—the steering wheel of my swing—began throbbing. Several bones got chipped. I struggled for about a month. My average dove into the .260s. Once I healed, I went on a 25-game hitting streak—the longest of my career and an Angels record. I cranked my average back to .319 by season's end. I finished third in the league. Best of all, our MVP-crammed lineup lifted us to another division title.

This being my fourth trip, I wasn't satisfied with getting to the playoffs. I turned 37 on the final weekend of the season. How many more chances would I have to win a World Series?

In Game 1 against the Brewers, Tommy John threw a complete game for us and we won 8–3. I smiled and went home without making a fuss. In Game 2, Bruce Kison was even better while throwing a complete game in a 4–2 victory. Again, I hustled out of the clubhouse. We still had to win one more of the last three games—that's when I would celebrate.

The '82 Brewers were known as "Harvey's Wallbangers," a nod to manager Harvey Kuenn and a ferocious lineup that included Robin Yount, Paul Molitor, Cecil Cooper, and Gorman Thomas. Robin was MVP. Gorman tied for the league lead in homers. Robin, Coop, and Gorman were all top five in RBIs. They could pitch, too—Pete Vuckovich won the Cy Young and Rollie Fingers was their closer. They'd won the most games in the American League. Their reward was hosting Games 3, 4, and—if necessary—5.

On the brink of elimination, they responded the way great teams do. In Game 3, their wily veteran Don Sutton shut us down. In Game 4, their offense came to life. They beat us 9–5, setting up a winner-take-all finale. Yet as we prepared for that game, many of us were worrying about what was happening back home in Orange County.

A power line went down in Gypsum Canyon, starting a fire. Santa Ana winds blew the flames toward Anaheim Hills and the homes where many of us lived. The wildfire was growing and we were across the country, unable to protect our property or help our friends and neighbors. My family was with me in Milwaukee, so I wasn't worried about their safety. I knew houses and everything else could be replaced. Still, it was a heck of a distraction.

We took a 3–1 lead off Vuckovich. In the bottom of the seventh, the Brewers went ahead 4–3. The score held that way going into the ninth.

I was due up fourth, meaning only one guy had to get on base for me to get a chance. I was not having a very good series—just three hits in 16 at-bats coming in. Today, I was 0-for-3 but reached twice on walks. I wanted a chance for one memorable at-bat. One swing that could help us win this game and this series. One whack like the drive in the ninth inning of an elimination game against Baltimore in 1979.

A leadoff single by Ron Jackson gave me hope. With two out and the tying run on second, I stepped in against Pete Ladd, a big, hard-throwing righty.

I'd only faced him twice. I flied out in September and struck out in Game 1. I'd also seen him pitch in Game 3. Based on those outings, I knew to expect plenty of fastballs.

I fouled the first pitch down the left-field line. The next pitch was a ball. Then I watched a strike. Sure enough, all were fastballs. With the count 1-2, I was looking for another. It came in waist high, then drifted to the outer half. I hit it hard, to the left side, like I'm supposed to do with balls pitched there. It hit the ground once and skipped into Robin's glove at shortstop. He had a routine throw to first. Coop caught it and was jumping for joy before I was anywhere near the bag.

That was it. My best chance at making the World Series. And I hit into the final out.

On the same field where Mike Hegan delivered the most painful moment of my career, this was the most disappointing.

Once we flew home and the fires were out, I found it tough to watch the Brewers and Cardinals play in that World Series. I started to wonder whether I would ever play in a World Series—or would I go down in history like Ernie Banks, Billy Williams, and other great players who always fell short. I was proud of my silver bats and other awards and honors, but my professional resume felt incomplete.

———————

In spring training of 1983, something seemed wrong with my swing. Then, when the season arrived, I caught the flu.

Was Father Time catching up to me?

Hardly.

Over my first 96 at-bats, I banged out 48 hits. That's a .500 average nearly a month into the season. The uncanny feeling from 1977—that mystical sense of being able to detect while a pitch was on the way that a fielder had shifted one way, then hitting it the other direction—was back.

There was plenty of buzz about this, although it was less intense than 1977. Maybe some of the novelty had worn off it since I'd already chased .400, or because George came even closer in 1980. Yet there was a twist to this: I was now 37 and five years removed from my last batting title.

In mid-June, *Sports Illustrated* put a huge closeup of my smiling face on the cover with the headline, .400! ROD CAREW IS AT IT AGAIN. I was still at it by the All-Star break. I carried a .402 average, marking the first time anyone got to the break with an average that high since Stan Musial was at .403 in 1948.

I maintained that glorious "4" at the start of my average until July 15—a few days later than in '77.

So, what was it? What was the secret that unleashed this? It wasn't Jackie's bat, like in '69. It wasn't Dr. Misel, like in '77. It was…

Nothing. I hadn't changed a thing. Not a single adjustment to my swing or my routine. While it would be a great story if I said that the one-hopper that ended the '82 ALCS prompted an offseason overhaul of my swing—that I found a flaw and fixed it—this was just a four-month hot stretch.

Then, everything came crashing down: my average and the Angels' season.

Gene had been fired a few days after the ALCS (Buzzie questioned some of his playoff moves) and replaced by John McNamara. Groove left via free agency. The knock on our '82 team was that we had too many older players, so the front office brought in some younger guys. All these new parts seemed to be meshing well; on the first Sunday after the All-Star break, we were tied for first place. But by the end of that week—the same week my average slipped below .400—we were in third place. We finished the month in fourth place.

We finished the season fifth, dragging a 70–92 record. We'd again followed a division title with a nose dive.

My average landed at .339, a terrific figure when you see it on the back of my baseball card but a bit disappointing considering what it was in July. Only Wade Boggs had a higher average in the AL. It also gave me 15 straight years of topping .300. The last American Leaguer to do that? Ted Williams.

As the season wound down, I considered retiring. The second-half slides by me and the team prompted the thought. My contract was expiring, too, making for a clean break.

"I'm tired of playing," I told Reggie.

"You can't be tired, man," he said. "You've got 3,000 hits almost in your hand. That's your ticket to the Hall of Fame."

"I'm not thinking about any of that," I said.

"You better start thinking about it," he said.

I went into the offseason 168 hits from 3,000. Reggie was right: if there was ever a milestone to care about, it was this one.

Accumulating 3,000 hits requires sustained greatness. The quick math: It takes 150 hits a year for 20 years, or 200 hits for 15 years. In my lifetime, it had been accomplished by the likes of Hank Aaron, Willie Mays, Roberto Clemente, and Stan Musial.

Considering I had 160 hits this past season, I likely would need two years. To be that close and give up would be silly, especially since this past season showed how much life was left in my bat.

I asked the Angels for a three-year deal. They declined. A November deadline passed, putting me into a draft of free agents. The way things worked back then, any team could've selected the right to negotiate with me. None did, apparently scared away by the combination of my age and my reported asking price of $1.5 million per year.

Although Buzzie dangled the idea of the Angels finding someone else to play first base, I ended up signing a two-year contract. When I arrived for spring training, I let everyone know I wasn't happy about how the front office treated me.

"All I ever ask is that people respect me," I told reporters.

Early in the season, I was hitting above .300 when I woke up one morning thinking I had slept wrong. My left arm felt numb and my neck hurt. I was in and out of the lineup for weeks.

My left arm felt useless at times. Or barely usable. I became a contact hitter by the strictest definition. Swinging with essentially one arm, I wanted the bat to meet the ball and let the impact of the collision drive it. In the field, I lacked strength in my glove hand. I caught fly balls like a Little Leaguer, using my right hand to help squeeze the mitt shut. I struggled to hold runners on first base. You're supposed to keep the glove in air, poised to receive a pickoff throw, but my arm fatigued after a few seconds.

The problem turned out to be a calcium deposit in the neck that was pinching a nerve. I finally went on the disabled list in August. I sat out 22 straight games. I made it through the rest of the season with the help of an electric stimulation machine, traction, and other physical therapy.

Had I stopped playing the final Monday of the season, I would've hit exactly .300. But I'd never sat to protect my average before and wasn't about to start now. I was in the lineup

for two more games and six more at-bats. I made nothing
but outs, dropping my average to .295.

At 38? With a bad neck? That's still dang good.

I finished the season with 2,929 hits—a nifty number for
someone who always wore 29 on his jersey. It also meant that
as soon as the 1985 schedule came out, folks started guessing
when I'd reach 3,000.

Would it come at home? Against which team? Another
conversation was how it would happen. Would I dump it
into left field, as I'd done for so many of my hits? Or would
it come on my other signature move at the plate—a bunt?
Or how about one more big surprise, like becoming the first
person to get there with a triple or a home run?

I just wanted to stay healthy. With the neck problem
resolved, I wanted to show that I could be the Rod Carew
of old, not an old Rod Carew. Something resembling the
early '83 model would get my average back in the .300s and
speed my progress to 3,000 hits. I could have the milestone
by June or early July, before the All-Star break.

Everything changed in early May. Playing Toronto, I slid
into home. My left foot crashed into the shin guards of catcher
Ernie Whitt. I came away safe but hurting. I left the game a
few innings later and went for X-rays. It showed no break.
Days later, my foot was still swollen and bruised. Another
X-ray showed no break.

I hobbled around for about 10 games. I knew it wasn't
getting better and I feared it might be getting worse. I didn't
want to go back to the team doctor because I figured all he
would do was take another X-ray. So I found my own specialist. A bone scan revealed a stress fracture. I missed 19 games

and probably should've missed more considering how I felt when I returned. I still had trouble pushing off. I could run straight, but changing directions was tough. My batting average reflected it: I went into July hitting .250.

With my pursuit of 3,000 hits slowed, my popularity faded, too. Eddie Murray overtook me in fan voting for the starting spot at first base for the AL squad. While that ended my streak of 18 straight elections, I still could've been invited as a reserve. But Detroit manager Sparky Anderson—who was in charge of the AL squad—chose Don Mattingly and Cecil Cooper as backups. So for the first time in my career, I got to enjoy an All-Star break at home with my family. I took the girls sailing and tried staying off my foot. I was only 15 hits away now, so the rest might do me good.

With all the downtime, I couldn't help but join the speculation about when, where, and how I might get No. 3,000.

We opened the second half with two weeks on the road. If I got rolling, I could get it in Toronto or Oakland. I would rather do it at home, of course. And guess who was coming to the Big A for our first series back home? The Twins. Tony was still their hitting coach and Harmon called games on TV. It would be so perfect for them to be there to celebrate with me and for fans in Minnesota to watch it live. A nice Plan B was in Minnesota a few days later. But that series in Minnesota might not even happen. Another strike was looming. It would begin after the games of Monday, August 5. This upped the stakes for me in the games coming out of the break.

Reggie warned me about what this stretch would be like. The year before, he'd been through something similar on the way to joining the 500 Home Run Club. No matter how much you stick with your routine and do the things that brought you to the brink of this feat, you can't escape the looming number. Everyone brings up the questions of when, where, and how. Forced into so many conversations about it, I ended up saying something that got twisted out of context.

Trying to emphasize that I wanted the hit to come in front of fans in Anaheim or Minneapolis, I used the phrase, "as long as it doesn't come in Canada." *The Globe and Mail*, the most circulated newspaper in Canada, had a field day with the quote when we got to Toronto. The blowback gave me something else to deal with, from reporters in the clubhouse to boo birds on the field.

When we returned to Anaheim for our series against the Twins, I was four hits away. And there were only four games left before the strike.

Two hits in the opener eased the burden. I was hoping for two more on Saturday off my pal Bert Blyleven.

In the fourth inning, I hit a blooper into left field for No. 2,999. Next time up, I hit a ball in about the same spot. Off the bat, I thought that was it. But shortstop Ron Washington snagged it over his shoulder with his back to the plate. It truly was a great catch. I flied out in my last chance.

Gene was our manager again that season, and he often rested me on day games following a night game. But he told me I would play Sunday. He knew how important every at-bat was, both for the sentimentality of doing it at home and because this was the second-to-last game before the strike date.

We were facing Frank Viola, a lefty who'd won 18 games the year before and would win a Cy Young Award a few years later. (Frank and I were also both signed by Herb Stein; in fact, we were his most successful signees.) I'd had decent success against him. I also thought about the fact my first career hit came off another tough lefty, Dave McNally.

In the first inning, I grounded out on a comebacker to Viola. I came up again in the third with one out and Brian Downing on second. With a 1-1 count, I did what the smart money said I would: I slapped it into left field for No. 3,000.

As I trotted the 90 feet to first base, complicated emotions washed over me—joy and pride, relief and exhaustion.

My teammates streamed out of the dugout to congratulate me. The Twins joined the crowd of 41,630 in giving me a long, loud ovation. I waved my helmet three times in thanks. I looked into the stands and smiled at everyone, including my three daughters.

Gene pried up the bag and handed it to me as a souvenir. Someone joked that after all my success stealing home, this was the first time I'd stolen first base. I was handed a microphone to speak to the crowd. I said, "I'm just glad it's over. I'm happy I could do it here so you fans could enjoy it."

After the game, reporters asked me to put it all in perspective—becoming the 16th member of the 3,000 Hit Club and the first since Carl Yastrzemski in '79; getting there in the second-fewest at-bats, behind only Stan Musial; joining Roberto Clemente as the only Latinos; and, since Puerto Rico is a U.S. territory, being the first born in a foreign country. Looking back at my remarks, they're pretty clichéd. But the thing about clichés is that they're usually true.

"When you're going into the class of people like Ty Cobb, Rogers Hornsby, Roberto Clemente, it's a great feeling,"

I said at a news conference, surrounded by family, including Michelle sitting on my lap.

We went straight home from the stadium. I didn't want to celebrate; I just wanted to savor how relieved I felt. I was eager for my first good night of sleep in weeks. (One other note about this day: Tom Seaver earned his 300th win the same afternoon, adding another link to our careers. The first came in 1967, when he was the NL Rookie of the Year and I won the AL honor.)

The strike indeed hit after the next game. Unlike the screeching halt in '81, this time we were only off the field for two days. I continued to support the union in its quest to improve things for the current generation of players and for generations to come—for the guys who would join me in the 3,000 Hit Club and for those who would try. But I knew my time was winding down. This was my 19th season. I liked the idea of reaching 20, and maybe another if I was still swinging the bat well. Although the Angels already had hinted they might not bring me back, surely someone would be glad to have me. With Calvin having sold the Twins, perhaps I could even return to Minnesota. But those were thoughts for the months ahead. We still had a pennant to chase. How great would it be if the season of my 3,000th hit also was the season that I finally got to the World Series?

We sure put ourselves in position. On October 1—the day I turned 40—we beat the Royals to take a one-game lead over them. Only five games remained.

Then, our offense fizzled. We were eliminated before the final day. At least my last hit of the season was a good one: a bunt. Yep, I still had the coordination and quickness to play another year or two.

My average for the season was .280, low by my standards but still among the best on the squad. I was especially proud of how strong I finished. Once I got beyond the burden of the 3,000th hit, I batted .310 the rest of the way—a stretch of more than two months.

"Pro, you'll be back," Gene told me. "You haven't lost a thing."

A few weeks later, I got a call from Mike Port, who'd recently replaced Buzzie as general manager of the Angels.

"We no longer need your services," he said.

Even though I'd been bracing for it, Port's words stung.

I'd long known baseball is a business. But there was still room to treat people well. There were still fans to please, too, and I believed Angels fans would've liked seeing me back out there, even in a part-time role. I would've taken less money to do that, too—and Port knew it. I was still ornery enough that I looked forward to proving him wrong.

With 25 other teams to choose from, I started thinking about where I might fit best. Surely a few teams would be interested, considering all I had to offer. In addition to a capable bat, my next employer would get my wealth of knowledge and my willingness to work with my teammates, especially young hitters. Signing me would be like hiring another coach. Since I likely was headed to the Hall of Fame, my presence could help sell tickets and, if nothing else, would ensure my new team's name got etched on my eventual plaque in Cooperstown.

Not a single team made a serious offer. Well, the Red Sox did—they wanted me to be their minor league hitting coach.

In May 1986, Giants general manager Al Rosen called to see if I was interested in backing up their young first baseman, a sweet-swinging, left-handed contact hitter named Will Clark. I was interested. But when I tried to envision it, I couldn't. I also remembered all the reasons I didn't go to San Francisco a decade earlier. In telling Al no, I realized this was it. My career was done.

I held a news conference at my house to make it official. I said I didn't want any fuss made over this, but the Angels insisted. A month later, they held Rod Carew Day. My No. 29 became the first retired jersey in club history.

A few months later, the Angels were a strike away from reaching the World Series. Instead of getting that final out, closer Donnie Moore gave up a home run to Boston's Dave Henderson. The Angels never recovered, losing that game and the next two. My heart broke for my friends. I lay in bed that night wondering how that series might have turned out if I'd been part of the club.

The following summer, the Twins retired my jersey. I joined Hank Aaron and Frank Robinson as the only players to have their number retired by multiple clubs. This time, good luck followed. The Twins went on to win their first World Series title. I was so happy to see my old roomie Tony get a championship ring.

———

There's one more layer to the unsatisfying way my career ended.

I wasn't the only veteran free agent left unemployed or forced to settle for a heavily discounted deal that offseason. It happened the year before, too, and again the year after. There were enough of us that it seemed like a fix was in.

A group of us shafted players filed a lawsuit accusing baseball team owners of collusion—that is, agreeing to work together to tamp down salaries. I was proud to be Plaintiff No. 1. Prouder still when an arbitrator ruled in our favor.

It was a somewhat empty victory. While I received a settlement check of around $780,000, I would've rather had another season or two of at-bats.

8

BATTING WIZARD

IN DECEMBER 1990, longtime members of the Baseball Writers Association of America received a thick envelope in the mail. It included a ballot to select the next crop of Hall of Famers and a lengthy summary of each candidate's career. The list included 21 guys who'd been on the ballot before and 24 newcomers. Among those appearing for the first time was a left-handed contact hitter from Panama.

Ballots arrived in about 450 mailboxes. How many of those reporters had I interacted with?

Better question: How many came away from those interactions cussing about how I'd treated them?

That was my concern. If this was a popularity contest, I didn't stand a chance.

During our Angels days, Reggie used to talk to me about making the Hall of Fame. With his outsize personality, and his 500-plus homers, he figured there couldn't be such a place

without him. He tried instilling that same belief in me, especially after I reached 3,000 hits. No way. All that confidence I
had at the plate came from being able to control the outcome.
This election wasn't just out of my hands—it was in the hands
of people I had alienated. Three baseball writers had flat-out
told me they would never vote for me.

Was my reputation really that bad at that time? Consider
these words written by two prominent BBWAA members.

In a profile that ran the day after my 3,000[th] hit, Mike
Downey of the *Los Angeles Times* wrote,

> Rod Carew does not want you probing him, prod-
> ding him, pretending to know him inside-out after
> borrowing a small piece of his precious time. Carew
> would just as soon you studied him in the batter's
> box, watched what he does for a living, form your
> own conclusions—ignorant as they may be—and
> leave him Garboesquely alone. We have here a man
> so enigmatic that you risk offending him by describ-
> ing him as enigmatic....
> Rod Carew is not always the most cordial fellow in
> the world, and often leaves you with nothing more
> than your thoughts about him. Take it from some-
> one who has attempted in three different years,
> in three different cities, to approach Rod Carew,
> speak with him, get to know him a little, wish him
> luck, only to be treated like a bug that has just
> crawled into the infielder's cereal. At various times
> in his life, were Rod Carew ever treated by other
> human beings the way he himself sometimes treats

human beings, he surely would have wondered what he ever did to make another man behave so insensitively....

Rod Carew the man remains fiercely private, intensely proud, affable with friends and aloof with strangers. He does not trust outsiders easily and often regrets it when he does....

Carew has not always been kind to the media and they have not always been kind to him. Now and then, Carew has opened up to the press, only to regret it afterward.

In a December 1990 column outlining his Hall of Fame votes, Dan Shaughnessy of the *Boston Globe* wrote of me, "This was a second baseman who bailed out on the double play.... Carew was accused of protecting his numbers, sacrificing power for average, and hitting .340 without helping his team. When he retired, nobody noticed."

Ouch. And that was from a guy who wrote he was voting for me.

Another reason I braced myself for disappointment traced back to the MVP vote in 1977. Despite my historic season, I received only 70 percent of the votes—and most of the same voters were part of this process.

Election required being named on 75 percent of ballots cast. It seemed quite possible that more than 25 percent of voters would seize this opportunity to get back at me. Waiting another year wouldn't be so terrible. Only 22 players had ever been elected in their first year of eligibility.

Since my doubts grew in fertile soil, the last thing I wanted to do on January 8, 1991, was sit around hoping for the phone to ring. So I went to work at the hitting academy I'd started after retiring. I was giving a lesson when I was summoned to the office for a call. Was it *the* call?

Sitting at my desk, under a blown-up image of the 1977 *Time* cover proclaiming me BASEBALL'S BEST HITTER, I got the good news. They were saving a spot for me in Cooperstown. My plaque would hang in the Hall alongside Jackie and Ted, Roberto and Hank, Babe Ruth and Ty Cobb. It was the highest honor of my professional career, the highest honor any ballplayer can receive. Getting in on the first try was even more validating.

As for the election itself, 443 ballots were cast, so it took 333 votes to get in. I got 401—more than 90 percent. Wow.

We popped champagne and it tasted delicious. Equally satisfying was sharing the news with others.

Just like the baseball writers put aside our personal differences and focused on my contributions to the game, I did the same by making my first call to Calvin Griffith.

Everything he did to launch my career outweighed what he told the Lions Club in Waseca and our other differences. I wanted him to know how much I appreciated his early support. I also wanted him to know the artist sculpting my bronze plaque would be etching on my head a Twins cap.

The next call was to my mother. We both shed tears of joy. She also said what she always said: "God is there for you. He's always going to be there. He's going to take care of you."

———————

The first two words on my Hall of Fame plaque are "batting wizard." The phrase stems from people describing my bat as a magic wand because it seemed as if I could say a few secret words and—presto!—put the ball wherever I wanted.

I also often heard people say I made the game look easy.

When *Sports Illustrated* brought together me and Ted Williams in 1977, he described my hitting as effortless: "When I first saw Carew in the late '60s, I didn't think he had the talent. He was a little too lackadaisical to suit me. He swung at bad balls, and he didn't make contact that much. He still looks lackadaisical. It's his style. He's so smooth he seems to be doing it without trying. Some guys—Pete Rose is one, and I put myself in this category—have to snort and fume to get everything going. Carew doesn't."

Another appreciation came from Jim Murray, the Pulitzer Prize–winning sportswriter from the *Los Angeles Times*. After the Angels were knocked out of the playoffs in 1979, my first year in Anaheim, he wrote a column lamenting the fact I had yet to play in a World Series. The story included these lines:

> Watching Rod Carew bat is like watching Bulova make a watch, DeBeers cut a diamond, Stradivarius varnish a violin, or Michelangelo do a ceiling. It's not sport, it's an art. It's not a contest, it's a recital. It's like watching a great maestro conduct a symphony. Rod Carew doesn't make hits, he composes them. Rod Carew bats .388 the way some people tie their shoelaces. Maybe with even less effort....

No one ever taught Rod Carew how to hit. No one
ever had to. No one ever had to teach Rod Carew
much of anything. Rod Carew stood as aloof from
life as he does from an outside curveball....
Carew never just hits a ball, he plays a tune with it.

I know Jim and Ted were complimenting me, as was the
Hall of Fame by calling me a wizard. Yet there's a difference
between making it look easy and it coming easy.

I had to do a lot more than just show up. I put as much
work into preparing my at-bats as Ted, Pete, or anyone else.

Another trait shared by hitters—not all great hitters, *all*
hitters—is confidence. Extreme confidence. Some people call
it "hitter's arrogance." Mine was higher than most. You need
that attitude because hitting is all about handling failure. As
the joke goes: "What do you call a baseball player who gets
out seven out of 10 times? A Hall of Famer."

I made outs in 67.2 percent of my at-bats. That translates
to a hit in almost every three at-bats. Here's how that confidence manifests: every time I went to the plate, I knew *this*
would be that one.

Again, I don't think that is unique. Consider Mario Mendoza, a shortstop who lasted nine seasons mainly because of
his slick fielding. Because his batting average usually hovered around .200, that figure became known as the "Mendoza
Line." That meant he got a hit every fifth at-bat. I'm sure
every time he stepped into the batter's box, he thought *this*
would be that one.

So, how did I do it?

How was I able to get hits more often than other guys?

How did I perfect my craft enough that even Ted Williams thought I made it look easy?

Glad you asked.

───────────

Any discussion about my swing starts with my stance. Or, more accurately, stances.

I changed pitch to pitch, at-bat to at-bat, game to game— so much that this, too, earned a reference on my Hall of Fame plaque. The line reads, "Used variety of relaxed, crouched batting stances to hit over .300 15 consecutive seasons."

I've heard many lyrical descriptions of my stance: calm, loose, sleepy, nonchalant. A kaleidoscope. A man crossing a narrow stream. Rival manager Dick Williams said pitching to me was like facing five different guys and 20 different swings.

The evolution began in Panama, when I first picked up a bat.

Because I followed the game on radio and through newspapers, I rarely saw the swings of big-league hitters. Maybe I caught a glimpse of Jackie or Ted on a newsreel in a movie theater, but it's not like I studied them on video. So the swing I developed was all mine.

I hit from the left side simply because it felt comfortable, natural. I tried hitting right-handed, like most of my friends, but it made me feel like a klutz.

My swing was so successful that no youth coach ever tried refining anything, even when they should have. For years, I swung with my left hand on the bottom by the knob and my right hand stacked on top. That's the setup for a righty.

Doing it as a lefty is what's called a cross-handed grip. I later learned that Hank Aaron hit that way growing up and even in the Negro Leagues. It wasn't until he got into the minors that a coach convinced him to switch to a traditional setup. I snapped out of it on my own long before I left Panama.

As for my stance, I got to the majors using a traditional upright pose.

Most successful hitters aim to be like robots. They build what they consider the perfect stance and the perfect swing and seek to repeat it every time. By having a single template, it's easier to detect and fix anything that gets out of whack. This all makes perfect sense. Until it stops working.

As I've mentioned, I struggled during my second season. The next year, Billy Martin helped me rebuild my swing and my game. That's when I started to really understand what I could and couldn't do in the batter's box. I soon found a new stance with more of a crouch. But it wasn't until a few years later that I discovered what a chameleon I could be in the batter's box.

It all started with Nolan Ryan.

I loved hitting fastballs and Nolan, of course, loved throwing them. Our battles weren't chess matches. It was more like arm wrestling. His strength against mine. It had all the ingredients for a great rivalry—the guy who became synonymous for strikeouts and no-hitters versus the guy known for making contact. Except, at first, I wasn't making it much of a fight.

Nolan dominated the early rounds because he kept firing high heat and I couldn't resist swinging. I also couldn't make good contact. I'd wave through the ball or hit it weakly.

I made my major league debut on April 11, 1967, getting a single in my first career at-bat. (Courtesy of the Minnesota Twins)

The day I tried out for the Twins, I wore Tony Oliva's No. 6. He eventually became my friend, mentor, and lifelong "roomie." Every June 29, Twins fans celebrate "Oliva–Carew Day" in honor of our now-retired jersey numbers. (Courtesy of the Minnesota Twins)

Harmon Killebrew was a gentle giant. He taught me "it doesn't cost anything to be nice." (Courtesy of the Minnesota Twins)

I led the AL in hitting in 1969, 1972–75 and 1977–78. Only Ty Cobb did it more often. Each year from 1973–75, my average topped both leagues. (Courtesy of Rod Carew)

I started the 1983 season with 48 hits in 96 at-bats. I was above .400 on July 15, a few days later than my MVP season in 1977. I finished with my 15th straight .300 season, a streak last done in the AL by another of my childhood idols, Ted Williams. (Courtesy of Angels Baseball)

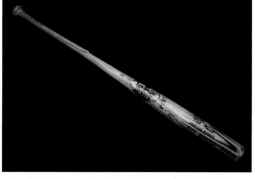

I used this bat for my 3,000th hit, an opposite-field single off Frank Viola on August 4, 1985. (Courtesy of the Baseball Hall of Fame)

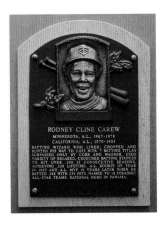

The greatest honor any player can receive is being inducted into the Baseball Hall of Fame. My plaque was unveiled in 1991, my first year of eligibility. (Courtesy of the Baseball Hall of Fame)

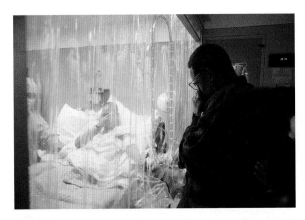

Before undergoing an umbilical cord blood transplant, my 18-year-old daughter, Michelle, told me it wasn't going to help her beat leukemia. Unfortunately, she was right. She died soon after at Children's Hospital of Orange County. (AP Images)

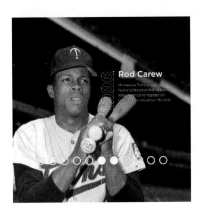 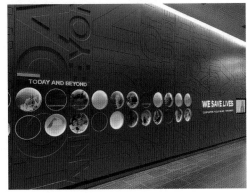

Michelle wanted to use her illness to raise awareness for the need to increase potential bone marrow donors, especially among minorities. The campaign she inspired was so profound that it's commemorated on a timeline of the history of Be The Match, the organization that used to be the National Marrow Donor Program. The organization also named its lifetime achievement award in my honor. (Courtesy of Be The Match)

Getting baptized by Pastor Rick Warren brought me closer to my faith. (Courtesy of Saddleback Church)

Here I was singing "Oye Como Va" on stage with my buddy Manny Rodriguez and his Carlos Santana cover band in the parking lot of Angel Stadium on September 19, 2015, the night before the heart attack that sent my life in an entirely new direction. (Courtesy of Rod Carew)

In my first public event since my heart attack and getting an LVAD to keep blood flowing through my heart, I was at Target Field for TwinsFest to announce Heart of 29, my campaign with the American Heart Association to raise awareness about heart disease. (Courtesy of the American Heart Association)

Rhonda and I having fun at the AHA selfie station at TwinsFest. (Courtesy of the American Heart Association)

I felt so good at TwinsFest that Rhonda and I climbed onto this one-of-a-kind Harley Davidson Road King designed with my name, number, and the Twins logo that was being raffled off for a hospice organization beloved by Harmon Killebrew. (Courtesy of the American Heart Association)

The Twins surprised—and overwhelmed—me by having everyone wear Heart of 29 T-shirts on the first day of spring training in 2016. We took a group shot, with me and Tony sitting front and center. (Courtesy of the Minnesota Twins)

The Twins honored our Heart of 29 campaign on their jerseys for several games in 2016. For the first, they also gave out a special bobblehead. (Jersey image courtesy of the Minnesota Twins/bobblehead image courtesy of the American Heart Association)

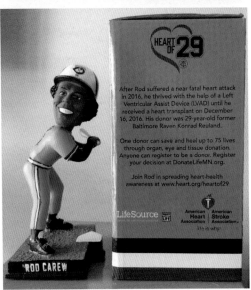

The Los Angeles Dodgers held a Heart of 29 celebration that included me throwing out the first pitch along with other families touched by heart disease. (Courtesy of the American Heart Association)

I started Heart of 29 in hopes of saving at least one life. That first life saved was former pitcher Clyde Wright, who'd become a close friend. The Angels celebrated us both during a Heart of 29 game at Angel Stadium. (Courtesy of Angels Baseball)

Mike Trout and Kole Calhoun were among the Angels players happy to see me during our Heart of 29 game at Angel Stadium. (Courtesy of the American Heart Association)

During the Heart of 29 game at Angel Stadium, I visited the Twins TV booth to spend time with Dick Bremer (far left) and Bert Blyleven (far right). We were joined by Tim Mead, the longtime Angels communications director who is now president of the Baseball Hall of Fame. (Courtesy of Angels Baseball)

Through my first 22 at-bats against him, I had five hits and 10 strikeouts. It was getting worse, too. After connecting for a home run in April 1973, I made seven straight outs—five of them whiffs.

I was a two-time batting champion at this point and headed for a third. Surely I could figure out a way to derail the Ryan Express.

I spent weeks working on different approaches. I started by standing taller. That brought my eyes and arms closer to the top of the zone. But everything else felt out of whack. So I tried the other extreme, a deeper crouch. This made it easy to lay off anything high because now it looked even higher. The challenge was keeping my body down as I took my stride. I eventually felt comfortable enough to try it.

On September 23, 1973, I struck out again in my first at-bat.

The next time up, I singled to left.

Then I singled to right.

When I stepped in again, Nolan smiled and screamed, "Stand up!" There may have been an expletive in there. It was music to my ears. Not only was I getting hits, I was getting into his head. I celebrated with a single to center.

I came up again in the ninth inning, with the bases loaded. I doubled to left.

Just like that, my career numbers against Nolan spiked to 9-for-27, a much more satisfying .333 average. Now our friendly rivalry was a fair fight. It turned out to be a draw: he struck me out 29 times, far more than any other pitcher. But I also got 28 hits off him, second most of any batter.

I wasn't about to customize a stance for every pitcher. But I sure liked the concept of mixing things up.

As I began tinkering, the main thing I wanted was a good look at the ball coming out of the pitcher's hand. This is where it all starts for a hitter. Seeing and recognizing a pitch early doesn't guarantee you'll hit it, but failing to do so makes it more likely you won't.

Ted always made a great case that hitting a baseball was the hardest thing to do in all of sports. Here's why: a 90 mph fastball gets to home plate in about 400 milliseconds. Hitters have only a fraction of that to decide whether to swing and, if so, where. The sooner and clearer we see the ball, the more slivers of time we have to decide.

The two variables of my stance were the placement of my front foot and how much I crouched. To a pitcher, this looked like an ever-changing width and height.

Based on where the front foot went, the stance was considered open, closed, or neutral. An open stance (with my front foot closer to first base) made it easier to hit an inside pitch. A closed stance (with my front foot closer to home plate) made it easier to hit the outside pitch.

The stance I used most is cast in bronze on an oversized statue outside Target Field in Minneapolis.

When I struck that pose, I planted my back foot at the rear of the batter's box, near the plate, and my right foot on the first-base side. My knees were bent and I leaned over them, crouching, my shoulders practically slumped. Another distinctive element was the position of my bat: flat, almost an extension of my shoulders. Ira Berkow of *The New York*

Times wrote that in this setup it looked like I was "plopped on a milk stool and handling an udder."

Another pose that kids loved to mimic was the one that looked like I was hitting during a hurricane. I crouched lower and leaned back, as if pushed by the high winds. My bat remained flat but was now down even with my waist instead of my shoulders.

I also sometimes broke out a version of my original stance, an upright approach that could've been used as a model for the batter figurine on top of a Little League trophy.

Shuffling my setups was a bit of performance art. Part bobbing and weaving à la Muhammad Ali, part chess strategy à la Bobby Fischer.

When the pitcher saw me in an open stance, it told him I was looking for an inside pitch. The obvious response is to throw it outside. But he had to wonder whether I was setting him up. Was I baiting him into throwing an outside pitch because that's what I really wanted?

The chess match element was fun because it added a new layer into the pitcher-hitter dynamic. As a hitter, I had to brace for different types of pitches thrown at different speeds in different locations. Now pitchers had to brace for—and interpret—my different stances.

Anything that distracted a pitcher from focusing on throwing strikes worked to my advantage. It's like Ali and the rope-a-dope. He didn't do that every fight, but everyone he fought knew that he might.

Long before Statcast provided exit velocity and launch angle, I had my own high-tech analytical tools: a pencil and a black pocket-sized notebook. This was how I charted every at-bat.

I started a new book every spring. Each pitcher I faced got his own page. When I faced a guy multiple times, I picked up where I left off last time. A typical entry went pitch-by-pitch: what he threw, where he threw it, and what I did with it.

"Curve. Inside. Took."

"Fastball. Outside. Knock to right field."

"Slider. Low and away. SO." (Unlike using K on a score-card, I went with SO for a strikeout.)

I also noted the situation: the inning, number of outs, score, how many men were on base.

I kept it in a corner of the dugout, stashed inside a glove. Referencing how a pitcher approached me in the past gave me an idea of what he'd do next time. The theory was simple: If he got me out in a similar situation last time, he'd prob-ably try it again. If I got a hit last time, then he'd probably do something different…unless deeper research showed this was a guy who rarely changed, regardless of the outcome.

Thanks to my research, I always knew what pitch was coming—or, at least, with my hitter's arrogance, I believed that I knew. I wasn't always right, of course. I got fooled plenty. But it was never because I guessed.

I eventually stopped tracking the pitchers I saw the most. It was a combination of knowing them and knowing I'd seen about all they could do. A great example is Catfish Hunter.

Catfish was among my favorite pitchers to hit against. He'd look at me and bark, "Let's go." He didn't nibble; he pounded the strike zone. This made for a great matchup. At

least, it often turned out great for me. I went 35-for-101 off
him, a .347 average. While I had more hits off Luis Tiant and
Jim Palmer (37 each), Catfish served up more homers (seven)
and RBIs (17) than any other pitcher I faced. But I'm bringing
him up now because his refusal to deviate from his pattern
led to one of my most memorable at-bats.

We were playing at Yankee Stadium. Before the game,
Thurman Munson passed me on his way to the bullpen to
warm up Catfish. Thurman patted me on the back and said,
"What're you going to do tonight, big boy?"

"I'll tell you when I get to home plate," I said.

Before Thurman could start his usual nuisances, like
throwing dirt on my feet and tugging at my shoelaces, I said,
"I'm going to call it every pitch. I'm going to yell it before
he releases it."

"Yeah, right," Thurman said.

Catfish went into his windup, reared back, and I said,
"Fastball, down and in."

When the fastball arrived down and in, Thurman said, "Are
you peeking at me with that funny batting style?"

"I don't have to peek," I said.

Catfish wound up and threw again, and I announced,
"Slider, down and in." When the slider arrived down and in,
Thurman jumped up and walked toward Catfish.

"He just called both of your pitches," Thurman screamed,
loud enough for Catfish and me to hear. "Let's knock him
down. I think he's peeking at my signs."

Catfish—the guy who always embraced our meetings—
told him, "No."

With the third pitch on the way, I screamed, "Fastball away—double down the left-field line."

When I got to second, I looked back at the plate. Thurman was steaming. The home-plate umpire showed his awe by bowing toward me.

At batting practice the next day, Thurman asked how I did it. I pulled out my black book and showed him my page for Catfish.

Catfish and Nolan were among 15 Hall of Famers I faced.

My cumulative average against them was .297, a bit below my overall average. That's to be expected. These are Hall of Famers we're talking about.

Yet the Hall of Famers I saw the most, I hit quite well.

I had at least 60 plate appearances against Catfish, Nolan, Palmer, Gaylord Perry, Ferguson Jenkins, and Dennis Eckersley. The lowest I hit against them was .301, off Nolan. The best was .362, off Fergie.

Fergie, Gaylord, and I happened to get inducted in the same class. I tagged Gaylord at a .316 clip, prompting him to once say, "Greaseball, greaseball, greaseball. That's all I throw him and he still hits them. He's the only player in baseball who consistently hits my grease. He sees the ball so well, I guess he can pick out the dry side."

Eck and I had some interesting encounters. It all started with him discovering my Achilles' heel, the pitch I'm embarrassed to admit that I struggled with the most: a heater down the middle. I was so accustomed to seeing pitches over the black that I froze when seeing something that juicy.

Eck was a rookie with the Indians when he rang me up on three pitches, all right down the pipe. After strike three, he screamed, "Go back to the dugout!" and pointed in that direction. Then he made the gesture pretending to brush a speck of dirt off his shoulder.

"Next time I see you, it's going to be different," I shouted.

It was. I hit a ball that went off his hand. In my next at-bat, he knocked me down. I answered with a home run.

"How does it feel to give up a hit to the American League's best hitter?" I screamed while rounding the bases.

This was 1975. I'd won four batting titles, including the last three, and was headed to another. This also was the season that Frank Robinson became player-manager of the Indians. Frank yelled to Eck: "Leave that man alone. You can't scare him."

My first game against Eck in 1976, I continued getting revenge. I got three singles off him—and stole second each time. The three steals matched my career high.

I finished with only five strikeouts in 60 plate appearances against him. Best of all, we wound up good friends.

I hated striking out.

To me, the worst thing in baseball is walking from the batter's box to the dugout after a strikeout. I know pitchers are going to get hitters out most of the time, but failing to put the ball in play is a humiliating way to go down. You're not forcing the fielder to make a play, eliminating the chance for an error. If you strike out with someone on base, you didn't move them over. More than three decades since my last at-bat, striking out still irks me—no matter how accepted it is in today's game.

Over my entire career, I averaged a mere two whiffs per week.

I also averaged just two walks per week. I wanted to hit my way on base.

There used to be a saying that guys from the Dominican Republic were free swingers because nobody ever walked off the island. This fellow Latino had a similar mindset. If a pitch was a bit outside the strike zone, but in an area where I knew I could hit it, I gladly took a whack. Why rely on an umpire to see things my way?

This is something else about the modern game that irks me. Too many guys go to the plate hunting for a walk. Or they'll wait for a certain pitch in a certain area. If they don't get it, they'll never take the bat off their shoulder, settling for a walk or strikeout. I don't understand that. Why leave the result up to the pitcher and umpire?

———————

I was never much of a scoreboard watcher.

That is, I rarely looked up to see my batting average. I also didn't check the standings to see how I stood against the league. It wouldn't tell me much.

The numbers were a reflection of how I was playing, and I knew that better than anyone. Besides, the numbers were based on what I'd already done. My focus was always the next pitch. Whether I was running hot or cold, I always viewed the next pitch as my next hit.

In the later years of my career, when video became more advanced, I didn't like studying my swing. Again, I had a good sense of how I was doing. In my early years, I bought one of those Bell and Howell 8mm video cameras that were popular for family vacations and birthday parties. They were tall and boxy, about the size and shape of early cell phones. Tony and I recorded each other's at-bats from the dugout. We carried a projector with us on the road to play the film in our hotel room. We'd sling a bedsheet over the drapes as a makeshift screen. But we were watching more than studying. There was no frame-by-frame analysis like guys do now.

When I looked at tape, it usually was to check one thing: the muscles on my right forearm.

If they were flexed, that was a problem. It meant I was squeezing the bat too tightly. Doing that lured me into the bad habit of swinging with my upper body more than with my hands.

My hands were the engine of my swing. They were most effective when they were nice and loose, like a twirler holding a baton.

When I first joined the Angels, I noticed the muscles in Bobby Grich's forearms always bulged. He was trying to squeeze his bat into sawdust. I told him to try rolling the handle loosely in his fingers. He quickly became comfortable with it. His whole upper body seemed relaxed as the pitch was on the way. His average soared 43 points that season (to .291) and he had career highs with 30 homers and 101 RBIs.

Knowing every aspect of my swing not only generated plenty of hot streaks. It also kept me out of prolonged slumps.

Over 2,469 career games, my longest stretch of consecutive games without a hit was eight. It happened once. My next-longest drought was four games.

I guess it makes sense that a guy who gets a lot of hits avoids making outs. But this speaks to my consistency. I wasn't a streaky hitter who could offset a bunch of 1-for-17s with some 8-for-10s. Day in and day out, the guys in the middle of the lineup could count on me to be on base.

When it came to the tools of my trade, I was mostly a Louisville Slugger guy. Specifically, models C243 and F147.

My first few seasons, I used a heavy bat—about 36 ounces. During spring training in 1970, I watched Al Kaline take batting practice, then asked to swing his bat. I was surprised by how light it was. I discovered Hank Aaron also used a lighter bat than I was using. Soon, I filled my locker with bats that were 34½ inches long and 32 ounces.

A trick I learned a few years into my career was changing bat sizes in August. By then, higher temperatures are baking a body that's also dealing with plenty of fatigue. I compensated by switching to a 34-inch, 31-ounce bat. The change is so subtle that it probably made more of a difference mentally than physically.

Whenever I got a shipment of bats, I inspected each one to determine whether it was worthy of accompanying me at the plate. The main thing I checked was the thickness of the bat handle. Like Goldilocks and her porridge, my bat handles had to be *just right*—not too thick, not too thin. (Although thinner than other guys liked their handles.) The test itself was simple. Wrapping my hands around a bat, I knew right away.

There are three places in your hand to hold a bat. The main point of contact is either along the fingers, the middle, or around the thumb. I liked coiling my fingers around the wood. That's probably why my hands were so sensitive to the thickness of the handle.

Bats are made by placing a cylinder of wood on a lathe and turning it. I found that bats turned by hand came out closer to my specifications than those turned by a machine. A rep from Louisville Slugger once asked if I had any requests; I asked for all my bats to be hand-turned. I could tell a difference by the next shipment.

Once a bat passed my inspection and made it into my locker, I became protective. Those sticks were my livelihood. I didn't like anyone messing with them.

Some guys slather bats in pine tar or rub the barrel with a bone to make it harder. I liked keeping my bats clean to avoid them carrying any extra weight. Plus, they looked better. Sometimes I kept bats propped near the door of a sauna. The dry heat baked out any imperfections in the wood, making it less likely to splinter.

Bats lasted longer for me than most guys. When mine broke, it was rarely from getting jammed at the handle. Mostly cracks came way down at the tip, as I mentioned happened with the bats that produced my 1,000th, 2,000th, and 3,000th hits.

The closest thing I had to a superstition was something else I've already mentioned—holding the bat with the label turned away. Seeing nothing but smooth wood gave me the sensation of a bigger hitting area. Considering that Ted Williams did this, too, there must've been something to it.

I never would have reached 3,000 hits if not for bunting.

That's not a comment. It's a fact—151 of my 3,053 hits were bunts.

In 1969, Billy Martin suggested I make bunting a bigger part of my game because he knew I had the basic skills required: hand-eye coordination and speed. Being lefty helped, too, because of the shorter path to first base. Billy told me that when I started dropping bunts, I'd only need a decent one because of the element of surprise. But he urged me to refine the skill because it would get tougher once defenses began expecting it.

As with my unconventional batting stance, my bunting style went against the norm.

Hitters are usually taught to "square around" to bunt. This means putting both knees even with the front of home plate, the bat lined up horizontally over the plate. I preferred something that felt more like my usual swing.

I started by pivoting my lower half toward the pitcher. By turning only my hips, knees, and feet, my upper body remained in its usual position. This let me see the ball the way I normally would. It also let me wait a tad bit longer before revealing my intentions. This kept fielders on their heels for a few more precious milliseconds. My legs also were now in position to start running toward first base.

While pivoting, I slid my top hand (the left hand) a few inches up the handle—only about three or four, not all the way to the label as preached by disciples of "squaring around." That hand worked like the rudder of a boat, steering the bat toward one line or the other.

The grip of my bottom hand remained as crucial as it did on a full swing. Holding the bat softly allowed it to absorb more impact, thus deadening the ball. Gripping it firmly sent the impact back out. I only wanted that when trying to push or drag a ball past a nimble pitcher. In either case, the goal was to "catch" the ball on the sweet spot of the bat.

Just like a ball hit high and deep is going to be a home run in any park, certain bunts are going to be hits no matter what. My target was a foot or so onto the grass beyond home plate, close to the chalk. No fielder could get there, pick up the ball, and throw it to first both accurately and with enough zip to beat me.

I spent 30 to 45 minutes a day in spring training working to place bunts. I maintained my sharpness with another 15 minutes per day during the season. That's a small investment for a big reward. Besides, it was fun. Bunting practice was like playing darts on a diamond. Instead of aiming at a bull's-eye on a wall, I'd put a small towel in one of those undefendable spots on both lines. To make it tougher, I'd try it against all kinds of pitches—high and low, in and out, fast and slow.

I broke out my new skill a month into the '69 season. Against the Orioles, I bunted for two singles against Mike

Cuellar. Brooks Robinson was their third baseman, so I was smart enough to drag both up the first-base line. Funny thing is, that's not what made this game so memorable. I also hit the first—and only—inside-the-park home run of my career.

My breakout season as a bunter was 1971. In late July, I bunted for two hits against Stan Bahnsen of the Yankees, got another the next day, and another a few days later. The next month, I got three over two games against the White Sox. After 13 bunt hits this season, the element of surprise was gone—which was fine by me. Having defenses worry about this was my aim all long. Just like the Muhammad Ali–Bobby Fischer element of changing stances affected pitchers, the threat of dropping a bunt gave me a mental edge against infielders.

Guys on the corners knew that setting up deep to cover more ground left them vulnerable to a bunt. And if they set up close to take away the bunt, they were more vulnerable to me slapping the ball past them. Pick your poison. So while the statistics show that I had 151 bunt hits, there's no telling how many more hits I had thanks to defenders caught out of position because they were wary of a bunt.

I bunted in almost every situation, including with two strikes or two outs. Probably the only exceptions were if we had a big lead (because it would look like rubbing it in) or if the bases were loaded. Men on first and third was okay, though. Three times, I drove in runs that way.

Multi-bunt games for me were like multi-homer games for sluggers.

I had 11 over my career. I even did it in back-to-back games in '73. Bahnsen was again on the mound for one and

Wilbur Wood the other. That was fitting considering that among all pitchers I faced, those guys surrendered the most bunt hits: six each.

In the final five weeks of my career, I bunted for hits four times. The first two came in Yankee Stadium, with Billy in the dugout. My final hit there—in the ballpark where I proved myself to Twins scouts by pounding balls into the upper deck—wound up being a bunt.

I already mentioned that my 3,053rd and final hit was a bunt. Well, in what turned out to be the final plate appearance of my career, I reached on a sacrifice bunt because of an error by the pitcher.

I have plenty of favorite bunt stories.

The first happened when Ken McMullen was playing third base for the Angels.

Ken scooted onto the grass and dared me to bunt at him. So I did, placing the ball so perfectly that he still couldn't throw me out. Next time up, he came in even closer and dared me to bunt again. So I did. Same result. He took off his glove and threw it down.

A few years later, something similar played out with Toby Harrah playing third for the Rangers.

He crept onto the grass and I bunted his direction anyway. I beat it out. My next time up, Toby crept in more, smiled, and said, "Try it again." I pivoted into bunting position, sending Toby rushing toward me. But I instead used a half swing to chop the ball over him. When the play ended, I stood on first and looked across the diamond. Toby reached up and tipped his cap.

In my 10 years as a big-league batting coach, I encouraged all hitters to work on bunting—not only as a way to get on base, but also as a way to work on tracking the ball. Practicing bunting is a great way to sharpen hand-eye coordination because it requires seeing the ball all the way from the pitcher's hand to the barrel of your bat. I never told anyone to become a bunter, like Billy did with me. I found that teaching bunting was akin to parenting. If it was my idea, they resisted; if it was their idea, they brought an open mind and a willingness. I had a few guys who worked on it in the cage until they were confident enough to try it in a game. From first base, they'd wave thanks to me in the dugout. They were so giddy you would've thought it was their first career hit and they wanted the ball thrown in.

When I go to spring training with the Twins these days, I often work with young, fast guys interested in adding bunting to their repertoire. I tell them it's like rebounding in basketball—desire and hard work are the main ingredients. But it can't be something you do in March and expect to be good at it all season. It takes daily work. Not much, but some.

With the way defenses shift in today's game, I'd like to see some of the big pull hitters more willing to drop a bunt. They don't even have to get all that good at it because their margin of error is huge. Since they often see only one guy on their opposite side, anything the pitcher can't reach will get them to first. I don't know why this remains rare. I guess it's machismo or the analytics guys telling them the math still favors swinging for the fences.

Oh well. Add this to the list of things I'm curious to see when the game will value again.

I want to clear up one thing about my playing days: chewing tobacco did *not* make me a better hitter.

A story went around that I always batted with a humongous, baseball-sized chew on the right side of my mouth because it pulled my cheek taut. This supposedly kept my right eye—the one facing the pitcher—wide open, thus giving me a better view of the ball. It's ridiculous. If that was the case, everyone would do it.

Somehow, the story caught on. I guess it became one of those things people wanted to think was true, like seeing my Chai necklace and believing I converted to Judaism.

I became a chewer in a wild, roundabout way. It started in the minors, while trying to cope with the heat and humidity in Florida and North Carolina.

All the sweating left my mouth dry. I guzzled water, but that left me feeling bloated. So I switched to Coke. I could easily chug 15 or 20 bottles in a game. Soon, all the sugar and caffeine hurt my stomach and began rotting my teeth. My dentist urged me to cut back. My search continued.

I don't like seeds, so I tried gum. It helped, but the moistness didn't last long enough. I somehow got the idea that I could extend the life of gum by mixing in something else as filler. Like cardboard. Why cardboard? I don't know. I was desperate. My story gets worse. I next tried toilet paper. When that didn't work, the only remaining option was the primary cash crop in the state where I was playing, North Carolina.

I tried snuff. It burned. So I went with a hunk of Red Man leaf tobacco. Problem solved. My mouth remained moist and the flavor lasted as long as I wanted. I often wrapped gum around it, which is how it blew up into something resembling a baseball inside my cheek. I enjoyed chewing, which is a shame considering the health risks and how much my family hated it.

But let the record show that I constantly moved my chaw from side to side. Even while hitting.

A journeyman named Alan Bannister once said I was the only guy he knew who could go 4-for-3.

That line is great for many reasons. A subtle one is that it reflects my hunger to pile up hits. I remember a game in Boston when Gene Mauch was my manager. A teammate who'd already had four hits made an out, then came back to the dugout laughing. He made some dumb joke indicating he didn't mind since he'd already gotten four hits.

"That's the difference between you and him," Gene said, pointing to me. "When he has five hits, he's looking for a sixth."

Is that selfish? Enough people said so that Dan Shaughnessy brought it up in his column evaluating my Hall of Fame candidacy. To this day, I don't understand the criticism. A guy who bats near the top of the lineup is supposed to be greedy about wanting to get on base so the guys in the middle of the lineup can drive him in. If that's a bad thing, then, yes, I'm guilty. And so are many of the other guys considered among the greatest players in baseball history.

It took a while for me to grasp that such a group included me. Fans hear players say that all the time, but it's true. In the midst of your career, you're too focused on the next pitch to absorb the big picture. You're aware of it, of course, but you lack the appreciation and understanding.

Once I accepted that I'd taken my final swing, I began evaluating my legacy. Looking over the stats, I was especially proud that at the time I retired...

My 3,053 hits were 12th most all-time.

My .328 average was 28th on the all-time list.

Only Ty Cobb and Honus Wagner had more than my seven batting titles. (Stan Musial also had seven.)

Then there were the All-Star appearances.

I was selected 18 times—all as a starter, all in a row. Only Hank Aaron, Willie Mays, and Stan the Man were honored in more seasons.

In 1970, when the vote was handed to the fans, Stan was retired, and Hank and Willie were winding down their careers. I was just getting started. So 15 of my selections came thanks to the fans. I set records for the most votes in a single year and for being the leading vote-getter the most times (four). When I retired, I'd racked up the most votes over a career, upward of 33 million.

To anyone who remembers hand-punching ballots in the stadiums—popping out those little chunks of paper we later learned were called "chads"—I offer my sincere thanks.

I'm often asked how I would do in today's game. I always say I'd hit about .280…but that's because I'm in my mid-seventies.

The real answer is complicated.

I have no doubt that, if I were in my prime, I would hit today's pitchers with the same success I had against my contemporaries. I think any player who stood out in his generation would be a star in any generation.

The real issue is, if I were breaking into the game today, would I stick with the style that got me to Cooperstown? Or would my style change to meet the demands of the modern game, meaning the analytically driven executives who value launch angle and homers and devalue singles, bunts, and steals?

My guess is, it depends on my age.

If I were a young kid with the traits I had in my youth, coaches would turn me into a slugger. My hitter's arrogance tells me I would have found a way to make it work. After all, I also would have access to all sorts of things we lacked, from better understanding of strength and nutrition to high-tech video and other swing-analysis tools.

But what if I were in the majors or close to it? What if I'd already developed my playing style?

I have to think the angry young man in me—a guy who was also fiercely stubborn—would insist on sticking with my own style.

I also think it would work. In fact, I think the game could use some guys who slash the ball from foul line to foul line, drop bunts, and are daring enough to steal home. Why do you need guys swinging for the fences at every spot in the lineup? It seems like a good idea to mix in a table-setter or two.

Surely there are plenty of guys out there capable of continuing the tradition I inherited from the likes of Ty Cobb, Stan Musial, and Ted Williams, a lineage that continued with George Brett, Wade Boggs, Tony Gwynn, and Ichiro Suzuki, among others. Here's hoping the guys with the algorithms can identify more such players and that front offices and managers give them the opportunity to join us.

––––––––––––

There's one final point I want to make about my success in baseball.

I've detailed many reasons for it, yet I've waited until now to share the one I consider most important. I hope this comes out the way it's intended.

I believe my ability to hit a baseball so well for so long was a gift from God.

Everything I accomplished was in service of showing Him my appreciation. That's why I was not driven by money or fame. My motivation was making God proud.

To clarify further, I don't believe God helped me hit Nolan's fastball. I don't believe He works that way. As I wrote about earlier, God doesn't choose winners and losers in these situations. I believe His role was providing me with the tools necessary to succeed. It was up to me to work hard to nurture that skill, to maximize it.

I also believe many people receive such opportunities. Some fail to recognize it. Others fail to refine it. You have to be lucky enough to get it, wise enough to take advantage, and disciplined enough to stick with it.

Tony Gwynn and I discussed this several times. I remember him nodding along as I said, "Well, it just doesn't come from us. Somebody helps. Our friend upstairs is always there."

When things were going well in my career, I often said a prayer of thanks to God. I always included the vow, "I will always work hard. I will make you proud."

Never did I question Him in bad times. Just like my mom taught me that God was there in the worst of times with Eric, I knew he was always there. Everything happens for a reason—including the fact I was given this gift. I didn't know why, but I knew one day it would be revealed.

———————

In July 1991, my family and I arrived in Cooperstown and checked into the beautiful Otesaga Resort Hotel. The view outside, on the veranda facing Otsego Lake, was breathtaking. So was the view inside: all the greats of the game— some I'd played against, some I'd only heard play on Armed Forces Radio. Walking through the lobby, I felt a tingly awe that reminded me of my first All-Star Game. My internal voice said, "I know I was invited here, but do I really belong here?"

Then I shook hands with Bobby Doerr, a superb second baseman on Ted's Red Sox teams. He greeted me with the line, "Welcome to the greatest fraternity in the world."

It was such a perfect icebreaker that I make a point of saying it to every inductee-to-be the first time I see them.

My speech was written well in advance, but my delivery still needed polishing. The day before, I spent about five hours practicing in my hotel room. The morning of, I continued rehearsing.

The majority of my talk consisted of thank-yous, primarily to my mom, Herb Stein, Calvin Griffith, Billy Martin, Gene Mauch, and Gene Autry. I also saluted my fellow honorees and, of course, my family. I made sure to point out that it was my daughter Stephanie's 16th birthday.

The presentation went great. I deviated from the script only once.

Right when I thanked Billy "for taking a young kid and turning him into a man," thunder roared. I smiled and said, "I know that the rumble that you just heard was Billy's message of saying that he approves of what's happening here today." The New Yorkers in the crowd loved it.

I closed with these words: "One of my first thoughts at being told of my election into the Hall of Fame was the natural awe of being recognized alongside Cobb, Ruth, Gehrig, and Jackie Robinson. But the Hall of Fame is more. It's all the kids who ever played the game. It's all the fans who ever bought a ticket. It's the first time you took your son or your daughter to a ballgame. It's Satchel Paige and Roberto Clemente. It's the Say Hey Kid. It's the Duke. The Hammer. Cool Papa. The Mick. Big Train. Pee Wee. Joe D, Teddy Ballgame, and many more. Thanks to all of you for moving over a little and making a space for me in your shrine."

Then they unveiled a shiny bronze plaque bearing my smiling face. Ever since the ceremony ended, it's hung on the wall of the Hall's gallery of greats.

This was it, the end of the road for my playing career. I reached the ultimate destination for anyone who's ever held a baseball. Yet my life's journey was far from finished. In many ways, it had yet to begin. And the fame and following I earned from playing baseball would play a large role in fulfilling what I learned to be my real purpose in life.

PART II

"You can't connect the dots looking forward; you can only connect them looking backward. So you have to trust that the dots will somehow connect in your future. You have to trust in something—your gut, destiny, life, karma, whatever. This approach has never let me down."
                        —Steve Jobs, in a commencement address
                                to Stanford University in 2005

9

BACK IN THE BIG LEAGUES

A BOUT SIX WEEKS after getting the call to Cooperstown, I left my hitting academy and once again reported to spring training.

With the Cleveland Indians.

This was an interesting time for the franchise. They were still the butt of jokes, such as in the recently released movie *Major League*. Yet they were building what would become one of the top teams of the 1990s. Omar Vizquel, Albert Belle, Carlos Baerga, and Sandy Alomar Jr. were already in the majors. Jim Thome, Manny Ramirez, and Kenny Lofton would soon join them. This core would lift the Indians to five straight playoff trips, making it all the way to the World Series in 1995 and '97.

One of the hopefuls on the early edge of the talent wave was a small, speedy, slap-hitting outfielder named Alex Cole. Alex could've been the inspiration for Willie Mays Hayes, the character played by Wesley Snipes in *Major League,* except the movie came out two years earlier.

The Indians sent Cole to my academy to work on his swing, his bunting, and his baserunning. Everyone liked the working relationship: Alex, the team's front office, and me. So we discussed me helping more of their players. I accepted a gig as a baserunning and bunting instructor in spring training, and working with minor leaguers during the season.

Spring training went well. My time with Alex seemed to be paying off, especially with bunting. In the towel drill, he got to the point where he could routinely stop the ball on a washcloth. Then the season began and he refused to bunt. Oh well.

A few weeks before my Hall of Fame induction, I went to the All-Star Game. Major League Baseball asked me to be the honorary captain of the American League. It was a tremendous honor, considering the honorary captain of the National League was Hank Aaron.

The game was in Toronto. On the field for batting practice the day before, Chris Berman of ESPN came over to me with a surprised look.

"What are you doing in *that* shirt?!" he said.

"I work for the Indians now," I said, thinking nothing of it.

For the game itself, I of course remained in an Indians jersey. To everyone watching, it probably looked as strange as it had to Berman. But the image meant a lot to the starting

catcher for the AL squad—Sandy Alomar Jr.—and his buddies in Cleveland.

"For many of us," Sandy said, "it was the first time we
were proud to be Indians."

Late in the 1991 season, the Angels got a new manager. The
front office hired Buck Rodgers, a guy I played with on the
Twins.

Buck had managed the Expos for several years. He'd tried
hiring me to be his hitting coach in Montreal, but I was too
comfortable in Anaheim. So he did the next best thing—he
sent guys to work with me in the offseason. Now that he was
taking over in Anaheim, he again started recruiting me to be
his hitting coach. He called every day, sometimes two or three
times a day. His sales pitch worked. My retired No. 29 Angels
jersey went back in circulation starting in 1992.

Great players rarely become great coaches. In fact, it often
works the other way—the worse a guy played, the better he
teaches. I guess it's a spin on the old saying, *Those who can,
do. Those who can't, teach.* Why do stars struggle to share what
they know? The reason cited most often is that we can't relate
to the struggles and limitations of other players. Put another
way: I went through a 15-year stretch where my lowest average was .305. Now I'd be working with guys who may never
hit that high.

There's a story about Ted Williams when he was manager
of the Texas Rangers. He took batting practice with his players in Fenway Park. He may have been in his fifties, but he

was still Ted Williams. The show he put on intimidated some players, humiliated others. Neither is conducive to getting the most out of your hitters.

My approach started with the simple premise that this wasn't about me. This was about *them*. I asked each guy what he wanted to improve. Slugging? Spraying the ball? Pulling more? Pulling less? Or we could go for an overhaul, figuring out what he did best and finding a way to do it every pitch. Those were the things I did with everyone who came through my hitting school, and it's what I promised Buck would do for the Angels.

———————

One of the main reasons I resisted previous coaching offers was to stay at home. Being with my family was part of it. But I also meant it literally. I didn't want to be on the road all the time.

I developed a fear of flying during my playing days. The less I could be on airplanes, the better. So in late May of my rookie season as a batting coach, I was thrilled we were going from New York to Baltimore by bus.

On the first of two buses—the one filled with coaches and other personnel—I sat alone in a window seat on the right side. A little before 2:00 AM, I was looking out the window as we rolled through a wooded, rural area on the New Jersey Turnpike. We were in the left lane of a two-lane highway and we drifted into the right lane. We kept drifting.

We banged into a guardrail. Time seemed to slow as we scraped against the metal barrier. It was like engaging gravity in a tug-of-war. Either the guardrail would win by slowing our momentum and keeping us on the road or gravity would win and we'd topple over, into the darkness.

Gravity won. We tumbled into a grove of trees, windows shattering and metal bending. Bad as it was, the limbs and branches broke our fall. Had we kept going, we would've wound up in a ravine.

The other bus pulled over. Chuck Finley was the first to reach us. He stepped in and the bus rocked. The drama wasn't done yet. We might still tumble into that ravine.

A highway patrolman soon lumbered onto the bus, rocking us again. Harder. His big concern was the carnage. Seeing twisted metal and bloody bodies, he leaned into his walkie-talkie and said, "We better get some bags over here."

"What do you mean, bags?" Buck screamed. "Get off of me. I'm alive!"

Twelve of us were hurt pretty bad. Buck suffered the most. He broke his right elbow, left knee, and a rib. He was out until late August.

My worst injury was whiplash. My teeth and jaw ached, too. The pain eventually went away. But ever since that day, I've dreaded bus rides as much as plane flights.

About a year later, an investigation revealed the cause: our driver fell asleep.

At the time of the crash, we were on a losing streak that had dropped us into fifth place in the AL West. That's where we finished the season. The next season, too.

A slow start in 1994 cost Buck his job. We weren't any better under his replacement, Marcel Lachemann, when the season came to a grinding halt. This was the year that the unthinkable happened: a strike wiped out the World Series.

Despite our disappointing results as a team, I thought I was making a difference. Our teamwide batting average went up each year I was in charge: from .243 to .260 to .264. I was especially proud of the progress by our best hitters.

Like Jim Edmonds. In my first spring training, people were claiming the game came so easy to him that he wasn't working very hard. I heard him tagged as "lackadaisical," the same damning word Ted Williams used when he first saw me. Jimmy's smooth left-handed swing didn't need much refinement. What he needed was confidence and encouragement. He grew up a long fly ball from the Big A and regularly came to games as a kid, so my support meant a lot to him. When he didn't make the Opening Day roster in '92, I said, "Just hang in there. You're going to be back up here." He sure was—for 17 superb years.

Tim Salmon blossomed alongside Jimmy. He was the AL Rookie of the Year in 1993 and was one of those guys who found something to improve on every season.

Gary DiSarcina wasn't as naturally gifted as those guys, but he was devoted to getting the most out of what he had. After hitting .247 and .238 his first two years as a regular, we fixed some flaws. He hit .260 and .307 the next two years.

A week before the strike hit, we called up Garret Anderson. I loved his swing from the start. As with all my pupils, I told him to tell me what kind of hitter he wanted to be, and

I'd help. At first, he aimed to keep the ball in the gaps. He became a consistent .300 hitter with about 80 RBIs. Then he said he wanted to start lifting the ball. He became a 25-plus homer, 40-plus double, 100-RBI guy without sacrificing much average.

When we returned from the strike in 1995, our roster boasted a collection of youngsters plus veterans like Chili Davis, Tony Phillips, and Rex Hudler. It was a winning formula. With about seven weeks left in the season, we led the division by 11 games.

Then everything that had been going right started going wrong.

The afternoon of September 10, we turned a five-run lead into a loss in extra innings. That shaved our division lead to five games. We were swooning and the Mariners were surging. Tensions were high in the clubhouse. When I came home that evening, I wanted to be alone. I busied myself by playing solitaire.

I was about to play another card when I heard, "Happy birthday to you…"

My birthday was three weeks away. But it was a biggie: No. 50. My family decided this was the perfect time for a surprise celebration.

Or maybe they just wanted to reveal my present: a Rottweiler puppy. We named him Hunter.

As we fussed over Hunter and nibbled on cake, Michelle and I talked about a paper she was writing for school.

She was a freshman at Cypress College, a community college in Orange County. Her assignment was about athletes who were good role models and those who weren't.

"You've got your dad—he's a good athlete and a good person," I said.

"Come on, Dad," she said with the dramatic sigh only a 17-year-old girl could deliver. "Be serious."

"How about Mike Tyson?" I said. "He's always in trouble. But that's what we hear. We would have to sit down and talk to him to see if that's true."

"Okay," she said. "What about a good athlete who also is a good person?"

"Nolan Ryan," I said.

"How do you know that?" she said.

"Because I know him, I've been his teammate," I said.

Now that she had her focus, she headed to her room to start working.

Later that night, I found her slumped over her computer. She said her head and back hurt. Her vision was blurry.

I carried her to bed thinking maybe she was fatigued. Or perhaps her allergies were flaring up. Hopefully a couple of Tylenols were all she needed.

When she got up the next morning, her head still bothered her.

10

PISH

———————

WHEN MICHELLE WAS A TODDLER, potty training proved…wet. She told us she'd had an accident by using a Yiddish term. "I pished again," she'd announce.

This was no shameful declaration. No "oops, sorry." To her, this was fun. A game.

She'd say it with a sweet smile and I laughed every time. She was my baby, the one who could get away with anything, and she was wrapping me around her pudgy little finger.

Her pishing became such a running joke that we nick-named her "Pish."

———————

One of the ways I tried to be the father I never had was by spending quality time with my three girls. Once we settled into California, I bought a sailboat for weekend outings and an RV for road trips. (We named the boat *Pishers Three*.)

The RV trips were, as the saying goes, as much about the journey as the destination. The togetherness brought us all closer. Rumbling down the highway, I loved looking back and seeing the girls talking, laughing, singing, playing games. Charryse was two years older than Stephanie, and Stephanie two years older than Michelle. They were a team, three friends who happened to be sisters.

Wherever we parked and set up camp, Michelle went exploring. Not seeing the sights. Her joy came from meeting new people. She reminded me of my old roomie Tony, or the legendary Will Rogers, in the way that she never met a stranger. Michelle connected with everyone she encountered because they sensed her sweet, gentle spirit.

At an RV park near the Grand Canyon, Michelle met a group of elderly ladies and fit right in. Weeks later, my five-year-old started getting mail from England.

"Honey, who are these from?" I asked. She reminded me about the ladies from the RV park. They'd become her pen pals. They exchanged letters and birthday cards for years. She enjoyed sending them 50 cents to buy tea.

"Daddy, they like to drink tea in England," she said.

On a trip to Baja California, Michelle rounded up something like a dozen kids and brought them back to our RV.

"Daddy, I brought some friends for dinner," she said. "We have enough food, don't we?"

After a visit deeper into Mexico, we discovered Michelle returned with only the clothes she was wearing and a bathing suit. She'd given everything else to kids who needed them more.

There was just something about this girl, something special. She had a wisdom that's rare in adults, much less children. Whatever the "it" factor is, she had it.

Everyone who spent time around her recognized it. From teachers and coaches, to parents of her friends and her English tea ladies at the RV park, people often told me, "She's such a wonderful girl."

Michelle's warmth extended to her posse of pets.

She cared for something like 18 cats. Many lived in our house and the rest were neighborhood prowlers. We turned our garage into her animal shelter. We parked our cars in the driveway to make room for all the litter boxes and bowls of food and water. We also always had many dogs. They all gravitated to Michelle, especially a German Shepherd named Atlas. He followed her everywhere, as her friend and her protector. When she took him for a walk, any stranger who got too close heard Atlas growling until they received Michelle's approval. When Hunter joined our family for my 50th birthday, he quickly joined the Michelle fan club, too.

Her love of animals—including a pet snake named Zebo—led her to start working for a veterinarian. The doctor said he'd never seen such a compassionate teenager. Especially when it came to death. As he prepared to put an animal to sleep, she had a knack for comforting them.

———————————

In the spring of 1986, while waiting to see whether I would return for a 20th big-league season, I became a softball dad. I volunteered as an assistant coach for Charryse's team and for the "Dangerous Dames," a team that included Stephanie and Michelle. The atmosphere was fun and relaxed—the way youth sports should be.

"I hope I can play good like you, Daddy," Michelle said.

If hitting is hereditary, Michelle got her mom's swing. Yet it hardly bothered her. She loved being a teammate and was an MVP in that role.

She offered an encouraging word for everyone headed to the plate and said something consoling whenever anyone returned to the dugout after getting out. While her teammates were in the field, she was up against the dugout barrier shouting support. Pulling for her friends came as naturally to her as hitting the ball the other way did for me.

Michelle was in third grade when I retired and she was a freshman in high school when I rejoined the Angels as batting coach. So I was around for more of her activities than I had been for Charryse and Stephanie. Is that why I felt closer to her than to her sisters? Did that make her my "pet," as I'd been my mother's? Maybe. But I also think it was Michelle's personality. *Everyone* felt close to her. That was one of her gifts. In the lunch room at school, she flowed between the most popular kids and the least popular. At a memorial service for Michelle, a girl and her mother introduced themselves to me. The mother wanted me to know high school had been rough on her daughter and would've been rougher if not for Michelle. Whenever Michelle saw this girl eating by herself, she joined her. Michelle always made sure this girl knew she had a friend. I later heard similar stories from others.

———

The day after my surprise 50th birthday party, my wife and Charryse took Michelle to the doctor.

We learned Michelle hadn't been feeling well for several days. She'd already visited this doctor and he'd ordered blood work. The results worried him. He sent everyone to the hospital to meet with an infectious disease specialist. They recommended I join them.

At the hospital, more blood was taken. Samples were sent to different laboratories. In case their worst fears were realized, doctors wanted it verified by multiple sources. As for what those worst fears were, Charryse spied it written on a piece of paper: "Suspect leukemia."

"We found something in your blood," the doctor told Michelle.

He explained that although Michelle was nearly 18, she would be treated alongside the kids at Children's Hospital of Orange County.

"Okay," she said. "That's fine with me."

I was crying. I wanted to scream. Yet Michelle hardly flinched. She didn't hit anything or try running out of the room. Neither her fight nor flight response was activated.

Of the many remarkable, extraordinary things I'd seen from Pish, this reaction—this lack of a reaction—topped the list.

And she was just getting started.

11

"DADDY, PLEASE HELP"

THE TESTS CONFIRMED the doctor's suspicions of leukemia. Only worse.

The version Michelle had—acute nonlymphocytic leukemia, or ANLL—was among the most aggressive.

This wasn't a diagnosis. This was a death sentence.

For the sweetest girl on the planet.

For my 17-year-old baby.

I don't know exactly how the doctor broke it to her. I missed it because I turned away and tuned out. It wasn't the most manly or fatherly thing to do, but I couldn't help it.

When I rejoined the conversation, I heard Michelle ask, "Do I have a chance?"

Yes, he said.

"That's all I want," she said.

Michelle's blood and bone marrow had been invaded by something called myeloid cells. They get in the way of normal white blood cells, red blood cells, and platelets.

Doctors said about 1,000 kids Michelle's age get diagnosed each year with ANLL. (It's also known as acute myeloid leukemia, or AML). About 50 percent got cured. The solution is reprogramming the source, the bone marrow, so it stops making the myeloid cells and starts making normal, healthy cells. This reprogramming can only come by transplanting someone else's bone marrow. But it can't be anyone's bone marrow. The challenge is finding bone marrow that matches genetic markers.

And there was Michelle's biggest obstacle.

Her body was a genetic gumbo: Panamanian–West Indies on my side, Caucasian-Russian-Jewish on her mother's. Obviously, there were two other people with the same mix. Charryse and Stephanie were tested right away. When we learned they matched each other, but not Michelle, it was like getting the ANLL diagnosis all over again. (My wife and I were also tested. As expected, we didn't match.)

We'd heard of parents in this dire situation having another baby to create a potential donor. This wasn't possible for many reasons. But it shows the extremes we were willing to go to—and how far we feared we had to go. Sadly, one of the main reasons this wasn't viable was the timeline: Michelle might not live long enough for a child to be born and grow old enough to become a donor.

If there was a savior out there, he or she would have to come via the National Marrow Donor Program.

More than 1.5 million people were on the list. This meant more than 1.5 million people were kind enough to donate a little blood so they could be considered as a possible match. Nobody already on the list matched Michelle. So we needed more people to join it.

Although I valued my privacy, I'd left the team in the middle of a pennant race, so an explanation was needed. Now that we had a diagnosis—and a need for the public to respond—we let the team spread the news and asked them to include a plea for help. We encouraged donations of money to the Pediatric Cancer Research Foundation and donations of whole blood or platelets to Children's Hospital, and requested that people call 1-800-MARROW2 to learn about joining the list of potential donors. It ran as a blurb in a few local sports sections.

———

Depending on your perspective, the oncology floor of Children's Hospital of Orange County was either incredibly depressing or amazingly uplifting.

I found it incredibly depressing. I saw kids left bald by chemotherapy. Others seemed shriveled. Some wandered the halls pushing IV poles. I flashed back to my days battling rheumatic fever at Gorgas Hospital in Panama. Cold dread raised the hairs on my arms.

Michelle found the scene amazingly uplifting. She felt surrounded by kindred spirits, kids like herself determined to beat this cruel disease. Michelle looked closely at the kids shuffling around with the IV poles and realized they were zigzagging because they were playing soccer.

"I'm going to be okay," she said. "No matter what happens to me, I want you to stay involved. Daddy, please help these kids."

———

The chemo hit her hard. Unable to differentiate between healthy cells and cancerous ones, the powerful drugs wiped them all out. This compromised her immune system, leaving her more susceptible to catching something her body might not be able to fight off. The rest of us were vaccinated for all sorts of things, from flu to Hepatitis B.

At Michelle's urging, I went back to work. The guys were happy to see me. It was nice to be part of something less important than life or death—even if these were pressure-packed games. Our late-summer swoon had turned a runaway division lead into a tight playoff chase. A bad road trip to Oakland and Arlington left us in second place behind the Mariners when we arrived in Seattle. That's where I was when a call came to rush home. Doctors found a tumor in Michelle's right eye, behind the optic nerve. It could leave her blind. They were about to operate.

The surgery went well. They saved her sight.

The next jarring episode was septic shock. Remnants of the bacteria killed by her chemo pooled together and attacked her body. Can you believe that? Even when she won, she lost. This episode escalated quickly. Her temperature shot up. Her blood pressure plummeted. Her heart rate bounced all over the place, from way too fast to frighteningly slow.

Once things settled, a doctor told me, "Your daughter has nine lives. She has used up three of them."

At least the chemo was meeting its primary goal. Her leukemia was in remission.

Knowing we were in for a long stay, I parked our RV in the hospital parking lot. The camper gave us a place to sleep, shower, and hang out when we weren't in room 306 of the oncology intensive care unit.

Charryse was a senior at Chapman College and Stephanie was a junior at UCLA. Neither wanted to be in class and wouldn't be able to concentrate if they had been. So both dropped out of school and spent each day at the hospital. I spent my 50th birthday there. This was where we'd spend Thanksgiving, Christmas, and more. Home is where the heart is, right? Like it or not, Children's Hospital essentially became our home.

In room 306, there was no way to pretend things were normal. The air was filtered to rid it of floating germs. We washed our hands each time we went in, scrubbing so often that our skin turned red and raw. We wore sterile masks over our mouths and noses. As a reminder that we were in a pediatric hospital, the white material was dotted with pink and blue teddy bears.

I'd sit for hours and stare at the monitors, watching her vital signs. In a batter's box, I could control how things would play out. Here? I'd never felt so helpless. Michelle could read it on my face. I'd walk into the room already upset and she would cheer *me* up.

A nice way Michelle and I passed our alone time together was doing crossword puzzles. She liked doing the ones in the gossip rags, particularly *National Enquirer* and *Star*. I enjoyed going to the grocery store each week to pick up the newest editions. I also kept a diary. I wanted to have a record of everything so that once she beat this, she could look back and know everything she went through, and how it looked and felt through our eyes.

Michelle wasn't afraid of dying. She wasn't afraid of anything.

We talked about this a lot. She understood that her genetic cocktail made a match unlikely. She accepted it. But she couldn't accept that so many other kids on the third floor—and in pediatric hospitals all over the country—might not get bone marrow transplants. She was especially frustrated at the dim outlook for kids with nonwhite skin. Her twin goals were getting more people signed up as potential donors and for many of them to be minorities.

She knew there was an obvious way of truly making a splash. During one of our late-night chats, she made her pitch. Echoing the words she spoke the day we checked in, she looked me in the eye, held my hands, and said, "Daddy, please help."

When your dying daughter makes a request like that, there is no choice.

After years of seeking the shadows—of ceding the spot-light to higher-wattage personalities like Tony and Reggie or to guys built to handle a burden like Harmon and Groove— it was my responsibility to become the frontman. I had to channel the strength of those men, and of my heroes. At the risk of overstating it, this was my chance to do something important for minorities like Jackie Robinson did. This was a time to be vulnerable and selfless, as Roberto Clemente so often was.

I had to use Michelle's story for the greater good.

My Hall of Fame career gave me a platform. *Not* using it would be a sin. So what if it made me uncomfortable? This was so much bigger than me. It was about Michelle. It was about all the other kids. It was about anyone and everyone with leukemia.

Mr. Reluctant was ready to become Mr. Expressive. The guy who dodged cameras and stiff-armed reporters vowed to embrace all media. I asked the hospital to hold a news conference.

Knowing that the TV and radio types were eager for a sound bite, I gave them one: "All the years I spent playing the game of baseball, right now it's one of my toughest at-bats."

Dr. Mitchell Cairo, Michelle's doctor and the hospital's director of bone marrow transplants, explained the medical challenge. He also described the numbers game: 1.8 million names were on the U.S. registry, plus another million world-wide, and only about 90,000 were black.

Once the news conference ended, once I'd taken this giant step outside my comfort zone, my biggest fear was letting Michelle down.

What if nobody responded?

What if people didn't care about my sick kid?

What if all we got was another blurb in the local sports section?

The response came swiftly. Calls, letters, and visitors to the hospital let us know that an army of do-gooders was mobilizing.

That weekend, we held our first donor drive. It was at a Planet Hollywood. More than 600 people showed up, including Garret Anderson, Jimmy Edmonds, Mark Langston, and Bert Blyleven. A few weeks later, we held another donor drive at the Farmers Market in Anaheim. Around this time, a player for the Mighty Ducks, Milos Holan, was diagnosed with another form of leukemia. He also needed a bone marrow transplant, so we held joint events. I took part in another drive at the Tustin Marine Corps Helicopter Station; once a Marine, always a Marine.

I filmed a public service announcement. I was joined by a man named Drew who survived thanks to a bone marrow transplant. We got to talking and I learned that he'd been treated at Children's Hospital, too. He even remembered his room number—306. We took that as a good sign.

ESPN ran a powerful feature on Thanksgiving. A few days later, newspaper readers across the country saw this:

> Dear Abby: Like so many others, I never thought I'd be writing a Dear Abby letter.
>
> My 17-year-old daughter, Michelle, has acute nonlymphocytic leukemia. Like too many other

children, she is in need of a bone marrow transplant. Her doctor has said she cannot survive unless
she receives a transplant with matching bone marrow. Time is running out for my daughter; the per-
centages are not in her favor.

There are 1.8 million wonderful people who are
registered potential donors with the National
Marrow Donor Program. None of them has bone
marrow that matches Michelle's. What makes our
daughter "different" isn't that she has leukemia, nor
is it because I am in the Baseball Hall of Fame.
Michelle must find the "needle in the haystack"
because I am African-American and her mother is
Caucasian.

People with African ancestry and other ethnic
minorities are underrepresented in donor pools.
The largest percentage of donors are Caucasian,
followed by African-American, Latino, Asian and,
finally, a donor with mixed black and white blood
types. The only donor who can give the gift of life
to Michelle and others like her is a person 18 or
older of mixed race—specifically African-American
and Caucasian.

Our prayer is that the awareness of our daughter's need, and the need of so many others, will
motivate people to action. We hope your readers
will step forward. The process is quite easy and
virtually painless. Donors share only a small por-
tion of bone marrow, and the body soon replaces
it. A simple blood test can determine whether

someone is a candidate to help Michelle and others like her.

Abby, we believe with today's technology and your wide readership, we can surely find that needle in a haystack. Time is short. The needle must be found today.

Not only for our daughter, but for all the children and adults in this country like her, my wife and I urge your readers to call 1-800-627-7692 to start saving lives today—before it's too late.

(Dear Abby's response)

My readers are the most caring and generous in the world, and I know they join me in praying for your daughter's recovery. Please, readers, call the number for the National Marrow Donor Program, 1-800-MARROW2, and obtain information on becoming a donor.

I had business cards printed with an image of me in my trademark batting stance and the following words:

Rod Carew

Help Michelle Find Her Miracle

Call 1-800-MARROW2

Share Life

I handed the cards to everyone I encountered, from folks in the line at the grocery store to parishioners at the black churches in Los Angeles that I visited to encourage them to join the registry.

One day, the Rev. Jesse Jackson came to room 306. Michelle was sleeping, so we looked in on her and prayed. Jesse then held a news conference pleading for more donors: "Make yourself available. For the life that you save today of your neighbor…could save your own child tomorrow."

I even chased down the phone numbers of reporters for several major newspapers and invited them to come hang out with us. I can only imagine the looks on their faces when they answered the phone and heard: "Hi, it's Rod Carew. Do you have some time to talk?" I brought them to room 306 and into my RV. I let my guard down and answered every question, no matter how personal or painful.

Within a month of our media blitz, the National Marrow Donor Program reported it had received almost 18,000 calls. In a typical month, it logged 3,000. In February, Dear Abby published a letter from the program's CEO. He wrote that the response to our letter that she published "has been greater than any other single print exposure of the NMDP's telephone number. Calls related to Michelle Carew currently total more than 47,000."

One day I awoke and realized something. The angry façade I put up as an abused child had crumbled. Once again, Michelle had done something that didn't seem possible.

This led to another epiphany. Maybe this was the reason God gave me my gifts as a ballplayer. Maybe this was what my life had been about all along.

———————

In the midst of Michelle's story capturing people's hearts, we nearly lost her. Two days after the donor drive at Planet Hollywood, she again went into toxic shock.

It was the final day of her fourth chemotherapy cycle. Things seemed so uneventful that my wife and I headed home to shower. Minutes into our drive, our car phone rang. Charryse called with panic in her voice. Things were going horribly wrong. Doctors and nurses were rushing in and out of Michelle's room. We turned around and zoomed back to the hospital.

Michelle's blood pressure had plummeted. Her temperature soared to 104—and kept rising. At one point, her eyes rolled back in her head. Someone shoved a breathing tube down her throat and she vomited. She saw me and said: "Daddy, I'm fighting. I'm fighting, Daddy."

I can still see the look in her eyes. Somehow, she conveyed to me that she was both scared but assured. I walked away to gather my emotions and tell God that I knew He was in control.

Her struggle worsened. Her heart rate, already low, drained like a countdown clock: 22...18...9, then a long flat line across the screen. The machine squealed.

"Don't leave us!" Stephanie screamed.

Jolts of a defibrillator brought Michelle back to life. Someone later said she was gone for an entire minute. It felt much longer to me.

By 10:00 PM, she was stable again.

The awful episode was triggered by a fungal infection. Doctors fought it for more than a month, giving her so many doses of a heavy-duty medicine that they needed permission from the Food and Drug Administration to keep giving it to her. Michelle wound up on that medicine for nearly two months.

Four days after the scare, Michelle turned 18. We celebrated with cake and a little party. Her favorite TV show was *Lois & Clark: The New Adventures of Superman*, and we played her a video of stars Teri Hatcher and Dean Cain wishing her a speedy recovery. When I remember that scene, I think of how wide she smiled watching that video. I treasure that memory.

A few weeks later, Michelle and I finished a crossword puzzle, then got to talking about the night she almost died. Or, rather, the night she died and was revived.

She wanted to tell me about it from her perspective.

She saw a man in the corner of her room. A glowing light surrounded him. He was her guardian angel. He was there to protect her. He would keep her safe and escort her when the time would come.

This confession of sorts left her in tears. As I held her and wiped her eyes, I also wondered. Could it be true? It was far more likely that the fungal infection and medications caused her mind to play tricks on her. After all, I'd had plenty of hallucinations when I fought rheumatic fever, and this was far more severe. Still, as a believer, I liked the notion that it might be real.

About once a week, my "flight" instinct kicked in. I had to get away. Late at night, I'd leave Michelle's room, get in my car, drive a few blocks to Interstate 5, and aimlessly keep going. This was my private time with God.

Early in this ordeal, I asked Him, "What did I do?" I knew Michelle never harmed anyone, so perhaps this was my punishment. I realized that made no sense. Once that phase passed, I thought more deeply about God's intentions.

I never argued with Him, though. Never got angry or blamed Him.

While others questioned why this wonderful, sweet child of God was forced to suffer, I didn't. I trusted that He had His reasons. My role model was my mother, who sustained her faith in the wake of Eric's brutal attacks on her and me. I thought of my mom singing "Amazing Grace" between punches. I heard her telling me the line that always resonated in my mind: "God is there for you. He's always going to be there. He's going to take care of you."

As the miles passed, I continued my lifelong conversation with God.

"I know you're doing everything you can," I said. "I know you are going to take care of her."

Sometimes I would drive as far as Nevada or Utah. I'd pull over and get out of the car. Gazing at the stars in the heavens, I'd wonder, "Where among them is Michelle going to be?"

Then I'd get back behind the wheel and steer back to room 306.

"Father," I'd say, "I know you only give us what we can handle."

The ANLL roller coaster continued. Michelle fought problems with every major organ: her heart, lungs, kidney, and liver. Her fever spiked. Her hearing dimmed. The chemotherapy continued to take a toll. Michelle didn't like seeing her hair fall out, so she took control. She cut it off. I secured her long braids in a bag and took it home, just like she asked.

In early February, her health stabilized. After five months in a sterilized room and 14 operations, she started going home for up to four hours a day.

When spring training rolled around, she suggested—no, demanded—that I be there.

"Daddy, go to work," she said. "The guys need you."

We agreed that I would spend weekdays on the fields in Tempe, Arizona, and weekends at Children's Hospital.

Before I left, I invited Mike DiGiovanna of the *Los Angeles Times* to spend time with us at the hospital and our house. His timing was great. Mike saw the real Michelle. Through his story, her plucky personality leaped off the page.

She said the best part of coming home was sticking her head out the window during the drive and "feeling the wind through my hair, whatever's left of it." She said she had to persevere or else "I wouldn't be able to spend all of Daddy's money." Similarly, she knew when she got platelets from Stephanie because "I have this urge to go shopping."

By now, the registry had grown by 25 percent—to more than 2 million candidates. It grew every year and other campaigns were helping, too. Still, many people were praising us for our role.

"It's scary that such a bad thing had to happen to wake people up," she said. "What if I didn't get leukemia? Would there be all these blood drives? I don't think so, and that's kind of scary. But because of me and my father, hopefully other people will have a better chance."

In my favorite quote of hers in the story, her sincere soul shined through: "I like making people smile, and I'll continue to do that. I don't think there's a day that goes by when I don't smile. Even when I cry, I smile."

12

BURYING MY BABY

———

DURING OUR MANY LATE-NIGHT CHATS, Michelle and I talked about all the things she would do once she beat leukemia. There were big goals, like becoming a nurse. And little ones, like finally playing in the snow.

Michelle was three when we moved to Orange County. We'd been back to Minnesota to visit, but never in the winter. Like some kids might dream of visiting Disneyland, my Southern California girl had a childlike fascination with what it would be like to experience a snowfall. I mentioned this to one of the many reporters who came by, Steve Wilstein of The Associated Press. His story opened with these words:

> Rod Carew muses wistfully about the snow his daughter Michelle has never seen, the falling flakes she's never tasted, the powder she's never scooped in her hands.

> Is there a way, he wonders, to make it snow outside
> her window in Room 306 of Children's Hospital?
> Get some machine and let her watch the snow float
> down magically in the brilliant Southern California
> sunshine?
> No, he says, she'd be wise to that, would tell him,
> "Daddy, it doesn't snow here, you have to go to Big
> Bear or Mammoth to see the snow for real."

The story ran in newspapers all over the country. A guy named Bob Decker read it and went to work. He set up his video camera and recorded two hours of snow falling outside his home in Denville, New Jersey. Then he mailed the videotape to Michelle Carew, Children's Hospital of Orange County, Room 306. We got another package from a woman whose hobby was craft making. She sent Michelle crocheted snowflakes.

In February, I went to a news conference at the hospital. The guests of honor were a seven-year-old girl who'd gotten a bone marrow transplant and the man who saved her life. The girl was so cute, so full of love and life and laughter. I remember her asking the donor if he liked Chinese food. Yes, he said—and why was she asking? Because before the transplant, she never did; now, she really liked it. Also honored at this news conference was a five-year-old who'd been the first leukemia patient in Southern California to receive another kind of transplant: blood from an umbilical cord.

Meeting him and his family, and learning about this option, was the reason I was invited to this event.

"A cord donation does not require a perfect match," the boy's father said. "This is the hope for the future."

When a baby is born, the cells and blood from an umbilical cord can be preserved and transfused into someone else. This was such a new procedure that only about 200 people in the world had received it. Seven were at Children's Hospital.

A few weeks later, it was obvious that the chemo and blood transfusions getting pumped into Michelle were starting to do as much harm as good. Something had to change to give her a chance. It was time for a medical Hail Mary. We agreed for her to become the eighth cord blood recipient at Children's Hospital.

As that was being set up, the transplant team brought other news. They found possible bone marrow donors. However, they were weak candidates.

What did we want to do?

Both options were flawed. Since there wasn't a better of the two, we went with the least flawed. We went with the cord blood.

Despite this being new technology, and thus a small sample size, Dr. Cairo said the chances of success were between 75 percent and 90 percent. Another deciding factor was the lower risk of rejection. After all that Michelle had been through, we couldn't bear the idea of getting new bone marrow and her body not accepting it. As a bonus, Dr. Cairo said we'd know within weeks whether the cord blood worked. Best-case scenario, she could be home in six weeks.

Before the procedure, Michelle and I were alone. She held my hand and said, "Daddy, I love you."

Then, she added, "I'm not going to come out of this."

"Come on," I said. "You're going to be okay."

"I know I'm not going to make it," she said. "But don't tell the others."

More jarring than the words was her demeanor. There were no tears, no sadness in her voice. It was more matter-of-fact. Something had changed, and she knew it. She wanted me to know it.

———————

The whole family gathered to watch as the cord blood flowed into her arm. We invited media to take pictures and video so the world could see the amazing possibilities provided by scientific research.

There was something magical about the idea that Michelle was getting a new chance at life thanks to the creation of another life. Seeing these new blood cells drain out of the IV bag and into her arm, I hoped that I was seeing my baby getting reborn. I hoped one day she would tell her children about this miracle that enabled her to become their mother. I hoped one day she would be a nurse who inspired patients with the story of her own incredible cure. I hoped one day she would roll around in the snow. I clung to these hopes no matter what she'd confided in me.

Dr. Cairo was right about the short timeline. We soon learned our flicker of hope had been a tease.

First, her kidneys failed. She went on dialysis, but this was clearly delaying the inevitable. The next day, the baseball season began. I went to Angel Stadium for the opener. I addressed the crowd, thanking them for everything they'd done for our family. Days later, I took another leave of absence. Michelle was back on a breathing machine. It was a matter of time.

That night, I went to the chapel and had my most difficult conversation with God. I spoke words that brought me both pain and comfort: "Father, please take her. She's ready to come home."

This, I believed, was why Michelle shared her insight before the cord blood transplant. She'd already let go and wanted to prepare me to do the same. She was ready for her journey. I accepted her wish and agreed not to interfere.

Her organs shut down over the next week. She couldn't speak, could hardly communicate. The most we got was a head nod, or a hand gesture. Shortly before sunrise on April 16, 1996, caregivers expanded her sterile, narrow environment. Germs weren't a concern anymore. We filled the space with family, friends, and the doctors and nurses who'd become like family. I held Michelle, kissed her, told her once more that I loved her, and said, "Have a safe journey." Seven months after I carried her to bed because of a headache and blurry vision, she was no longer suffering. God had a new star in the heavens, another rose for his garden.

She was at peace, and so was I.

When we nearly lost her during the toxic shock episode in November, I tried to imagine what it would be like to see my baby die. This wasn't what I expected. I thought there would be nothing worse. But in the months since then, and especially the last few weeks, I'd seen worse. I'd been bracing for this conclusion since that night in the chapel when I asked God to take her. I took solace in knowing she was in the arms of the heavenly Father, and that I would see her again one day.

The countless people who'd followed our story deserved to know her saga was done. We let the hospital announce her death that morning and we held a news conference in the afternoon.

That night, the Angels were playing at home. Beyond the fence in right field, they covered the No. 29 sign commemorating my retired jersey with a banner that read, PISHER 1977–1996. During pregame ceremonies, the video board showed pictures of Michelle and a statement we released thanking everyone and again encouraging donations and joining the registry. Our note also said, "We hope tonight parents everywhere spend a moment with their children, give them a hug for Michelle and realize the special gift they have." Then everyone stood and bowed their heads for a moment of silence. We later learned that all MLB games that night included a moment of silence.

When the national anthem started, I walked out of the tunnel, up the steps, and onto the field in street clothes. Only the most observant people noticed as I stood next to our manager, Marcel Lachemann. I didn't stay long. Just long enough to hug my friends, thank them, and let them know I was okay.

Two days later, we held a memorial service at our shul, Temple Beth Shalom. More than 1,000 people showed up, including Gene Autry and Reggie. Chili Davis and Rene

Gonzales were among the pallbearers. I spoke briefly. I wanted everyone to remember her at her best. I said, "If she saw someone who didn't have a smile, she would take hers off and put it on them." And I shared what I'll miss most, the simple joy of hearing her say "I love you, Daddy." She never outgrew that term of affection. It was among the many ways she blessed me.

Southern California wasn't her final resting place. For that, we flew to Minnesota.

We held another service at B'nai Emet Synagogue, in the same sanctuary where 18 years earlier she received her Hebrew name: Tigra Shifra. Tigra means strife and shifra means beautiful. I swallowed hard upon remembering that.

"What a beautiful name it was," Rabbi David L. Abramson said. "Goodness knows she fought like hell. And the beauty of her soul shone through the darkness of despair and will continue to shine in the days and the years ahead."

Stephanie told of the difficulty she herself had making friends in high school. "I'll be your friend," Michelle had told her, and she became a great one. "She took care of me," Stephanie said. In Michelle's excruciating final days, Stephanie said she told her sister, "If you need to go, you go." She also encouraged Michelle to make some friends in heaven until we could join her. Stephanie walked to Michelle's casket, put a yellow rose on it, leaned into me, and sobbed, "This isn't happening, Daddy."

After remembrances from Charryse, a cousin from Minneapolis, and several friends from California, it was my turn.

I spoke about *It's A Wonderful Life*. I drew a parallel that came to mind months ago, after Michelle said, "Daddy, please help."

I compared myself to the Jimmy Stewart character. Like George Bailey, I was a flawed man in need of a new outlook on life, a new appreciation. Michelle played the role of Clarence. She was the angel who made me see the world in a different, better way. And like the movie tells us that every time a bell rings, an angel gets its wings, every time I hear a bell ring, I'll think of my angel.

"I will never question God for taking her from us at such an early age," I said. "I only thank Him for letting us have her for that time."

———————

She was laid to rest in the United Hebrew Brotherhood Cemetery, in the same neighborhood as the hospital where she was born. Her casket was buried near the grandfather who inspired her name.

The skies were gray and it was cold for this time of year, even for Minnesota. We planned to keep it private—only family and close friends. Then we reconsidered. Just like we'd felt the need to hold a news conference in California on the day she died, we decided the fans and media here deserved to share this solemn event. Despite the weather and the late announcement that this would be public, more than 500 people joined us. Tony was one of the pallbearers. So was Kirby Puckett, who throughout the season had shown he was thinking about us by writing No. 29 on his hat.

For her final journey home, we packed some things that would make her comfortable. We put inside the casket a handful of pens and pastel-colored papers because she loved to write and draw. She wore one of her favorite T-shirts. It was purple, her favorite color. Those small gestures meant a lot to us. But it was nothing compared with what happened during the burial.

It snowed. Not heavy and not for very long, just enough for everyone to absorb the power of the moment. I looked up to the heavens and thought, *Now she is at peace.*

———————

I drove the RV back to my house. Days and nights no longer revolved around Children's Hospital.

Yet the world we returned to was a vastly different place.

I spent some time in her room. I looked at her music collection and laughed. While all her friends were listening to rap, she loved Motown. I went through her beloved T-shirts. I pulled out a few that I wanted—purple ones, mainly, especially those still carrying her scent. They're in my closet to this day. We eventually donated most of her clothes, but not any shoes. This was purely symbolic: in my mind, no one could fill her shoes.

Charryse channeled her grief into designing Michelle's tombstone. The main piece is wide, beautiful, black marble with a rounded top. Carved into it are these words:

MICHELLE SIARRA
CAREW
TIGRA SHIFRA
NOV. 18, 1977 (JEWISH STAR) APRIL 17, 1996
HER STRENGTH AND COURAGE IS
AN INSPIRATION TO US ALL

The main piece sits atop a wider, rectangular piece of the same marble. Extra room was intentionally created where the pieces come together as a place to put stones, per the Jewish tradition of visitors leaving rocks instead of flowers. The base carries another tribute: HER SMILE WAS LIKE SUNSHINE THAT BRIGHTENED OUR LIVES AND TAUGHT US TO TREASURE THE MEANING OF LOVE. The back is striking, too. Two eternal flames are etched in gold, atop a profound observation by Michelle's grandmother: SHE WENT TO SLEEP AND WOKE THE WORLD. I visit my baby every chance I get when I'm in Minneapolis.

The Angels honored her memory by creating the Michelle Carew Community Courtyard a few steps inside Gate 3 of Angel Stadium. There's a big circular concrete bench, with an inner ring of flowers and, inside that, a statue of Michelle and her loyal dog, Atlas. A plaque reads:

THIS COURTYARD WAS DEDICATED SEPTEMBER 17TH 1999
IN LOVING MEMORY OF MICHELLE CAREW.
HER SPIRITED BATTLE AGAINST LEUKEMIA RAISED
AWARENESS OF THE NATIONAL MARROW DONOR PROGRAM
THROUGHOUT THIS COUNTRY. IN THE PROCESS, HER
LEGACY HAS SAVED COUNTLESS LIVES. 'WHEN SHE
WENT TO SLEEP, SHE WOKE UP THE WORLD.'

I stop by to say hello and pat Michelle on the head every time I'm at the stadium.

Keeping my vow of continuing to help kids battling cancer, we held the first annual Rod Carew Children's Cancer Golf Classic six weeks after she died. My former Angels teammate Doug DeCinces was already involved in an annual event for another organization. He took over the launch of this, and it was a hit from the start, pumping more money into the Pediatric Cancer Research Foundation. We've held the event every year since.

We also continue to tout the National Marrow Donor Program. At the time of Michelle's death, the registry had about 2 million names. The organization is now called Be The Match and the registry is more than 20 million strong, with roughly 300,000 cord blood units available. In the lobby of its national headquarters, which happens to be a few blocks from the Twins' ballpark in Minneapolis, a timeline of the organization's history features a section on Michelle. I'm also honored that they named their lifetime achievement award after me.

Michelle's alma mater, Canyon High School, already had an annual softball Tournament of Champions, but it was renamed the Michelle Carew Classic. The team also created in her honor an award for their most inspirational player. It's not given out each year, though—only when someone comes along who meets the standard she set.

Congress called, too. A few months after Michelle passed, I spoke to a joint committee on Capitol Hill about the importance of funding scientific research. Other advocates included U.S. Army General Norman Schwarzkopf, a survivor of prostate cancer, and Travis Roy, who was paralyzed from his neck down during his first college hockey game. Back in California a few days after I testified, I was in my car when my business manager and good friend Frank Pace called. He'd just gotten word that lawmakers approved an extra $800 million for scientific research funding. The timing was great. This was my 51st birthday.

I looked up through my open sunroof and said, "Thanks, Pish."

———————

Michelle's death transformed me, but not in the ways people would expect.

I didn't question my faith. I reaffirmed it.

Instead of shutting out the world, I opened myself to it.

Most of all, seeing her stare down death showed me how to overcome the demons of my past. If she didn't dread cancer coursing through her blood and bones, then why was I still carrying my dread from nearly 40 years ago? Why did I maintain the persona of a boy looking out his apartment window and seeing his father coming up the stairs drunk and angry, wondering whether tonight he'd whip me with his belt or the iron cord? So I stopped. Just like that, I let it go. My entire personality changed—for the better.

Soon, there were other, bigger changes.

———————

An ordeal such as the demise and death of a teenage daughter either brings a husband and wife closer together or tears them apart. Michelle's death tore us apart.

The foundation of my marriage already had cracks. The weight of this tragedy exposed deeper flaws.

Each of us responded differently to this new void in our lives. An example involves an invitation to spend time at a children's hospital in San Diego.

The request came from a friend of Tony Gwynn. At her urging, I visited the rooms of kids who were going through treatment and hung out with others in the playroom. I found this fulfilling. I knew I was doing what Michelle would've wanted me to do. My wife didn't feel comfortable there. She didn't seem to feel comfortable anywhere, at least not when I was around. We tried group therapy and counseling. Nothing worked.

The only solution was a divorce. Yet it proved to be even more devastating. Charryse and Stephanie followed their mother's lead. Without Michelle there to talk some sense into her sisters, they cut me out of their lives.

Now, the four people most important to me were all out of my life. Michelle had apparently been the glue holding us all together.

My family of five was down to one.

13

STARTING OVER

O N A SUNNY DAY during spring training in Palm Springs, California, the usual gentle breeze turned into a harsh, cold wind. If you didn't have a jacket, you were in trouble.

I looked into the stands near our dugout and saw two women in trouble. They were at the end of a row, huddled together for warmth. Wearing short pants and sleeveless shirts, they were no match for the chilling gusts. It was particularly bad for the blonde woman on the outside, who was taking the brunt of it. Gary Pettis noticed them, too. Then he realized he knew the gal shielding her friend. They took their kids to the same pediatrician.

I found two tan windbreakers in the dugout and asked a batboy to deliver them to the women.

"These are from Rod," the kid told them. "He says you look cold."

After the game, the ladies returned the jackets and thanked us. I invited them to join Gary and me for a drink. The four of us had a nice, brief visit. I eventually got the phone number of the woman Gary knew. Looking at her number, I laughed.

Her last four digits were 3053. That's the number of hits I had in my career.

———————

The year Michelle died, the Angels finished in last place.

We went through three managers that season, then got another in the winter. Terry Collins took over and I remained the batting coach. He guided us to second place each of the next two seasons, 1997 and 1998. His demanding style caught up to him the following year. He lost the clubhouse and ended up resigning as we bottomed out again. The next offseason, the Angels decided to clean house. Mike Scioscia took over as manager and he replaced the entire coaching staff.

I wasn't a free agent for very long. My pal Davey Lopes got his first managing job and talked me into joining him in Milwaukee.

This was a huge move for me. I was going to a new team in a new city and a new league. The Brewers had switched from the AL to the NL a few years before. But with all that was going on in my private life, it was a good time to get away and try something different. It was quite the plot twist to try improving my life in Milwaukee's County Stadium, site of the two most miserable moments in my career. This was where Mike Hegan slid into me and where I grounded out to end my last and best chance of playing in the World

Series. Funny thing was, the upcoming 2000 season would be the last in County Stadium. I could wish it good riddance in person.

Milwaukee reminded me a lot of Minneapolis. The people were friendly and the weather was similar. As for the club, we had the usual mix of young guys and veterans, some who were open to what I was teaching, some who weren't.

Looking back, the Brewers of that era were ahead of their time. It's not a compliment.

We had the lowest batting average in the majors but set franchise records for home runs and extra-base hits. The next year, we moved into Miller Park. One of the features was the mascot going down a slide every time a Brewer homered. Guys seemed hell-bent on making that happen. They took even bigger swings and connected even less. We set a major league record for strikeouts. Worse, we became the first team ever to have more strikeouts than hits. I hated watching this, much less being associated with it. The difference between the mindsets of me and these hitters couldn't have been wider. No matter what I tried, they didn't listen. It was as if we were speaking different languages.

When I took off my uniform after the final game, I knew this was it. After 18 seasons as a player and 10 more as a coach, my big-league career was done. I'd had enough of the February-to-October grind. This was a chance to walk away on my terms, unlike the way my playing days ended.

Most of all, I had other plans. With the blonde gal in the tan windbreaker.

Rhonda Fedden came from a large, close-knit family with roots as deep into Orange County as the orange trees that prompted the name. Both arrived in the mid-1800s.

She grew up in Laguna Niguel, back when that bustling area had only one stop sign between Interstate 5 and the Pacific Coast Highway. Her dad had five siblings and her mom had three. That makes for lots of aunts, uncles, and cousins— close to 80. The way the ages were spread out, Rhonda is only five years younger than one of her uncles. She has a younger brother, and is close enough to some of her cousins that they might as well be her siblings. Pretty much everyone remains within a short drive of each other. Family, obviously, was a major part of her upbringing. As was church.

She was raised Catholic. During Lent, even as a young girl, she had to give up something important—lemons, usually. She still remembers the agony of going 40 days without them. Also during Lent, her family went to church every single day, with young Rhonda required to wear a dress and cover her head. In eighth grade, she got confirmed. Her parents said that from then on, she could attend any church she wanted as long as she went somewhere.

After Saturday-night sleepovers at her best friend Lori's house, Rhonda started going with Lori and her dad to Calvary Chapel. Wearing jeans and sitting comfortably on the ground, she heard Pastor Chuck Smith tell folksy stories in plain English. There was no mention of fire and brimstone, no dire warnings about what happens if you sin. Nothing to feel guilty about. Instead of being told to fear God's power, the vibe at Calvary was to be in awe of God's great deeds. Prayer was about creating and sustaining a personal relationship with

God. Faith was a customizable experience for each person, not a series of dos and don'ts that apply to all. Everything about this spiritual lifestyle made sense to her. This, she realized, was the church for her.

At home, the emphasis was less on quoting Jesus and more on living like Him. When a neighbor was in need, they helped. When a plane crash killed three football coaches at Cal State Fullerton, leaving 14 kids without dads, Rhonda and her friends sold tickets to a football game held as a fundraiser. Every Thanksgiving, she and a posse of relatives fed and distributed clothes to those less fortunate at missions in Santa Ana. They returned every Christmas with toys for the children. It wasn't until she was an adult that she learned there were people who *didn't* instinctively do such things.

I mention all this because, from my perspective, she was raised right. Her morals and principles ran deep. It was a heck of a foundation to build on. It would be a heck of a family for me to join.

Rhonda also was proudly part of a long line of tomboys.

As kids, she and Lori were always climbing trees, playing hide-and-seek in the orange groves, or joining the boys in baseball, football, and kickball. They played a version of street baseball they called "Indian baseball." Instead of a home plate, there was a bat on the ground. Instead of pitching, a ball was rolled into that bat, popping the ball into the air for the batter to hit it. Like me, she swung from the left side.

In the fall of 1971, Rhonda and Lori were old enough to join their dads to watch the L.A. Rams every Sunday afternoon. When football season ended, they switched to basketball. That was the year the Lakers won 33 straight games. That also was the first year that girls at their school could wear pants. Rhonda, Lori, and another friend named Cookie decided to pay homage to the Lakers by wearing dresses for 33 straight days. It's a trivial thing, but she tells the story to show her commitment. And she was just warming up.

The Lakers went on to win it all that season. Once the NBA Finals ended, Rhonda and Lori switched their devotion to baseball. They also had an a-ha moment: while the Rams and Lakers were in Los Angeles, there was a baseball team in Orange County. Not only could they root for the Angels, they could go to their games. So they did. These 12-year-old girls persuaded their parents to ferry them back and forth to the Big A, dropping them off in time for the first pitch at 8:00 PM and picking them up after the final out.

Tickets were only $4 for field level, and good seats were always available. These girls babysat, washed cars, polished silver—"whatever someone would pay us money to do," Rhonda said—to save up for season tickets in 1973. Add in money received as birthday and Christmas presents and they were able to buy them. That's how Rhonda became a season-ticket owner at age 13. She's had them every year since. When we watch the replay of my 3,000th hit, she always points herself out. In the view from behind the pitcher, you can see her four rows behind home plate, sitting with two friends, her hair in a vintage 1980s perm with bangs. She even saved the ticket stub from that game, thinking it may one day be a nice collector's item.

Early on, she and Lori went to as many games as they could get rides to and from. Once they were old enough to drive, they caught almost every game through high school and college. They made sure to be there on the nights Nolan pitched. The atmosphere was always electric because of the way he could dominate. There was also the hope of seeing a no-hitter. Rhonda and Lori saw several. Plenty of near misses, too.

Her favorite season was my first as an Angel. That was our "Yes We Can" year, the one that ended with us going to the playoffs for the first time. The 1985 season was pivotal for each of us—my last as a player and her last as a regular. The real world started demanding more of her time.

Rhonda graduated from the University of California, Irvine with a degree in psychology. She wanted to teach deaf children at the John Tracy Clinic in Riverside. She was accepted into their training program, but not until the spring semester. To earn money until then, she took a marketing job. She liked it so much that it became her career. She also got married and had two kids: a daughter named Cheyenne in 1987, then a son named Devon in 1989. In 1991, she got divorced and started her own marketing company. Her ex-husband moved away from California, giving her custody of the kids but no child support.

As a single mom and business owner, she went to Angels games whenever she could. She always followed along, though. Reading about Michelle's diagnosis, she shuddered at the thought of something like that happening to her kids. She remembers the day Michelle died. It was Devon's seventh birthday.

In December 1995, after I made the plea for people to join the registry and shortly after the local hockey player also was diagnosed with leukemia, Rhonda attended a donor drive cohosted by the Angels and Mighty Ducks. She stood in line and gave blood to get on the list. Over the years, she's been contacted twice about possibly donating bone marrow. Both times, someone else turned out to be a stronger match. She's hoping for another call and the opportunity to save a life.

———————

As I began spending more time with Rhonda, I saw many of Michelle's best traits in her, all the way down to her fondness for cats. I often tell Rhonda, "Michelle would've loved you."

By the time I resigned from the Brewers, I'd fallen in love with her. I was ready to settle down.

"Let's go to Hawaii," I said. "Let's go get married."

"Okay," she said.

We exchanged our vows on December 22, 2001, at the seaside chapel of the Grand Wailea Maui. It was a simple, casual ceremony. Cheyenne and Devon were part of it, as were some of the closest members of Rhonda's family. Better yet, what was now my family, too.

———————

When Cheyenne and Devon Jones returned from Maui and started the spring semester at Saint John's Episcopal School, they did so as Cheyenne and Devon Carew.

Once Rhonda and I told the kids we were getting married, they said they hated the label of stepdaughter and stepson.

"Then what should I call you?" I asked.

"Daughter and son," they said. "We want you to adopt us."

Being part of a loving family meant everything to me, and these terrific children wanted me to be their dad? I couldn't have asked for more. Still, out of respect to their birth father, I sought his permission. To my delight, he gave it.

Having already seen three girls go through the angst of their teen years, I was somewhat prepared for what Cheyenne would experience. But Devon was my first son.

Eric was a distant memory now. He'd been out of my life for many years and my experience with Michelle helped me overcome lingering angst from his evil parenting. In other words, there was no chance of him infecting my relationship with Devon. I was concerned, though, that it might be difficult for him to carry my last name onto a baseball field.

"If baseball's not for you, don't worry about it," I said.

He couldn't have cared less.

Devon had been in diapers when his birth father left. So I wasn't replacing anyone in his life. I was filling a void. The interesting thing is, he went a long time without realizing the void existed. He found so many father figures among his uncles and cousins that it took until he was in third grade to notice that other kids lived in the same house as their dads. Once he discovered that hole, it seemed awfully deep. Now he had me.

Because of Rhonda's job, I often took Devon to school and picked him up. Every morning and afternoon, he greeted me with a hug, a kiss, and the wonderful line, "I love you, Daddy."

"When you're 13, 14 years old, you're going to be too embarrassed to hug and kiss me anymore," I'd tell him.

"What do you want to bet?" he'd say.

I'm glad I never took him up on it.

14

A BLESSED LIFE

WHEN I WORKED FOR THE BREWERS, they were owned by the family of MLB commissioner Bud Selig. Bud lived in Milwaukee and we had a good relationship. Good enough that in August 2001, he invited me and my business manager Frank Pace to join him on his private plane while flying to Cooperstown for Hall of Fame weekend.

The Brewers were nice enough to let me slip away to attend the induction of my pal Kirby Puckett. During the flight, Frank and I told Bud that I would be resigning at season's end. I added that I wouldn't take a job with another team because I no longer wanted to work every day. However, I was willing to consider helping him.

I knew Bud was looking to grow the game internationally. Between being a Hall of Famer and Spanish being my native tongue, I figured they might have a role for me. Months later, Sandy Alderson—MLB's executive vice president for baseball operations—asked me to become a special adviser for international player development. I gladly accepted. Over the years, I traveled to Puerto Rico and around Latin America, and roamed as far as Australia and Italy.

On that same trip to Cooperstown, Frank befriended Dave St. Peter, then a senior vice president for the Twins. They began discussing the possibility of my rejoining the organization. Meanwhile, Twins TV play-by-play guy Dick Bremer began lobbying the front office to bring me back in some role. Finally, in 2003, around the time Dave got promoted to team president, I formally returned to the organization I considered my professional home. Among my duties was lobbying the state legislature to help build a new outdoor ballpark in downtown Minneapolis. (It took years, but Target Field opened in 2010.) The best part of our arrangement was getting to spend about a month each year at spring training in Fort Myers, Florida. That meant hanging out with my old roomie Tony and working with young hitters. I threw batting practice, gave bunting lessons, and offered pointers on baserunning. I was happy to do anything manager Ron Gardenhire wanted.

In 2009, I also rekindled my relationship with the Angels. Dave and the Twins were kind enough to allow me to do some work locally as an ambassador for my hometown team. There was less to it than my involvement with the Twins, but it was equally meaningful. It also brought everything full circle. I was now connected again to both teams that retired my No. 29 jersey and I got to represent MLB. I loved it. Judging by my interactions with fans, they enjoyed having me around, too.

When I married Rhonda, her marketing firm's biggest account was the residential building company U.S. Home, a subsidiary of the Lennar Corporation. Lennar bought her company a year later. As part of the deal, she agreed to stick around for at least five years.

Her obligation ended in early 2008, around the time I was leaving for spring training. "I want to go to spring training every year," she thought. Then the subprime mortgage crisis hit, collapsing the housing market. Rhonda didn't like the idea of encouraging home buying under those circumstances. Seeing as she already was looking for a good time to leave the company, the choice became easy.

Now that we were both retired, and the kids were out of the house, we were fortunate enough to have the financial freedom to do whatever we wanted. This meant seeing more of the world. We'd already taken vacations fishing in Alaska and petting whales in Mexico. Now we'd see other places and add to our unusual travel tradition.

While some people bring home snow globes or coffee mugs to remind them of places they visit, we collect wedding pictures—our own, of course.

Whenever we visit somewhere scenic, we pick out a gorgeous spot and renew our vows. It's hard to top our original setting in Maui. But we've come close in Tahiti, Turks and Caicos, Bora Bora, and Puerto Rico, and back on my home turf in Panama. To this day, I love flipping through photo albums and remembering our various ceremonies.

All travel and work plans were scheduled around my golf tournament benefiting the Pediatric Cancer Research Foundation.

Continuing my promise to Michelle to help save lives means everything to me. The biggest piece of that is the golf tournament. I also remain involved with the Leukemia and Lymphoma Society, City of Hope, and Be The Match. Some of my favorite days of each year are spent with those organizations.

At Rhonda's urging, I also became involved with organizations that care for women and children who are victims of domestic abuse. We joined the board of Hillview Acres Children's Home, a safe place they could escape to when home life is dangerous. (Sadly, it closed in 2011.) I've also worked with other groups in Southern California, such as Eli Home, and given speeches at schools around the country. I tell my story and offer to meet afterward with anyone who would like to talk. In those private chats, I answer every question; nothing is off limits. I'm also a good listener for anyone who wants to share their story. Sometimes, they just want a hug.

I'm not ashamed of being an abuse victim. It's an important part of who I am, and of how I became the man I am today. I hope I can inspire people to escape a bad situation. If they've already gotten out, I want them to know they can rise far above it. I also want men to understand the damage they cause when they terrorize the people they're supposed to love and protect. Conversations about this subject are always emotionally draining, but I'm glad there is less of a social stigma around it than when I was growing up.

Whenever I talk about the abuse I endured, I always make it clear that the hero of my upbringing is my mom.

In 2010, my mother passed away. She was 89. The world is a lesser place without her. But I know there's another angel in heaven, hand in hand with Michelle.

———————

Early in my relationship with Rhonda, I shared the words from my mother that helped sustain me, the lines that have echoed through these pages like they've echoed through my life: "God is there for you. He's always going to be there. He's going to take care of you."

Rhonda smiled and nodded. She understood. Because it was a perfect complement to the analogy she's long used to explain God's role in our lives. She came up with it as a young girl, when she was trying to square her beliefs with what she was hearing from the priests and nuns at Catholic school. It was part of the questioning that would lead her to Calvary. The inspiration came from hanging out with her friend Lori and her family, which is only fitting since they're the ones who took her to Calvary.

Lori's mom liked to make tapestries. She'd spend weeks at her loom, carefully weaving bunches of colorful thread over and under each other. All the girls could see was the tangled underside of the project. It made no sense. From this angle, they couldn't detect patterns or shapes. Anticipation grew over what she was making. A boat? A beach? A sunset? The more bizarre it seemed, the longer it took, the greater their fascination. It became a fun guessing game. Then, finally, the day would come when she finished looping, knotting, and tamping. It was time for the big reveal. She'd flip it over and it was always something completely different than they expected. Better, too.

One day, Rhonda saw the parallel. Each tapestry created by Lori's mom was like each life created by God.

Our lives are made of many colorful threads, all looped, knotted, and tamped over the years. Sometimes the threads fit together smoothly. Other times, it's a struggle. Often, it looks like a mess. Outsiders see no discernible pattern or shape. The image isn't revealed until it is finished. For some, like Michelle, the revelation comes after only 18 years. For others, like my mom, it takes 89 years. None of us knows how much time we have on Earth. Only God knows. He knows from the start of each project how long it will take. That is, from our birth, He already has our final image in mind. Such a notion can provide serenity in tough times.

"Everybody asks, 'Why, God, are you putting me through this horrible event? What did I do to deserve it?' It's because we don't understand the purpose of that thread," Rhonda said. "Every day—when we're enjoying the highs and suffering through the lows—more threads are being added to our tapestry. We don't know what's coming. It can't be revealed until all the threads are in place. Once you get to heaven, you'll get your tapestry. You'll turn it over and it will all make sense."

To me, her analogy matched my mother's words. To her, my mother's words fit her analogy.

We continued talking about our views on faith and found them remarkably similar. Neither of us likes following a set of rules established by a particular religion. We just want to follow God.

Rhonda marks God's presence more closely than me. The big ways He guides us, such as us finding each other, are easy to spot. She's also keenly aware of the small ways. For instance, whenever we come across something most people would consider a coincidence—like the last four digits of her phone number matching the number of hits in my career— Rhonda says, "There are no coincidences. Those are God winks." Read this book closely and you'll find many, big and small. They start at the very beginning, with Mrs. Allen being on the train when I was born.

The biggest way our faith differed was how we practiced. Simply put, she was a churchgoer and I wasn't.

She remained at Calvary until Cheyenne and Devon started going to Saint John's Episcopal School in Rancho Santa Margarita. Living near there, the three of them began worshiping at the Saint John's Episcopal Church.

Her rule for the kids was the same she followed while growing up: you can go to any church you want, as long as you go somewhere. Often, they had Saturday-night sleepovers at their friends' homes and would join those families at church on Sunday. She started hearing how much they enjoyed Saddleback Church and Pastor Rick Warren. They said the message there resonated more than what they were hearing at St. John's. Rhonda could only shake her head at how her history was repeating with her children. She eventually decided to see what all the fuss was about. Like her first visit to Calvary, she instantly knew this was where she belonged. That was in 1994, the year before Rick gained worldwide fame by publishing *The Purpose Driven Church,* the precursor to his phenomenally successful *The Purpose Driven Life: What on Earth Am I Here For?*

Rhonda and the kids liked going to Saddleback on Saturday evenings. She never pushed me to join them. Maybe she was using the old trick of letting it be my idea. And it was. One day, I asked if I could tag along.

"Of course," she said.

I, too, felt connected right away. Everything I heard aligned with my beliefs—those formed at the Episcopal church I attended as a boy in Panama, reassembled over my years around Judaism and further refined through the soul-searching I did during and after Michelle's ordeal. Over the years, Pastor Rick's messages have touched on many of the themes my mother taught me. My bond to him and Saddleback strengthened.

The day before Easter in 2010, I walked into the baptism pool on the patio outside the worship center. With my arms crossed against my chest, Rick guided me backward into the water and back up again. I proudly affirmed my love and obedience of Jesus Christ, my Lord and Savior.

———————

For one of our earliest anniversaries, Rhonda gave me golf lessons.

Although I had my weekly trip to the movies with her uncle, she thought I could use another excuse to get out of the house and hang out with other guys. The idea made sense, but I wasn't interested. Despite hosting a tournament, playing golf never seemed to be my thing.

I first tried in 1982, while with the Angels. Gene Mauch loved golf and thought I would be good at it. To get me started, he bought me a set of clubs.

I went out for a round with some teammates. I sliced my first three shots, sending them directly into the water. I drove my cart to the area where the balls went in. As I searched for them, my frustration started to boil. I began thinking about the fact my job was a relentless pursuit of hitting a white ball. Why spend my free time waking up at 6:00 AM to hit and then chase another, smaller white ball? I threw my golf bag into the water and went home.

About 10 years later, I tried again. I bought a set of clubs and went to a course with Doug DeCinces and Bobby Grich. Again, I sliced my opening tee shot. At this course, that meant it went into the woods. As the ball flew through the trees, I heard, "Quack, quack, quack." Not from a real duck, of course, but from a laugh box one of them pulled out. I heard it enough times that day that I quit again. Instead of sending these clubs to a watery grave, I took them up the loft in my garage. I pulled out a long spike and pounded it through the bag, pinning my golf gear to the wall to prevent me from taking it down again.

After I married Rhonda, I started joining my buddy Jimmy Duran when he played golf. All I did, though, was drive the cart. I eventually saw him hit enough long drives that I wanted to give it one more try. I cashed in the lessons Rhonda gave me.

The golf pro explained how the wrist snap in golf is different from in baseball. Once I understood that, I started working to control it. As anyone who's played the game knows, it only takes a few perfect shots to get you hooked. I was soon playing regularly, with Jimmy and with others. As Rhonda originally intended, I found new groups of guys to hang out with. I got into a foursome with Chris Ferraro, the insurance guy who ended up warning me about the symptoms of a heart attack and urging me to get help right away if I felt any of them. I got into another foursome with Lou Sauritch, a guy I befriended when he was a photographer for a baseball card company. (I have a knack for collecting friends in unusual ways. Jimmy went from a UPS delivery guy spooked by my German Shepherds to best man when I married Rhonda.) I also started to enjoy playing in my own tournament.

Golf offered a perfect mix of camaraderie and competition.

Baseball was me against the pitcher. In golf, the competition was myself and what I think I'm capable of doing. Just like I had to learn my best approach to hitting a baseball, I had to learn my golf swing. Funny thing is, the adjustment that unlocked my ability in golf was the same as in baseball—stop trying to crush the ball and start focusing on precision. While nobody has referred to my golf clubs as magic wands, I became pretty good. I started consistently shooting in the mid-80s.

Because my Orange County gal despises cold weather, there's usually a golf course wherever we go on vacation. We were in Arizona when I nailed my first hole-in-one. It was lucky. So was my second. And especially my third.

I hit a low line drive that headed for the green and, we all presumed, well beyond. I was playing with Dennis Kuhl, the chairman of the Angels. He told me to hit another ball in case we couldn't find that one. When we got to the green, everyone looked for my original tee shot. We couldn't find it. Then Dennis walked by the hole and screamed, "Hey! Here's your ball!"

I was up to six aces by the time I teed off at Cresta Verde Golf Course the morning of September 20, 2015.

PART III

"If you're alive, there's a purpose for your life."
—Pastor Rick Warren

15

THE PROMISE

BEFORE I COULD even begin processing that I'd survived cardiac arrest and a widowmaker heart attack, the folks at Riverside Hospital were getting me ready to go home.

They took me off a breathing machine after two days. Hours later, they removed the balloon pump that was helping my heart do its job. I was eligible to have the pump for five days, but the lead cardiologist thought it was no longer necessary. I even took my first actual steps on the road to recovery, getting out of bed and walking with the aid of a physical therapist. A nurse said the only reason I was in intensive care was to protect my privacy.

Rhonda felt relieved. The clogged arteries in my heart were now clear, with stents ensuring smooth blood flow. The removal of equipment and getting me out of bed were clear signs that I had "dodged a bullet," as I'd told her. She and Devon were thrilled with everything—my progress, the care I was getting, and especially the doctor. His aggressive approach fit my style. Let's get this taken care of and get me home. The way things were going, we might even make our flight to Italy in a few weeks.

We were told that as my heart healed, my ejection fraction would increase, which would help my breathing. For now, I needed a little oxygen, but that was no big deal considering all I'd been through. The cardiologist mentioned that my heart was enlarged, but he figured that came from the shock of everything else. It should calm on its own. Since this was all new to us, we treated his words as gospel. It made sense and he seemed so confident. All the other doctors and nurses agreed.

The Sunday after I checked into Riverside, I was checking out.

"Two weeks of light activity," the doctor said. "After that, no restrictions."

Our flight to Italy left in exactly a month. Could we go?

"The way I look at it," he said, "you should live your life to the fullest because you never know what's coming around the corner."

———————

Riverside Hospital was more than an hour from our house, so we needed a nearby cardiologist. We began our search by calling Frank.

A good friend of his, Deborah Proctor, was an executive at St. Joseph Health. She recommended Dr. Sanjay Bhojraj at Mission Hospital. Rhonda called his office the first thing the next day, which was a Monday.

The doctor at Riverside had suggested that I put in those two weeks of light activity before meeting my new cardiologist. But when the scheduler said Dr. Bhojraj had an opening on Wednesday, Rhonda took it.

Those few days in between were uncomfortable. Rhonda took me outside for walks around our cul-de-sac and everything hurt. Every breath was a struggle, even with oxygen from a tank. Was I relying too much on this extra oxygen? A nurse at Riverside said my shallow breathing might be more mental than physical. Often, she said, people who survive a heart attack are too scared to take a deep breath. It takes time to trust your body again, she said. My skin tone also seemed off, but we had no idea how someone should look 10 days after a heart attack.

When we headed to Dr. Bhojraj's office, I left the oxygen at home. We'd been told that I could take it off whenever I wanted, and it seemed like a hassle to drag it to a doctor's office.

As we ran through all this with Dr. Bhojraj's nurse, we figured she heard stories like this all the time. Yet she seemed to tilt her head and crinkle her forehead. When she asked for the list of my medicines, our naivete showed again. We didn't know we were supposed to bring it.

"We thought you got all the details from Riverside," Rhonda said. She then called the pharmacy for the list of medicines while the nurse went to get Dr. Bhojraj.

He walked in, introduced himself and immediately said, "I really don't like what I'm seeing. I think you should go over to Mission's ER and get checked out."

"He was just discharged!" Rhonda said. "What happened to two weeks of light activity then no restrictions? What do you mean he needs to go to the ER?!"

Dr. Bhojraj calmly said I might need "a tune-up." Since they didn't have any records from Riverside, this would be an opportunity to run their own tests.

It was an ingenious display of bedside manner.

In the ER, a doctor mentioned something about my congestive heart failure.

My what? It was the first time we'd heard that phrase.

Although the diagnosis sounds like a heart is giving out, he explained that the "failure" is the heart's inability to pump blood like it should. This can lead to swelling, often in the lungs. That was why I could hardly breathe. That was why my skin tone was off. That was why my heart was enlarged.

Rhonda began asking more questions. The answers painted a completely different picture of everything we'd been told at Riverside. It quickly became clear that two weeks of light activity might have killed me. There was no time to get angry about how much we'd been misled. The focus was on how these better doctors would heal me. Rhonda also vowed to no longer passively trust the advice from the supposed experts. She'd question everything, making sure she understood the reason behind each decision. She would become as much of an expert as she could.

Dr. Bhojraj said he needed more test results before he could set a treatment plan. Meanwhile, he got me hooked up to another balloon pump. My heart certainly needed the help.

The next thing I remember, it was Thursday. And that day was October 1, my 70th birthday.

Devon and his girlfriend, Mary Zuromskis, came to visit. So did my friend Allen Tom from the Angels and his girl-friend, Elena. Elena baked me a birthday cake. She was getting ready to light a candle when Rhonda screamed, "NOOO! He's on oxygen! You're going to blow up the place!" Her moment of panic ended up giving us all a good laugh. We needed that.

On Friday morning, Dr. Bhojraj arrived with a diagnosis. I didn't merely have heart failure, I had severe heart failure. The left side of my heart was damaged beyond repair. It could no longer keep me alive.

I needed a major operation. Doctors either would implant something called a left ventricular assist device (an LVAD), or I'd get a heart transplant.

"Wait a minute," Rhonda told Dr. Bhojraj. "That first thing you said, I don't know what it is. That second thing is the last thing I want to hear."

The LVAD, he said, was a machine that would take over the blood-pumping duty of the left side of my heart. He didn't want to give too many details about it because of his other big piece of news: Mission Hospital wasn't equipped to handle either operation. We had to choose where to go next. He said our best options were Keck Medicine of USC in Los Angeles or Scripps Health in San Diego.

Rhonda asked Dr. Bhojraj for a recommendation. He made it clear there was no bad choice. That said, he'd done his residency with an excellent heart failure specialist at Scripps. He knew and respected several other doctors there. Scripps also had a cardiovascular institute that had opened only a few months earlier. It became an easy choice.

For Rhonda, that is. My brain shut down when Dr. Bhojraj said "severe."

Everything else he said scared and overwhelmed me.

As soon as Dr. Bhojraj left the room, my old flight response kicked in. I wanted to get out of there. I told Rhonda to let me go home to die.

She called Devon and Mary and warned them that I was having a panic attack. She asked them to come help calm me down.

I began lashing out. I tried peeling the EKG pads off my chest and the IV lines out of my arms. Nurses pumped the antianxiety drug Xanax into my system. They put an alarm on the bed that let out a scream if I got up. I went through stretches of calm followed by fits of rage. I wasn't speaking coherently. The sounds I made were more like grunts and mumbles.

Devon arrived and pinned me down so nurses could inject more Xanax.

"You can't go anywhere," Devon said. "We've got to get you to another hospital."

When the transport team arrived to take me to Scripps, I took them on, too.

Once they got me into the ambulance and started driving away, all the Xanax finally kicked in.

_____

As Rhonda made her way to Scripps, the word that resonated in her mind was "transplant."

Two years earlier, she came within an hour of undergoing a liver transplant. A lifelong reliance on Tylenol to deal with neck pain and headaches—caused by three car accidents between ages 15 and 25, as well as injuries from being a competitive gymnast through college—caught up to her in a violent way. Acetaminophen toxicity caused her liver to shut down. Her situation was acute enough that a donor organ was lined up and ready to be implanted. Her body began recovering just in time to avoid it. Still, that was "only" a liver. This was *a new heart*. It seemed so dire. So desperate. So risky. She considered it a last resort—a medical Hail Mary along the lines of what the cord blood transplant had been for Michelle. She was rooting for an LVAD, even though she had no idea what that meant.

During the drive, she received a call from my new cardiologist, Dr. Ajay Srivastava, the guy who previously worked with Dr. Bhojraj. Dr. Ajay was at a conference in Connecticut but he wanted to begin discussing my case. He explained that Dr. James Heywood would handle things over the weekend, and that we'd soon meet Dr. Dan Meyer, who started the LVAD program at Scripps.

I awoke on Saturday at Scripps Green in La Jolla. While I was still fuzzy on the medical details, I was aware enough to recognize that the people at this hospital were doing the same damn things that had been done at Riverside and Mission— echocardiogram, electrocardiogram, and another balloon pump. It got me thinking that they'd run out of things to try.

By Sunday morning, I'd convinced myself that nothing could be done to save me. I feared they were keeping me alive for the sake of it. I didn't want that. I didn't want to be a burden on Rhonda and the kids.

Rhonda wasn't at the hospital yet, so I asked a nurse to get her on the phone.

"I want you to make me a promise," I told Rhonda. "If nothing can be done, let me go. Let me die. I'm ready."

"Yes," she said. "I will not hold on and keep you alive just to keep you alive. But you have to make me a promise, too. If there is anything that they can do for you, you will let them do it."

"I promise," I said.

Rhonda hung up feeling terrible for me. She knew my default perspective is seeing the proverbial glass as half empty. She knew my tendencies to shut down and flee. And she knew it was all justified. My life was in jeopardy.

However, she had the advantage of knowing that the glass was half full. She trusted that we were in good hands with Dr. Ajay and the Scripps team. She knew we'd have answers soon. Drs. Ajay, Heywood, and Meyer were reviewing all my test results and meeting to discuss them. We'd know tomorrow morning whether I needed an LVAD or a transplant.

Then Dr. Ajay threw us a curveball.

He recommended an LVAD *and* a transplant.

To Rhonda, needing both operations indicated I was close to dying. Our conversation from the day before rushed to her mind. She'd promised not to go to extreme lengths to save me. Would she have to tell Dr. Ajay no?

Color drained from her face. Her legs wobbled.

Devon and Mary were on the other side of my bed. Mary noticed Rhonda getting woozy and rushed to her side. Rhonda probably would've fainted had Mary not held her.

Actually, Dr. Ajay explained, this was good news.

A transplant is not the medical equivalent of a baseball team being down to its last strike. The upside was actually better than an LVAD. Many heart transplant recipients get 10 or even 20 quality years added to their life. Yet, for several reasons, I wasn't a good candidate for a transplant. Not now, at least. But I could be, down the road. So it made more sense to let an LVAD power my heart for a while. Once time passed and the rest of my body improved, then we'd look into getting me on the transplant waiting list.

This was exactly why the LVAD was invented—to buy time for heart failure patients until a donor heart could be found. As a "bridge to transplant," it was made to keep people alive for days or weeks. As technology improved, the bridge held up much longer—years, even. Some people who were in the clinical trials for the device I'd be getting were still alive after more than a decade.

As this sunk in for Rhonda, she looked at me.

I was smiling.

I didn't understand the particulars, but I knew we finally had a plan. I was out of limbo. No more same old, same old.

Even if this operation didn't work, at least they were trying something.

And, as always, I heard my mother's words: "God is there for you. He's always going to be there. He's going to take care of you."

Before they could schedule the LVAD operation, there was one more test. Not for me, though.

The LVAD team had to make sure Rhonda and the kids were capable of caring for me.

Of course, this wasn't framed as an evaluation. It came in the form of explaining how an LVAD works and what the patient needs.

First off, someone would have to be with me during recovery and beyond. That was an easy yes. Rhonda wasn't going anywhere. Devon and Mary also vowed to be available as long as necessary. He was working for AT&T and his bosses had given him permission to work remotely. Mary was studying to become a veterinarian but wasn't currently in school or working.

Next question: Could we stay within San Diego County until the LVAD team released me from their care? Another easy yes.

The last hurdle was making sure my loved ones could grasp the basics of caring for an LVAD patient.

An LVAD requires constant monitoring and maintenance. Many things could go wrong. Knowing what to do and when to do it is crucial. They watched a PowerPoint presentation that gave them an overview.

The staff could see that my family was ready, willing, and able. To be clear, this was standard protocol—not something done because there were concerns about Rhonda, Devon, and Mary.

With that box checked, we switched hospitals yet again. We moved to Scripps Prebys Cardiovascular Institute, the fancy new facility Dr. Bhojraj mentioned. I would become only the 34th person to get an LVAD there.

Dr. Meyer and his team cracked open my chest, hooked up my new hardware, and sewed in a pouch for the mechanism to hang. Blood no longer flowed through the diseased part of my heart. It was rerouted to flow through a device called a HeartMate II. This left me without a heartbeat. Instead of a heart squeezing and contracting, making the thumping sound, an LVAD creates a constant flow, like water rushing through a garden hose. Similarly, it makes a whooshing sound. A wire called a driveline ran from the component inside, out the right side of my belly, and into a controller. That's the brain of the device. It had two wires coming out of it, each going to a battery. Those batteries powered the device that powered my heart.

The operation was projected to take eight hours. It took six, an indication of how smoothly it went. Dr. Meyer and his team felt good about everything. Then, while I was being transferred from the operating room to the recovery room, my brain glitched—I suffered a seizure. As my body spasmed, I bit down so hard that I knocked out two teeth.

In all his years doing LVADs, transplants, and other such operations, Dr. Meyer had never had a patient suffer a seizure. I'd never had a seizure, either. Dr. Meyer ordered all sorts of tests. They offered no explanation. They also showed no reason for concern. Dr. Meyer was confident the only long-term impact would be the need for some cosmetic dentistry.

While I was in surgery, Rhonda was comforted by Devon, Mary, Frank, and the small circle of people who knew what had happened. Once I was safely in recovery, the group filtered out. Left alone with her thoughts, Rhonda finally considered how drastically our lives had changed over the last 18 days.

I'd gone from singing on stage with Manny to nearly dying in the cath lab at Riverside Hospital. I'd been sent home and told that we could probably still visit Italy, only to wind up in three more hospitals.

Who knows what would've happened had we listened to the original doctor's instructions and waited two weeks for a follow-up appointment.

So much remained uncertain about my future. But right now, Rhonda could exhale a little. We'd made it this far.

Soon, her mind shifted into overdrive again. With the LVAD safely inserted, she began projecting the timeline for a transplant.

No matter what, we had to wait until at least April. I was in a six-month hold not because of the LVAD, but because of my tobacco habit. Although I long ago gave up the humongous wad from my playing days, I'd remained a regular chewer.

What can I say? The nasty habit comforted me. Now I was paying the price. Rules required that a transplant recipient be tobacco-free for six months. By the time I'd be eligible, I would be closer to 71 than 70, another potential problem.

Dr. Meyer looked Rhonda in the eye and said, "He *will* get a heart."

He'd been in this field for more than 25 years. He knew how the process worked. He knew how I stacked up to other candidates; he'd just literally held my heart in his hands. If he felt this strongly about my prognosis, then that was good enough for us. Well, for Rhonda. She didn't discuss this with me for a long time. My focus was adjusting to life as a bionic man.

People who've had both an LVAD implant and a transplant say recovering from the LVAD is far more difficult.

I spent about a month at Prebys building up my strength. My room overlooked the baseball fields at UC–San Diego. Being the offseason, there were no games to watch, just occasionally some people playing catch.

One afternoon, Rhonda, Devon, Mary, and I each made our bucket lists. Our top item was for me to get a new heart. Rhonda and I also picked a few more vacation destinations. I still owed her a trip to Italy. I also wanted to visit Trinidad and Tobago, which is where my family came from before moving to Panama, and Scotland, so I could play a round at the birthplace of golf, St. Andrews. My wildest entries were skydiving and getting up close with sharks in the ocean. I'd seen on TV that people get into metal cages and drop down deep for amazing encounters. That was pretty far-fetched for a guy who currently needed all sorts of preparations just to get in the shower.

After a stint at a rehab hospital, we moved into a house on Coronado Island, right across the street from the Coronado Golf Course. Some friends let us stay at their place while they were away. A physical therapist visited regularly and we continued seeing the LVAD team at Prebys. We waited for them to give us permission to move back home.

Rhonda and Devon babied me, which was fitting considering my helplessness. They made me meals and sometimes fed me. I wore diapers they had to change. I cried a lot. I slept a lot, often fitfully. When I lost consciousness, my anxieties often ganged up on me and took over. My recurring nightmare isn't even true; it's a blend of two moments on the day I nearly died. The reality is that paramedics treated me at the golf course, but they never used a defibrillator to restart my heart. That happened later, in the cath lab, during my stent procedure. But in my nightmares, I see the paramedics working on me in pro shop of the golf course. The guy on top of me is screaming, "We're losing him, God damn it, we're losing him!" He gets out the paddles to save me and…that's when I wake up, cold, wet, shaking, hollering for help. In a caregiver support group, Rhonda was told to let it play out. It's an unfortunate part of the coping process.

Rhonda was less tolerant of my reluctance to do physical therapy. I had three sessions a week, plus I was supposed to get moving around the house or go walking through the neighborhood. Like I'd once been an angry young man, I now turned into a grumpy old man. I didn't want to move.

Everything hurt. What if something went wrong? Just let me be.

But doctors said I could do all these things. I *should* do them.

"You're not sick," Rhonda kept telling me.

That was the part I struggled to accept. How could I consider myself healthy—or, at least, "not sick"—when I had a machine keeping me alive? When I got plugged directly into a wall socket every night?

We still weren't ready to tell the world what had happened. But we shared the details with more of our trusted friends.

When Dave St. Peter heard, he flew out from Minneapolis. He told me the Twins would renew my contract regardless of whether I would be healthy enough to work for them. It was a kind, unexpected gesture that we very much appreciated. Hall of Fame president Jeff Idelson came, too. He vowed to put the Hall's support behind me in any way they could.

Frank insisted on telling my ex-wife. He thought it was only right that word get to Charryse and Stephanie. If they were ever going to revive our relationship, the time was now. Sure enough, Stephanie came to visit me at Prebys.

I hadn't seen her in at least 10 years. Rhonda, Devon, and Mary greeted her, then headed out so we could be alone together. Stephanie stayed for about an hour. She sat next to the bed and held my hand. It wasn't a big, tearful reconciliation but it was a nice start.

"My wife's a very nice person," I told her. "You would like her. Please show her some respect."

In the following months, Stephanie and I remained in touch. I got her a job with my friend John Boggs, the agent best known for representing Tony Gwynn and Ichiro. Once Stephanie started working, I stopped hearing from her.

Charryse used me even more blatantly.

She called to say she was coming to visit. Then she called to say she was having car trouble. Rhonda knew how much this relationship meant to me, so she did everything she could to make things work. That included spending hours on the phone with Charryse and her obnoxious boyfriend (who was screaming in the background) to try getting her the money. Charryse never did visit me.

I hope my daughters eventually return to my life in a meaningful way. I want to share with them holidays and birthdays, as well as lazy afternoons. That's on my bucket list, too.

16

"HONEY, WE'VE GOT A LOT OF WORK TO DO"

SKIPPED OVER SOMETHING that happened between the violent panic attack at Mission Hospital and my panicking again two days later, when I asked Rhonda to promise she wouldn't go to extraordinary lengths to save me.

It occurred during my first full day at Scripps Green. I'd spent the morning going through the tests that would help doctors decide whether I needed an LVAD or a transplant. Then I returned to my room and settled in for the day and a half of waiting until we got the answer. My mind drifted to the part of my saga that Rhonda and I were struggling to understand.

How could I have been so healthy one minute, so sick the next?

Shouldn't we have seen a heart attack coming? Did we miss any signs? Did I downplay any symptoms?

No matter how many times we reviewed the days and weeks leading up to that fateful morning at Cresta Verde, we couldn't come up with any answers.

Months before, a physical showed I was in very good health for someone pushing 70. Yet I had a ticking time bomb in my chest.

How many other people did, too? If I went to the other cardiac patients on this floor, how many of them also got blindsided?

And what about all the people who have warning signs but don't immediately recognize them and get help right away? How many die each year because their heart goes out before they even know there's something wrong with it?

Any time the subject turns to disease and dying, I of course think about Michelle. And it was on this Saturday afternoon when everything clicked.

"Honey," I said urgently, getting Rhonda's attention. "We've got a lot of work to do."

"Work?" she said.

"I don't want anybody to go through what I'm going through if I can help it," I said. "If we start getting the word out, maybe people will start getting their hearts checked. Even if they're okay, they still need to know the warning signs of a heart attack."

I wanted her to call Marcia Smith, a terrific reporter at the *Orange County Register,* and my longtime friend Jim Hill of CBS 2 in Los Angeles. Through them, I would try doing for the fight against heart disease what Michelle did for the fight against pediatric cancer. Even if we saved only one life, it would be worth the effort.

Rhonda agreed. She also offered some wise advice.

In her role as my loving wife, she told me I wasn't up for that yet. I needed to save my strength. And as a former marketing wiz, she said we needed to think through this more.

With Michelle, we had the specific plea of adding names to the donor registry. What would our message be this time? With Michelle, we used the National Marrow Donor Program as our trusted resource. Who would we partner with this time? With Michelle, I was the face of the campaign, giving interviews and attending events. I couldn't do that now, at least not yet.

By late October, though, the LVAD was in. My recovery was going well.

It was time to get to work.

———————————

When we shared the idea with Frank, he again knew a terrific person for us to consult.

Dr. Gerald Marx was a pediatric cardiologist in Boston and a longtime volunteer for the American Heart Association. Two years before, the AHA named him Physician of the Year. He was was one of Frank's best friends since grade school.

Jerry connected us with the right people at the AHA. Soon after, several executives from the organization's national office visited us at the house in Coronado. They listened to what we wanted to accomplish and had great ideas for how to make it happen.

The aim was simple: awareness. By telling my story, I hoped to jolt people into action. If a Hall of Fame ballplayer who looked and felt fine could be walking around with a severe heart problem, maybe they were, too. Once I had people's attention, I would steer them to the AHA.

The next step was figuring out how to break the news. Yet again, Frank knew the perfect person.

Steve Rushin grew up in the 1970s in Bloomington, Minnesota—home of the Twins—and I'd been his favorite player. He went on to become one of the best sportswriters in the country, working for one of the most prestigious publications, *Sports Illustrated*. He flew out to visit with us. Rhonda, Devon, and I went through all the details from Cresta Verde until now. We also discussed my plan to work with the AHA.

His story was going to come out after Thanksgiving. Then we learned that Marcia Smith was calling around about my heart problems. She didn't have enough details to put out a story. But we feared it was only a matter of time until she did.

That close call was a reminder of how lucky we'd been to keep our secret for this long.

The timing helped. I usually keep a lower profile this time of year anyway. I hadn't skipped anything that would've required me to explain my absence. For instance, missing the Light The Night walk would've been a big deal; luckily, that was the day before my heart attack. Had the Angels or Twins made the playoffs, people would've wondered where I was. Both had been in position to make the playoffs at the time of my heart attack, but neither did.

Something else that worked to my advantage was the fact I rarely call people back or reply to text messages. So when days and weeks went by and I hadn't gotten back to anyone—even those who'd reached out for my 70th birthday—my friends thought nothing of it.

The reason we cherished our privacy was purely practical. We had enough going on trying to deal with the stress and uncertainty surrounding my health. Even after I got out of the hospital, we needed to concentrate on figuring out life with an LVAD. We weren't ready for the time or energy required to handle the attention we expected the story to generate. An endless stream of people calling and visiting because they care about you is a nice problem to have, yet it can still be a problem.

The post-Thanksgiving time frame seemed about right. But now that Marcia was closing in, and Steve already had all the details, we moved up the release date.

Mid-morning on the Monday before Thanksgiving, SI.com published a story headlined ROD CAREW OPENS UP ABOUT HIS PRIVATE LIFE AND HIS NEAR-DEATH EXPERIENCE. Minutes later, Heart.org—the American Heart Association's website—published a story headlined BASEBALL GREAT ROD CAREW WINNING FIGHT FOR LIFE.

The news sped around the sports world with the velocity we expected. To handle all the interview requests from reporters, Frank set up a conference call for that afternoon. Speaking from the Coronado house, I was weak, weepy, and overwhelmed. Because I wasn't sharp on many of the details, Rhonda fed me a lot of lines. She sometimes passed me handwritten notes as if we were in grade school. Delivering the main reason why I was speaking up came easily. I said, "I just want you guys to understand how fatal this can be. Get yourselves checked. Don't wait for it to happen. Everyone looks at me like I was healthy, but I was unhealthy. And, man, it got me."

After keeping the story secret for so long, it was nice having it out in the open.

However, the same day ESPN and MLB Network reported that I'd nearly died but was now recovering also turned out to be the day I suffered my first setback.

———

Following the conference call, I went to Prebys for routine blood work and a checkup.

Dr. Heywood looked over my test results and said my blood count was low. That was a sign of bleeding somewhere in my gastrointestinal tract.

"We'll do our best to get you home for Thanksgiving," Dr. Heywood said.

"You mean he has to be hospitalized?" Rhonda said. "He just got out!"

While we knew GI bleeds were common in LVAD patients, nobody told us that resolving them required checking back into the hospital.

The bleed likely had sealed on its own, Dr. Heywood explained. If so, my blood count was low only because it was early in the healing cycle. I got the standard transfusion of fresh blood as a booster. But since this was my first GI bleed, they had to run all the tests to try finding the source. I ended up undergoing an endoscopy, then a colonoscopy, then swallowing a capsule with a camera in it so they could watch it progress through my system in hopes of pinpointing the problem that way. They didn't find anything. I was released the morning of Thanksgiving.

Rhonda's Aunt Di and Uncle Wayne prepared a delicious meal in their kitchen and drove it down to the house in Coronado. Cheyenne came, too. It was an unusual, memorable Thanksgiving feast. While not the most ideal of circumstances, we made the most of them. Looking around the table, I thought about the sacrifices each person made to be here. Then I started thinking about everything Rhonda, Devon, and Mary had done for me the last two months. I tried expressing how thankful I was. I hope my tears were good enough.

On December 22, we celebrated again. It was our 14th wedding anniversary. And it was the day we returned home.

Something else happened that day.

Marcia Smith broke the news of the first life saved because the man had heard my story.

———————

Clyde Wright was a left-handed pitcher who reached the majors two years before me.

He threw a no-hitter in 1970 as part of a hot streak that turned him into an All-Star that summer. In that game he gave up the hit that resulted in one of the iconic plays in All-Star history: Pete Rose plowing through catcher Ray Fosse to score the winning run for the NL in the 11th inning. Clyde won 22 games that season. He won exactly 100 over his 10-year career, the first eight spent with the Angels.

In our head-to-head meetings, Clyde usually got the best of me. I hit only .264 over 53 at-bats against him. It wasn't only because of his screwball. It was because he didn't let me get comfortable in the batter's box. Clyde never threw at my head or anything dirty, but he sure liked to come inside around my knees. That kept my feet dancing.

He remained in Orange County after his career. (His son, Jaret, pitched 11 seasons in the majors. He's best remembered for starting Game 7 of the World Series as a rookie for the Indians in 1997.) Clyde and I became friendly while I was playing with the Angels. That's when I started my usual greeting for him—pointing to my knees. He'd always smile and laugh. When I started working for the Angels again in the late 1990s, Clyde was doing community relations for the club. We saw each other practically every time I was at the ballpark. Rhonda and I always enjoyed spending time with him and his wife, Vicki.

Like most people, Clyde didn't know what had happened to me while it was playing out. But over that same time, he attended the funerals of two former teammates. Ed Sukla passed away following a long battle with cancer. Dean Chance died suddenly of a heart attack. Their deaths got Clyde thinking about his mortality. Losing Dean hit him especially hard. They'd once been young stars in the prime of their lives together. In August, they'd relived great memories when Dean went into the Angels Hall of Fame. Then Dean was gone. Soon after, Clyde read about my close call.

Clyde knew he was a few years older than me and not in as good shape. He thought back to some episodes where long walks left him feeling short of breath. Maybe there was more to it than age or indigestion.

He went for a checkup and doctors found four nearly clogged arteries. He had a time bomb ticking inside his chest, like I'd had. He underwent a quadruple bypass operation and was home a few days later. By heeding my advice, my buddy and his family avoided the pain and suffering that my family and I knew all too well.

When Clyde called to share the news, I went through a burst of emotions: sad for what he'd been through, glad for his recovery, proud for having played a role. When I hung up and dried my tears, what I felt most was pride. This completely validated everything I looked forward to doing with the American Heart Association. My aim was saving at least one life. We'd already done that, and it was someone I loved.

I still greet Clyde by pointing at my knees. He now greets me with a big hug and a kiss on the cheek. He refers to me as his brother. Every February 20, he calls to thank me for helping him have another birthday.

A few days after we returned home, Christmas arrived.

I wasn't able to go to Saddleback for the midnight service, like we usually do. Instead, we stayed home and I continued my lifelong conversation with God.

I spoke to God plenty during my medical journey. Many times when I tuned out the doctors, I tuned in to Him. I never questioned why this was happening to me. I knew it was more threads being woven into the tapestry of my life. I told Him so.

During these conversations, I kept remembering the visit from my guardian angel while I was in the cath lab at Riverside Hospital. It wasn't just that I clearly saw this mysterious figure. It was that I awoke with the memory of seeing him before I understood the timing. This vision occurred while my heart was stopped and doctors were trying to revive me. Like Rhonda says, there are no coincidences.

God spared me for a reason. Was that reason because I was doing good work for Him? Was it because I could do more?

As we went into 2016, I looked forward to finding out.

17

HEART OF 29

———————

ON NEW YEAR'S DAY, I set three goals for 2016:

1. Go to Minneapolis in late January for a Twins fan event.
2. Go to spring training a few weeks later to work with Twins hitters.
3. Go to Cooperstown in July to welcome the newest Hall of Famers to our club.

Of course, I'd gladly scrap those plans if a new heart became available. But getting a transplant was mostly beyond my control. Making these trips was largely up to me. Doctors said I could, provided I followed all the rules. That meant taking my medicines, keeping up with physical therapy, and mastering everything that comes with having an LVAD. I knew I would; Rhonda would make sure of it.

I began calling her my drill sergeant. Some days, she was tougher on me than the guys at Marine boot camp had been.

To inspire me, all she had to do was remind me about Clyde Wright. Or Dave Henderson, the jolly outfielder everyone called "Hendu." He died of a heart attack right after Christmas. He was only 57.

Through the American Heart Association, I learned that about one in every nine Americans—the equivalent of one person in every baseball lineup—faces some form of heart disease. It's the top killer of Americans every year, among men *and* women. I had no idea it was that lopsided. Maybe my serving as the messenger would help get people in and around baseball to pay closer attention to the importance of heart health.

My campaign with the AHA needed a name. Twins community relations director Bryan Donaldson came up with The Heart of 29, a nod to the jersey number I wore my entire career. Dave St. Peter suggested dropping the "the." Bingo, we had the perfect name. Once I was sure I could make it to Target Field for TwinsFest, the team's winter fan festival, we turned that into the kickoff for Heart of 29.

I've never been much of a vest guy. With the LVAD, I had no choice. It was about function, not fashion. The black vest I had to wear was customized for this purpose. It had pouches against each side of my rib cage to hold the batteries powering my device. I wore it outside my clothes.

I also had another fashionable accessory: a purselike bag for backup batteries. The LVAD folks recommended I give this constant companion a nickname. Considering I needed it with me at all times, I chose the same pet term I use for the most indispensable person in my life: Honey.

The trip to Minneapolis was the first time I left California since getting the LVAD. We filled an entire suitcase with LVAD-related gear. We had to get used to this since our plans for the year were all about traveling.

At the airports on both ends of our flight, I was happy to use a wheelchair. When we got to Target Field for TwinsFest, I was again offered a ride.

"No thanks," Rhonda said. "He'll walk."

She wanted fans and media to see how I strong I was. Her real aim was for me to realize it.

I did, too. Right away.

Being in a ballpark again got my adrenaline flowing. So what if it was the dead of winter and snow blanketed the field? Even the hallways of Target Field soothed my soul.

When we got to the concourse area set up for our event, an overflow crowd already was gathered. I worked my way onto a stage with my buddy Dick Bremer, the team's TV play-by-play announcer. I struggled to get comfortable in a tall, stiff leather chair. The problem wasn't the chair. I was trying to control my thoughts and emotions.

I leaned back, grimaced, and swallowed hard. I warned everyone that I'd probably cry. Then I told the story of my heart attack and everything since. Dick was the perfect emcee, shifting gears to the introduction of Heart of 29.

"I don't want this to happen to anyone else," I said. "If this is the only way that I can help, by sharing the things that I've gone through and crying like a baby in front of I don't know how many people, then it's worth it. From here on in,

I hope that I will be reading stories about people getting their hearts checked and doing okay."

After signing autographs for fans who'd donated to our campaign, then a news conference in the press box, I was supposed to head back to the hotel and rest. But I was feeling good. I wanted to hang out a little longer. I visited the booth where AHA folks were handing out information. Nearby was a booth with a one-of-a-kind Harley Davidson Road King—designed with my name, my number, and the Twins logo. It was being raffled off for a hospice organization Harmon always supported. I climbed aboard the bike and insisted on Rhonda joining me.

I returned to the stadium on Sunday for another meet-and-greet, then again Monday for more interviews. A local media member who survived a life-threatening heart problem a few years before shared the details with me for the first time. For various reasons, he'd kept it quiet and needed to continue keeping it private. He wanted me to know how much he appreciated me using my story for the greater good. To show his thanks, he gave me a pair of heart-shaped cuff links he'd worn since his recovery.

All weekend, a video crew hired by MLB Network followed me. They were gathering footage for an hourlong special called *Rod Carew: The Fight for His Life*. Much of the material came from an interview I did at my house with Bob Costas. It aired a couple of weeks later. Minutes into it, Rhonda's phone began lighting up again. Jim Palmer called first. Then Bobby Grich. More ballplayers reached out, all with the same message: *You're making a difference. Keep up the good work.*

Days later, the baseball world got yet another reminder about the urgency of my message. A heart attack claimed Tony Phillips, a guy I coached in 1995. He was the leadoff hitter and spark plug of that memorable Angels team. He was only 56.

Near the end of February, Rhonda and I arrived in Fort Myers, Florida, for spring training. I was as nervous and excited as a rookie.

I started coming to the Sunshine State in 1965, right after signing with the Twins. I'd been here as a cocky kid expecting to make the club (only to learn otherwise) and as a reigning MVP looking to knock off the rust from a long winter. I'd been here as a hitting coach and, for the last decade, as an alumni coach for the Twins. Now I was back as a guy lucky to be alive.

Packing for our monthlong visit, I thought about being so far away from my medical team for so long. It was fine by them, though. Rhonda took care of everything. My records were sent to Tampa General Hospital, the nearest LVAD facility, just in case. Since that hospital was two hours away, Rhonda carried a copy of my records in the event I needed treatment elsewhere. She'd also arranged for me to visit a clinic for blood draws every few days.

Unpacking in our Fort Myers hotel room, I realized I'd been so focused on bringing all my LVAD gear that I'd forgotten my glove. Oh well. I wasn't going to teach defense anyway. I went back to putting things away when I heard something frightening.

My controller was screeching.

"Honey!" I screamed.

The only time I'd heard the device make this noise was while learning how to use the equipment. We were taught that the machine only makes two sounds: a loud, terrifying squawk with a red light that means there's a major problem and you must call 911 right away, and a milder, cautionary chirp with a yellow light that means the batteries are low and need charging. This was only the chirp. I'd gone beyond the recommended 12 hours on the batteries. I needed to swap them out or plug into the wall. Rhonda knew right away that it was only a battery issue. She calmly got the backups.

The night before the first full-squad workout, Rhonda and I enjoyed dinner with my roomie Tony and his wife, Gordette. He and I decided that the next morning we'd follow our normal workday routine during spring training: I'll be outside his place at 7:00 AM and he'll be running late.

Only, I overslept. Then I couldn't find his condo. I had to call him for directions. For all my excitement over this day, rookie jitters got the best of me.

At the stadium, we had a long walk to the clubhouse. I was eager to sit down when I noticed a clubhouse attendant wearing a rose-colored T-shirt with the Heart of 29 logo. I smiled and kept going. Soon, I noticed that everyone was wearing the shirt.

I vaguely recalled Dave St. Peter or Bryan Donaldson saying something about making Heart of 29 T-shirts. Nobody said anything about having them ready for Day 1. Or about everyone wearing them. I couldn't wait to get into the coaches' dressing room and slip on mine.

In my excitement, I pulled it over my LVAD gear. Looking in the mirror, I realized how much more sense it made to present myself to the world like anyone else. This may seem like a small thing, but it changed my outlook. I'd come to Florida hoping to feel more like my old self and now I'd taken a big step before breakfast on the first day of work.

Soon the clubhouse was cleared of everyone but players and coaches. It was time to get down to business. Manager Paul Molitor delivered his opening address, the speech that sets the tone for spring training and the entire season.

Early on, Molly introduced all the alumni coaches. Even though most of us were pretty well known, it never hurts reminding the players that we know what we're talking about. He saved me for last. He told everyone about my 3,053 hits and about the time I nearly hit .400; he told them about my 15 straight seasons of hitting .300 and making 18 straight All-Star teams; he told them about my bunting and base stealing, especially my knack for swiping home. And he told them about everything I'd been through since September and how it led to the T-shirts everyone was wearing. He ended by telling the guys how lucky they were to have me here.

They responded by giving me a standing ovation.

The meeting wrapped up after about an hour. Before heading out, the team photographer crammed together all 90 or so of us. He stood on a ladder and somehow managed to get a picture of everyone wearing the Heart of 29 T-shirts. I was right in the middle of the front row, the center of attention.

Normally, that would make me uncomfortable. This time, it felt pretty terrific.

I headed down the tunnel to the batting cage still buzzing with excitement. I was trying to get back into coaching mode when I heard, "Honey!"

Seeing Rhonda surprised me at first. What was she doing here? How'd she even get here? I had our rental car.

"Dave set it up," she said. "He sent a car."

I was excited for her to see everyone in the T-shirts.

"Dave told me they were doing it," she said with a smile. "That's why he wanted me to be here."

Once we got to the field, I spoke to all the reporters while guys were getting loose. I was soon feeling so good that I borrowed a glove and played catch. Rhonda watched for about an hour, then was ready to head back to the hotel.

"Are you going to throw batting practice?" she said.

"No," I said, laughing. "A man's got to know his limitations."

"Don't overdo it, okay?" she said. "But have fun."

I did. For four weeks, I made it through pretty much every day of practice. I went to most of the home games, although not always until the end. That was typical for me, though. The biggest change now that I was powered by an LVAD was my afternoon nap. It was more common and lasted longer.

———————

The Twins started the season on the road. A week later, I was in their dugout at Target Field, waiting to be introduced to throw the first pitch for the home opener.

Looking at the outfield wall, I noticed a Heart of 29 logo as big as any paid ad. Another classy touch by the organization. Then I looked up at the video board. They played a video in memory of people with ties to the organization who'd died since the end of last season.

"Honey," I said, squeezing Rhonda's hand. "I was almost in that video."

I was still thinking about that when they announced my name. Fans began cheering. More than 40,000 people stood and clapped. Tony came out, too, to deliver me the ball. With Joe Mauer catching, I fired a strike.

The Twins declared their next game a "Heart of 29" game. They debuted new red jerseys and wore patches of our logo on the right side of their chest. They asked their opponents, the Chicago White Sox, if they'd like to wear the patches, too. They accepted. Even the umpires agreed to wear them.

The ceremonial first pitch was tossed by two heart disease survivors, a woman named Barb and a man named Seng. After the throws, I went out to greet them. I gave Barb a hug, then turned to Seng. Like me, he had severe heart failure. Now he was five years removed from a transplant. He was so full of life that he wrapped his arms around me and tried lifting me off the ground. I was startled at first, then laughed. I hoped to be that energetic once I got a new heart.

———

The coming months were a whirlwind for our campaign.

After another trip to Target Field for the AHA's Heart Walk, we took the show elsewhere in baseball. The Dodgers invited us to spread the word to their fans during a game against the Angels. They even distributed baseball cards the AHA made featuring a picture of me early in my career on the front and heart-healthy tips on the back. There was a great ceremony on the field before the game, capped by me throwing out another first pitch. My catcher was Dodgers closer Kenley Jansen, a heart patient himself. We were joined on the mound by several other survivors—including Dravyn Johnson, a one-year-old transplant recipient.

While at Dodger Stadium, I went to the radio booth to greet Vin Scully, who was in his final season. I also saw Kenny Landreaux, one of the guys who went to the Twins in the trade that sent me to the Angels. As I was leaving the stadium, a man stopped me to tell me his heart story. Then he asked where he could get more information. Encounters like that showed me our message was being heard.

The Angels were the next team to spotlight Heart of 29. For this first pitch, my catcher was Clyde Wright. It was so nice to share his story to a stadium full of people. The Angels were kind enough to schedule this game against the Twins. They brought along their Heart of 29 patches and wore them on their hats during batting practice. During BP, the Angels wore Heart of 29 patches they made. Many of my former Angels teammates were at the stadium. It was great seeing them for the first time since my heart attack. But the person I was most excited to see was a fan: Dr. Dan Meyer, the surgeon who put in my LVAD. He'd moved to Dallas but scheduled a family vacation to Disneyland to coincide with this game.

Dr. Dan Meyer went from being the surgeon who implanted my LVAD to a close friend and trusted adviser. Rhonda and I were so happy he and his family joined us for the Heart of 29 game at Angel Stadium. (Courtesy of the American Heart Association)

Tony and Gordette Oliva with Rhonda and me at the 2016 All-Star Game FanFest. (Courtesy of the American Heart Association)

Mark Bonney (right) was among the first responders from the Corona Fire Department who saved my life the day of my heart attack. He attended the All-Star FanFest along with my cardiologist, Dr. Ajay Srivastava, and Jennifer Nowaczyk, the coordinator of the Scripps LVAD program. (Courtesy of the American Heart Association)

I was so happy to be joined by Rhonda, Devon, Cheyenne, and the Olivas when Major League Baseball announced that the AL batting champion award would be known as the Rod Carew American League Batting Champion Award. (Courtesy of Rod Carew)

In the Red Sox dugout at Fenway Park during a Heart of 29 Game, I showed off my gear to manager John Farrell and hitting coach Chili Davis, who also is a longtime close friend. (Courtesy of the American Heart Association)

My final big outing with my LVAD was my annual trip to the Hall of Fame. I held a news conference promoting Heart of 29 and was happy to be joined by Dr. Gerald Marx (red shirt). Jerry helped connect us with the American Heart Association. (Courtesy of the American Heart Association)

Rhonda; Devon; his girlfriend, Mary Zuromskis; and me beneath my plaque in the Hall of Fame. (Courtesy of Rod Carew)

They said recovery from a heart transplant was less painful than recovering from receiving an LVAD. They were right. In January 2017, I was on the fast track to recovery. (Courtesy of Rod Carew)

To this day, I'm amazed that this device—the actual HeartMate II LVAD that was my in my chest—helped keep me alive for 14 months. (Courtesy of the American Heart Association)

Mary and Ralf Reuland listen to the heartbeat of their late son, Konrad, in my chest. (Courtesy of the American Heart Association)

Mary spent her final hours with Konrad listening to his heartbeat. After Mary heard his heart beating in my chest, Rhonda asked her whether it sounded the same way. Mary smiled and said, "I've got it memorized." (Courtesy of the American Heart Association)

"Welcome home, Konrad," Ralf said when he heard Konrad's heartbeat. (Courtesy of the American Heart Association)

Ralf, Mary, and Austin Reuland with Rhonda and me. We're all family now: the Careulands. (Courtesy of the American Heart Association)

Ten months after getting a new heart, I became a grandfather for the first time. My best days now are those spent with AviBleu. (Courtesy of Rod Carew)

Konrad Albert Reuland
Son – Brother – Friend

✝

April 4, 1987 – December 12, 2016
Taken Too Soon, Forever In Our Hearts.

On what would've been Konrad's 30th birthday, Rhonda and I visited his grave to say a prayer and offer our thanks for his selflessness. (Courtesy of the American Heart Association)

I was home one day when I got a call from the commissioner's office. The All-Star Game was coming up in San Diego, and they invited me there. They were going to turn the NL batting title into the Tony Gwynn National League Batting Champion Award. And they wanted to name the AL version after me.

It just so happened that we already were planning to be in San Diego for Heart of 29.

The day before the game, at the All-Star FanFest, we held an event that included CPR training for kids. As a group of Little Leaguers practiced giving compressions to manikins, my old roomie Tony got down on the ground and joined them. It was quite a scene. My favorite part, though, was seeing Mark Bonney, one of the paramedics from the Corona Fire Department who treated me at Cresta Verde. Other honored guests included Dr. Ajay and Jennifer Nowaczyk, the coordinator of the Scripps LVAD program.

The next day at Petco Park, Devon and Cheyenne joined Rhonda and me on the field for the ceremony. Having the kids there was important to me.

I retired before they were born and I'd been in the Hall of Fame for about a decade when I met them. While they'd been with me in Cooperstown and at other events, they'd never seen my career celebrated on a stage this big.

When emcee Dick Enberg made the announcement—which had been a secret until then—fans rose and clapped. I instinctively turned and waved in all directions. I must not have been prepared for this because the moment overwhelmed me. My mind flashed to the fact I'd gone from nearly dying to getting a standing ovation at an All-Star

Game. Then I thought about my buddy Tony Gwynn, the hometown hero who died of cancer a few years ago; this would've meant so much to him. I was so lost in my thoughts that I didn't even smile.

MLB commissioner Rob Manfred greeted me in front of a prototype of the award itself: me in my crouched batting stance, my top hand holding the bat loosely and the bat practically an extension of my shoulders.

"This is really well deserved," Manfred told me.

That trophy is now on display in my house, on a table next to my favorite chair. Despite the big unveiling, MLB has yet to present it to a batting champion.

Baseball continued to be my best therapy.

The events themselves kept my body and mind going. Between trips, Rhonda pushed me to remain active to make sure I could attend the next event. Still, there were some medical challenges. I was retaining way too much fluid in my ankles and legs. Also, I had episodes where my brain seemed a bit loopy. I often failed to come up with the word I wanted. Sometimes I couldn't think of a simple word, like flower.

She asked the LVAD team about consulting a neurologist. No need, they said. The LVAD and blood thinners left me with a lower blood cell count, which likely was to blame for the cognitive issues. However, they had no explanation for another strange change that came over me each night.

I used to be a snorer. Since Coronado, I'd begun talking in my sleep—in English and Spanish. These weren't mumbles, they were full conversations. Sometimes I gave batting lessons. Other times, I gave speeches encouraging people to get their hearts checked. Rhonda found it frustrating but, ultimately, easier for her to tolerate than my snoring.

GI bleeds remained an issue as well. They forced me into three more hospital stays, but always briefly. In fact, they got shorter each time.

In the grand scheme of things, these were minor issues. None would keep me from getting a transplant. I'd also easily kicked my tobacco habit. I hadn't even been tempted to chew since doctors told me to stop.

We'd decided to pursue the transplant at Cedars-Sinai Medical Center in Los Angeles. The choice was relatively easy, considering Cedars-Sinai handles the most heart transplants each year in the world. I especially liked the hospital's batting average: over a recent five-year span, 91 percent of recipients lived at least a year with their new heart. And people who make it one year generally live long beyond that.

As July rolled around, we began talking to the Cedars-Sinai transplant team about when to schedule my evaluation, the test that would determine whether I could qualify for the transplant waiting list. They couldn't set a date yet. But they said it was getting closer.

Soon, that would be our sole priority. That meant it was time to wrap up our travels.

———————

Our final journey had three legs, starting in Minneapolis for the Twins Hall of Fame induction weekend.

As chairman of the selection committee, I'd had the privilege of sharing the good news with the two honorees back in January. I always love making that call, and this year I had the pleasure of calling Torii Hunter. Of all the guys who've come through the Twins since I returned to the organization, he's perhaps the guy I've become closest friends with. The relationship grew when he played for the Angels. Longtime radio voice John Gordon was also chosen. Now, before a game in mid-July, I handed each of them a blue blazer with the Twins Hall of Fame crest.

Next, Rhonda and I went to Boston for our final Heart of 29 game.

Like the Dodgers, the Red Sox were kind enough to spread our message despite having no connection to me. They just recognized a good cause worthy of their support.

Fenway Park had been one of my favorite places to play. Red Sox fans always treated me well, which I know is rarely the case for black guys. Before I went on the field, a team employee brought me a white jersey. It had RED SOX across the front with a Heart of 29 patch over my heart; my name and the number 29 were on the back. I hadn't worn a jersey at the other stops, even in the stadiums of teams that had retired my jersey. I gladly buttoned it up.

In the dugout, I went straight to Red Sox hitting coach Chili Davis. Back in his playing days, he came to my hitting school to work on his swing. Then he became one of my pupils on the Angels. During Michelle's fight for life, he came to the hospital and our donor drives for the registry. He'd even been one of Michelle's pallbearers. He'd come to visit me in the hospital after the LVAD operation. As we chatted, I noticed a Heart of 29 patch above his heart. I looked at Rhonda and she was smiling. She'd helped arrange this with the Red Sox and their opponent, the Twins.

Over the years, I'd gotten to know many Boston players, in part because they also have spring training in Fort Myers. Dustin Pedroia lit up when he saw me. He was eager to tell me that his father-in-law got an LVAD three years ago and was doing great. Next came David Ortiz. I've known Big Papi since he broke in with the Twins. I hated when they let him go and wasn't surprised when he turned into a star in Boston.

"I love you," he told me. "I'm pulling for you."

My Twins friends got quite a kick out of seeing me in a Red Sox jersey. In the TV booth, Dick Bremer and my old teammate Roy Smalley teased me plenty. My former Angels teammate Fred Lynn, a Red Sox Hall of Famer, happened to be in the ballpark, too. Freddy also got a laugh out of seeing me in a Red Sox jersey.

"We could've used you here," he said.

Another special visitor was Dr. Jerry Marx, Frank's childhood friend who helped get me connected with the American Heart Association. Jerry also would be joining us for the final leg of this trip—induction weekend in Cooperstown.

———————————

Of all the people I could reach with my message about heart health, I hoped my fellow Hall of Famers would be the most receptive.

The AHA worked with Jeff Idelson's team and the local hospital to provide heart screenings inside the Otesaga Resort

Hotel on Saturday and Sunday. Jeff also suggested that Rhonda
and I send a letter promoting this to the Hall of Famers who
said they were coming. Our note read, in part:

> In just a few weeks, we will all be together again
> in Cooperstown, enjoying our annual reunion of
> the greatest fraternity in all of sports. We earned
> the right to be part of this club in our younger,
> stronger days and now we get to reap the rewards
> every July. If you are anything like me, you spend
> all year looking forward to this get-together.
> Last September 20, that pleasure—along with every-
> thing else I hold dear—almost was snatched from
> me.... I've learned a lot during this ordeal, including
> something I need to share with you.
> Heart disease is mostly preventable. It can often be
> caught before you end up in a situation like mine.
> This is why I want to ask you to do me a favor.
> This Hall of Fame weekend, set aside about a half
> hour to get your heart checked. Your wife, too....
> I know our time in Cooperstown is brief, and I
> know there are many other things you'd rather do
> while there. But there's no down side to this small
> investment of time. You'll either get the informa-
> tion needed to stop problems before they start, or
> you'll get the peace of mind of knowing you're OK.
> That's a win either way.
> Do you remember when Mickey Mantle was fight-
> ing for his life? He told everyone, "Don't be like

me." Well, that is my wish for you. Don't end up a victim of heart disease like me.

I plan on returning to Cooperstown for many years to come. Please get your heart checked so you can keep coming, too.

Brooks Robinson was the first to get screened. He'd dealt with an irregular heartbeat for 17 years and was happy to have a mini-checkup. When he went back to the lobby, he encouraged Gaylord Perry to get checked. Gaylord came and brought some friends. (Gaylord being Gaylord, he declared, "It's about time Rod did something for me after all those hits I gave him.")

Bert Blyleven and his wife, Gayle, got checked. So did some of the younger guys, Tom Glavine and John Smoltz, and their wives.

Around lunchtime, I held a news conference to promote Heart of 29, with Dr. Marx joining me on the stage. Rhonda, meanwhile, spoke at the annual luncheon for Hall of Famers' wives. People who were there said she was amazing. The best evidence was the line of women who went straight from the luncheon to the screening.

I signed autographs in the afternoon, then went back to my room to rest. I felt zonked.

This was a busy day at the end of a stretch of busy days. And it was really hot. After a nap, I had Jerry check me out. Fearing dehydration, he got me some Gatorade and told me to drink lots of water.

The evening began with a parade down Main Street, culminating at the museum, where we went inside for a party in the room with all the plaques. My ride in the parade was a pickup truck. Sitting in the bed with Rhonda, Devon, and Mary, I heard fans hollering the usual stuff ("Love you Rod!" "Looking good!"). Then I heard, "Thanks for being alive." Something about that line struck me. I didn't just sob. I went into a shoulder-shaking, jaw-trembling bawl unlike any in the last six months. I spent the rest of the ride trying to regain my composure. When we stopped in front of the museum, I needed two strong people to help me out of the truck.

On Sunday, I knew something was still off.

I made it to the induction ceremony for Ken Griffey Jr. and Mike Piazza. But when it was time for me to walk onto the stage, my back hurt and I felt weak. I didn't trust my balance. I needed help getting to my seat. Since everyone knew I was being kept alive by a machine, they thought little of this. I knew better. Watching from the crowd, Rhonda hoped it was only dehydration.

In the evening, I attended the event I look forward to most each year: the private dinner exclusively for us fraternity members. The only tears I shed this time came from laughing so hard.

I left Cooperstown with a big smile. I'd gone 3-for-3 on my list of things to do in 2016.

Now it was time to get home and see about getting a new heart.

18

WORSENING. WAITING.

AROUND THE ALL-STAR GAME, Rhonda noticed my outlook was dimming.

She's always described me as a glass-half-empty guy. Now I was going through stretches where there was hardly anything in the glass.

I twisted things into worst-case scenarios. Like the power going out in our house and the LVAD batteries running out. What if we're not home, the batteries die, and I don't have Honey? I thought about being like Walter Payton and dying while on a transplant waiting list. Even if I got a new heart, what if my body rejected it? I still wasn't afraid of dying, but I thought God might soon decide my time was up. I reminded Rhonda of our promise—no extreme measures to keep me alive.

I was aware enough about my unhappiness that I saw a psychiatrist. He prescribed an antidepressant. I visited him a few more times, mainly to regulate the dosage. I wanted to talk about my moods, so I started seeing a psychologist. At first, talking to her relaxed me. Then the demons squeezed my mind shut. I refused to share my feelings with the woman I was paying to listen to me talk about my feelings. I started thinking, *I can handle this.*

———————

After Cooperstown, the focus was supposed to be getting an evaluation from the transplant team at Cedars-Sinai.

But when we got home, my body was as frazzled as my mind.

Rhonda feared another GI bleed was to blame. I'd had enough of them that we'd bought a machine to check my blood count at home.

It was low, but not low enough to confirm a bleed. Rhonda called Dr. Ajay and he said to keep monitoring it. After a third straight day of the number slightly dropping, he had me check in to Scripps.

When the infectious disease doctor examined me, we knew there was more to this. Something was wrong; they just weren't sure what. More tests on Friday failed to answer the question.

Late Saturday night, after Rhonda left the hospital, I was talking to a nurse when my speech became scrambled. I couldn't form a sentence. She asked me to put on my glasses. I put them in my mouth.

A CT scan showed a brain bleed. I went right into surgery to drain the blood from above each temple. The doctor who called Rhonda said it was a simple operation. Still, it counted as brain surgery.

Like the GI bleeds, the brain bleed was caused by blood thinners.

I needed the medicine because LVADs have a tendency to cause blood clots. Yet while reducing the risk of one problem, these blood thinners were causing other problems. This made four GI bleeds and a brain bleed.

"That's it—no more blood thinners," Rhonda told Dr. Ajay. "Over my dead body, he's not getting any more blood thinners!"

She asked if there was a way to screen for symptoms of clots, like an early detection system. He said there was.

"Good. Let's start using that," she said. "Otherwise we are never going to get an evaluation because he's always going to be in the hospital dealing with a bleed."

———————

All brain surgery patients at Scripps are required to go through rehabilitation at the traumatic brain injury unit in Encinitas. My transfer was delayed by a urinary tract infection.

Once I got to Encinitas, I started yelling at nurses. I tried escaping my bed.

This wasn't another panic attack. It was something far more sinister. We just didn't know what it was.

My rage forced caregivers to tie my arms to the bed rails and my feet to the end of the bed. That only made me angrier.

"You can't keep me strapped down in here!" I screamed.

At night, I declared that the Marines were coming to break me out and take me to Camp Pendleton. I talked about living in a shack and becoming a terrorist. I told Rhonda that if she tried to get in my way, I was going to chop her into a million pieces and leave her in the corner.

When anyone tried taking me for tests or therapy, I accused them of trying to take me to the dungeon where they were going to turn me into Frankenstein's monster. The only therapist I trusted was a woman named Paige. On her days off, I rudely told the others to get away from me.

For Rhonda, this was the most traumatic part of the entire saga—and it had nothing to do with the horrendous things I was saying. She feared I had brain damage. Was this the real reason they'd transferred me to the traumatic brain injury unit? Most of all, she saw this ending my chance of getting a transplant.

Rhonda felt like doctors and nurses weren't telling her all they knew and she had no allies to rely on for insight. After three frustrating days, she stalked Dr. Stephanie Joseph, who was in charge of the unit. Rhonda found Dr. Joseph in a hallway and blocked her path.

"What is going on?" Rhonda said. "My husband is not getting better. He is getting worse, and I'm being told that this is part of the healing. What are you keeping from me?"

"I understand you are upset," Dr. Joseph said. "This is exactly what we expect when you have a urinary tract infection on top of a traumatic brain injury."

"But he doesn't have that anymore," Rhonda said. "They didn't let him come here until it was gone."

"Well, he relapsed," Dr. Joseph said. "It's possible he never completely healed. Sometimes UTIs show in behavior before they show in bacteria."

So that was it? A measly UTI? This wild episode was caused by something that, comparatively speaking, was so minor?

Whew!

My ridiculous rants continued, but now Rhonda considered them a source of amusement. Seeing her snicker added to my rage, so she tried hiding it.

Doctors eventually found the right antibiotic to wipe out my infection. My demeanor changed and, soon enough, my blood count rose to normal levels. My mood improved, too.

Well, except for the last few days before I went home.

―――――――――

My golf tournament was on the final Monday in August.

I constantly asked to be released in time for it. When it looked like I wouldn't, I begged for a day pass. Cried for it. They put me off like a parent would a child—"We'll see how it goes."

Rhonda considered my persistence a good sign. My brain was clear and I was getting ornery again.

They didn't let me go. Rhonda pinch hit.

She told everyone I was dealing with a bleeding issue. She explained that doctors decided it would be best for me to rest. Her cool, breezy demeanor sent the message that she wasn't worried, so they shouldn't be either. As with her speech to the wives in Cooperstown, she knocked it out of the park.

Frank called to let me how great everything went. When Rhonda returned to the hospital, I accused her of turning me into Wally Pipp.

"Wally Pipp?" she said.

I told her the story of the first baseman for the Yankees who took a day off because of a headache. A rookie replaced him in the lineup. Lou Gehrig ended up playing the next 2,130 straight games.

———————

Rhonda had long since given up her notion of a transplant being the worst-case scenario. It had become her sole focus.

She understood that a new heart was the only way for me to regain a normal life. Her views were shaped through talks with Dr. Meyer. Now working in Dallas, he'd become a trusted adviser and good friend.

To get me on board with the transplant, Rhonda worked on me in her usual way. Rather than making a case to me, she talked about it to others in front of me. She knew I would eventually absorb the message.

She had another reason for becoming more insistent about getting me on the waiting list. One she didn't dare mention.

———————

The L in LVAD stands for left. That was the side of my heart it was powering.

Now my right side was failing, too.

The first clue came earlier that summer, when I started swelling again. The fact I was swelling in different places from before made Rhonda worry that it might be coming from a different source. Dr. Heywood ran some tests that confirmed it. The good half of my heart was in the early stages of heart failure.

Rhonda knew all this before our last trip. It was part of the reason she recommended clearing our schedule after Cooperstown. It also had been weighing on her mind through the episodes at the Hall of Fame, the brain bleed, the meltdown later traced to the UTI and the slow recovery from it.

Medically, none of these recent issues would affect my eligibility for the transplant. All we'd lost was time. But now, time was of the essence.

With no blood thinners to keep me from clotting, and the right side of my heart giving out, I needed a new heart more than ever. Yet I couldn't get on the waiting list without an evaluation. And I still didn't have an appointment for it.

19

THE GREATEST GIFT

CEDARS-SINAI SCHEDULED my transplant evaluation for September 23, 2016.

Or, as I saw it, a few days after the first anniversary of the day I nearly died.

Although I knew the stakes were high for this appointment, I didn't fully understand. Rhonda did, and her mind was racing. The wild cards were my age and antibodies accumulated from all the blood transfusions following my various bleeds.

Numbers, though, were only part of the evaluation. Dr. Meyer told Rhonda this meeting was more like a first date. This was a chance for the transplant team to look me over, talk to me, get an idea of what a new heart would do for me. This had nothing to do with my status as a Hall of Famer and everything to do with showing that I was an otherwise healthy, alert, active 70-year-old who'd never abused drugs or alcohol and had a strong family support system. Those were the reasons why after giving me the LVAD, Dr. Meyer had insisted to Rhonda, "He *will* get a heart."

Our evaluator was Dr. Michelle Kittleson. Her big concern was my kidneys.

This both was and wasn't a surprise.

Back in April, when I'd gone six months without using tobacco and thus became eligible for an evaluation, Dr. Ajay ran some tests to essentially prescreen me for the evaluation. He discovered that my kidneys were a bit weak.

My kidneys were fine while I had the LVAD. But if I got a transplant, one of them probably would fail under the stress of the antirejection medicines I'd have to take. Because a transplant is supposed to return a person to a high quality of life, it would be counterproductive to give a limited resource like a heart to someone who would wind up in dialysis. Realizing this could be an issue with the evaluators, Dr. Ajay changed some of my medicines in hopes of strengthening the kidneys before the evaluation.

Waiting for my kidneys to improve was among the reasons we'd initially waited to schedule the evaluation. Then came all the bleeds, which both delayed things further and led to all the transfusions. And all the transfusions possibly stirred up trouble with the antibodies. Rhonda was on top of this stuff, not me. She was far more concerned about the antibodies than the kidneys. But now Dr. Kittleson considered my kidney problem an obstacle.

"That does not mean that we couldn't work around it," Dr. Kittleson said. "I will need to talk to my team about it."

That wouldn't be until next Friday.

Meanwhile, Dr. Ajay started looking into other transplant centers. Just in case.

———————

Rhonda woke up every morning wishing it was Friday.

For the first time, our roles had reversed. I was counseling her. I kept reminding her that everything was in God's hands. We talked about not being able to peek at the tapestry while it's in progress and how frustrating that can be.

We both read books of daily devotionals. This week, I noticed her spending more time in those pages. One afternoon, she closed the book, turned to me, and said, "I don't think God would've put you on this journey and let you get to this point only to turn you away."

Around noon on Friday, I was in the kitchen when Rhonda walked in with an interesting look on her face.

"I heard from the heart team," she said.

"You did?!" I said.

"Yes," she said, flatly.

"Not good news," I said.

"Why would you say that?" she said.

"Well, just by the look on your face and the tone of your voice," I said.

"I just want to do this right," she said. "You've been accepted!"

However, there was a catch: I also needed a new kidney, and that meant needing approval from another set of evaluators. We could take comfort in knowing that the kidney team usually followed recommendations from the heart team. However, it would be two weeks until we could meet them and another two weeks until their decision.

The next day, I turned 71. No need to guess what I wished for when I blew out the candles.

On October 27, the kidney team accepted me for transplant. I was going on the list. Soon. I had to wait two more weeks for them to determine my spot in the batting order, so to speak.

The tiers are 1A, 1B, and 2. There are further levels within 1A, marked by letters A through E. LVAD patients are generally slotted as 1B. However, Dr. Meyer projected me as a 1A-(E) because of all my additional risks: the right side of my heart was failing, I'd been off blood thinners for three months, and I wasn't getting any younger. While my age was initially considered an obstacle to getting on the list, now that I'd been approved it should be a reason for them to hurry.

It's important to note something about Dr. Meyer. While we were biased toward his opinion because he'd become our friend, he also was highly respected by his peers. A few months before, at the annual event for the leading organization in the field of transplantation (the American Society of Transplantation's Cutting Edge of Transplantation conference), he gave a presentation titled "Overview of New Donor Heart Allocation

Tiers." In other words, Dr. Meyer was among the leaders working to improve this very process. He was helping determine how to set a heart transplant waiting list.

———————

The Friday before Thanksgiving, we were having dinner with Di and Wayne when the phone rang. It was the transplant coordinator's office. They had my status.

1B.

"I'm probably the first person you called who wasn't happy to hear that," Rhonda told her. "Do you know the risks he has right now?!"

Rhonda snapped into what our family calls her pitbull mode. She rattled off all the reasons we expected a 1A-(E) listing.

"No, ma'am, I was not aware of the risks," the woman from Cedars-Sinai said. "When someone gets listed and classified, we're not looking at their information. We're just making phone calls to let the patient know what the classification of their listing is. I will talk to Dr. Kittleson."

———————

As all this played out, I began wrapping my mind around the fact that this was really happening. I was about to get a new heart. As weird as it was having a gizmo in my chest, it seemed even weirder to think that I'd be inheriting a stranger's organs.

I had an idea of what it might be like from talking to transplant recipients during my time at Prebys. But that was a while ago, when this was a long way off. I wanted to talk to someone new. A friend connected me with Kent Tekulve, the former All-Star closer for the Pittsburgh Pirates who'd had a transplant two years earlier. Kent eased some of my concerns about the discomfort of the surgery and recovery. He also got me more excited.

"You think the Hall of Fame call was the greatest call you've ever gotten?" he said. "Won't even compare."

Around this time, we also went to several services at Saddleback. After one of them, we spent time in private with Pastor Rick. He'd just started delivering a series of messages around the theme of "Seeking God for a Breakthrough." We then held hands and prayed for my breakthrough.

The Sunday following the 1B call, we returned to Saddleback. That happened to be the day Pastor Rick kicked off his series. The message was called "Praying and Fasting for a Breakthrough."

We saw another pastor we knew and shared the latest news with him. Two days later, we received this email:

> Hey Rod!
> Thanks for letting me pray for you on the patio a
> couple weeks ago. I heard that we've had a break-
> through in getting you on the list!
> That's great! Please keep me up-to date.
> Rick

Once Dr. Kittleson took a closer look at all my risks, she too believed I deserved a 1A-(E) listing.

She also worked to help me get it.

The standard drill involved presenting a case to a team of 40-plus people at Cedars-Sinai. It took a unanimous vote to then ask for a change in status by the United Network for Organ Sharing, the guiding body that oversees all transplants in the United States. To help speed my process, she flipped the order. She asked UNOS whether they would make the adjustment. Told they would, she easily secured the unanimous vote. Again, this wasn't a case of anyone looking out for a Hall of Famer, it was simply an example of a doctor advocating for a patient she believed in.

The evening of December 9, the coordinator called to say my status was revised to 1A-(E).

Our world now revolved around waiting for "the call."

We'd repeatedly been told there was only a four-hour window to get the organs from the donor into the recipient. So we had to be ready at any moment.

We packed suitcases and put them in the trunk. In the glove box, we put the list of people we promised to call on the way to the hospital. Our biggest concern was traffic. It could take up to three hours to get from our house to Cedars-Sinai. If the call came during rush hour, we would use a private helicopter. Rhonda had a company on standby. She'd already arranged for the helicopter to land in the field behind the cul-de-sac at the end of our block.

Both of us expected the call to come in the middle of the night. We slept with our cell phones on the bed between us.

When I got up during the night, I checked that the phones were still there, fully charged and with the ringer at full volume.

The next day, a Saturday, I did a lot of thinking.

My biggest sensation wasn't fear. Or excitement. I was tranquil. I knew God was in control.

That led me down another line of thinking. For me to get new organs, someone else had to die. My family's joy would come from another family's tragedy. I'd known this all along, of course, but it always seemed abstract. Now that I actually was near the top of the list, it was different. That concept was now a reality. Rhonda reminded me that we'd been counseled to accept that there's nothing we could do for the other person. We should focus instead on how wonderful a person was to have made the selfless decision to help someone else—in this case, me—after dying. I would be part of that person's legacy. In fact, our local organ donor recovery network is called One Legacy.

By Sunday evening, I'd gone from months of being detached to paying too much attention. I was trying to wish the call into existence.

"I hope they didn't forget about me," I said.

"It's only been 48 hours," Rhonda said.

By Wednesday, we'd settled into the waiting game.

I had appointments with Dr. Ajay, Dr. Heywood, and the entire LVAD team in San Diego. Although it would take us another 90 minutes away from Cedars-Sinai, we never considered skipping it. Even this close to getting a new heart, I still had to care for my current one.

They were as excited as we were about the 1A-(E) status. They realized this could be our last LVAD checkup. We talked about what I might do with the LVAD once it was out of me. They mentioned that inside the device were two rubies. Yes, the actual precious jewel. I promised Rhonda that it would become part of a ring or necklace for her.

The visit left us in such a good mood that on the drive back, we stopped for lunch, something we rarely did.

We got home around 4:30 PM. Rhonda went upstairs and I was in the kitchen when my phone rang. It was an unfamiliar number with a 310 area code. The same area code as Cedars-Sinai. My eyes widened and my hands shook. Rhonda was downstairs again by now, so I handed her the phone. It was a small dose of my flight response kicking in. I wasn't going to run away, but I was panicking.

"Honey," I said. "I think you might want to answer this call."

Indeed. They'd found a match. I would be getting a new heart and a new kidney. We didn't have to rush, though. They asked us to try getting to the hospital by 9 PM. The operation wasn't going to happen for another day anyway. We wondered what happened to the four-hour window, but let that go.

Kent was right. This was better than the call from Cooperstown.

Cheyenne, Devon, Mary, and Frank joined us at the hospital. For once, the mood in my hospital room was pure joy. We joked about swapping out my bad organs for good ones.

I could hardly remember Rhonda looking so relaxed. She'd been right about God not sending us so far down this road without letting us reach our destination.

After waiting all day Thursday, they wheeled me into the operating room around midnight.

We were originally told I would have separate operations. The heart would be transplanted first, then they'd watch me for up to 18 hours until they were sure I was ready for the kidney. During our wait, they said there was a new plan. The procedures would be done back-to-back. All told, it was supposed to take 17 hours.

It went so well that it only took 13.

20

SAVING LIVES, TOGETHER

ONCE MY NEW HEART and kidney were in, surgeon Fardad Esmailian went to let Rhonda know the good news.

As they went over the particulars, he raved about what a great heart I'd received. He joked that they had to stuff in the kidney because it was so large. Rhonda asked what he could share about the donor. All we knew so far was that he was an exceptionally healthy, local man in his twenties who'd died at UCLA Medical Center. Could he at least share the specific age?

"29," he said.

Goose bumps rose on Rhonda's arm.

Another God wink, she thought.

While I was in recovery, Rhonda kept thinking about this new meaning for "Heart of 29."

Then she started thinking about the flip side—the fact that a mother was going through the horror of having lost a 29-year-old son. It hit her especially hard because Cheyenne was 29 and Devon was 27. She said a prayer for my donor's family. She recalled our conversations about this and the advice from the counselors. But, again, it now felt more real. How could we ever reconcile our joy with their grief?

She also thought about another family grieving over the loss of a 29-year-old son. Konrad Reuland went to Saint John's Episcopal School with Cheyenne from sixth through eighth grade. Devon was there those years, too, in a younger grade. Devon and Konrad's younger brother Warren had been basketball teammates; they were still Facebook friends. Over the years, we'd heard that Konrad had become a star football player, even making it to the NFL. His name had come up Wednesday night during our drive to Cedars-Sinai and several times again as we waited on Thursday. People wondered whether I might be getting his heart. It seemed so random. We didn't understand the connection.

During the 13 hours of my operation, Rhonda sifted through all the calls, texts, emails, and Facebook messages that had accumulated on her phone since we got "the call." She saw so many references to Konrad that she finally Googled him. She learned that he'd died of a ruptured brain aneurysm. She also saw that he died on Monday. This was Friday. With the four-hour window to get a heart from donor to recipient, I couldn't possibly have received his heart and kidney.

Too far-fetched, she thought.

I began rehab the day after my transplant.

A therapist helped lift me off the bed. I was reminded of what I'd heard from people who'd had both an LVAD and a transplant—recovering from the transplant is easier.

My heart was so strong it felt like I had a Ferrari in my chest. In the 14 months of the LVAD, I never had a heartbeat, just a whooshing sound. Now, this powerhouse was roaring.

After I got the LVAD, Rhonda used to always tell me, "You're not sick." Because, temporarily, I wasn't. Now, I truly wasn't. My body was working better than it had in more than a year. Once I recovered from the surgery itself, I'd be a new man.

And I had a stranger to thank for it.

I began asking Rhonda about my donor. What did we know about this angel who'd given me these gifts on his way to heaven?

About two weeks later, after a magnificent Christmas, Rhonda kept getting messages from Mike Cohen. He was one of the insurance agents I used to play golf with. He was part of the foursome with Chris Ferraro, the guy who'd taught me the warning signs of a heart attack and urged me to get help if I ever felt any of them.

Mike wanted to talk about whether I might have Konrad's heart and kidney. Rhonda said she'd heard the theory, but it wasn't possible.

"The Reulands think it's true," he said. "Konrad's mom, Mary, wants to talk to you. She would love for you to call her."

"I would love to call her, too," Rhonda said. "But I can't. I don't want to get anyone in trouble."

The cardinal rule for organ donation recipients is not to contact the donor's family. Considering what our donor had done for us, following this rule seemed like the least we could do for them. There was a nuance here in that Rhonda didn't think the organs came from Konrad. Still, she wasn't taking any chances. Any contact would have to come through One Legacy, or from his family reaching out to us.

So Mike asked if he could give Rhonda's phone number to Mary.

"Of course," Rhonda said.

———

News of my transplant generated calls from everyone we knew and plenty we didn't. Rhonda got into the habit of only answering calls from a few people. The rest went to voicemail.

Checking her messages one morning, Rhonda heard: "This is Mary Reuland. And I think your husband may have my son's heart and kidney. Give me a call back."

The message was several days old. Rhonda returned the call immediately.

"Please don't think I was avoiding calling," Rhonda said. "I just didn't recognize the number."

Both were nervous. Each feared saying the wrong thing.

For Rhonda, it was all about survivor's guilt; her husband lived because Mary's son died. Her voice needed to carry the right tone.

For Mary, it was all about this being possibly her only shot to share what she'd learned. If she came on too strong, she might get turned away and never get to hear Konrad's heart beat again.

Mary went first, explaining the events that led her down this path.

At Konrad's funeral, people kept asking her whether his organs went to me. She found it as befuddling as we had when folks asked if I was getting his organs. Just like Rhonda eventually found a quiet moment to look up why everyone mentioned Konrad, Mary eventually Googled me.

What she learned matched the scant details from her end: on December 16, Konrad's heart and left kidney went to a 71-year-old man from Orange County who was treated at Cedars-Sinai. On this call, Mary confirmed to Rhonda that Konrad had been an exceptionally healthy, local man in his twenties who'd died at UCLA Medical Center.

Before parsing those details, Mary had more to share.

Growing up, she watched and went to many Angels games with her dad and brothers. I'd been her favorite player. She opened packs of baseball cards hoping to find ones with my picture on it. She remembered seeing me at Saint John's. She especially remembered an afternoon when Konrad was 11. He climbed into her car after school and blurted, "You're never going to believe who I met today! I met Rod Carew! He played for the Angels!" For a kid who wanted to become a professional athlete, this was such a big deal that he talked about it all night. Whenever anyone mentioned something about their day, Konrad interrupted, "Yeah, but did *you* meet Rod Carew today? *I* met Rod Carew today!"

In the final hours before Konrad was declared brain dead, Mary kept her right ear on his chest. She listened to his heartbeat thumping over and over. This was how she said goodbye to her oldest child, a precocious little boy who'd grown into a wonderful man. When she had to leave him, she told the representative from One Legacy, "Whoever gets this heart better deserve it. Because Konrad had a good heart." So when she Googled me and found that the circumstances lined up, she kept opening more links to see whether I was worthy. Reading about the Heart of 29 campaign proved it. Reading about Michelle took everything to a new level. Even if I didn't have Konrad's organs, we were bonded by having buried a child. You never get over that. She considered herself lucky to have spent 11 more years with her firstborn than I had with my baby.

Also during her final moments with Konrad, Mary told the One Legacy rep that she wanted to know who got his heart so she could one day hear his heartbeat again. It was too soon, however, for One Legacy to start their process of connecting the families.

As Mary spoke, Rhonda wished this story to be true, too. The scant details we had about our donor and their had about the recipient of Konrad's heart sure lined up nicely.

Yet Rhonda still considered this a puzzle with some pieces missing.

So they spent the next few weeks trying to find them.

The hunt started with the timing. How did the four-hour window get stretched to four days?

The simple answer is, it didn't.

Although Konrad was declared brain dead on a Monday, machines kept his body alive while matches were sought for all his organs. Because his fatal injury was limited to his brain, and because he was so healthy, there were lots of matches to be made. When we got the call on Wednesday, they said we could take our time because they knew the heart would be the last organ removed. That wasn't until late Thursday night, shortly before I was rolled into the operating room.

Next question: How did we match? Why didn't his heart and kidney go to one of the patients ahead of me?

The linchpin was hepatitis B.

Konrad had been exposed to it. This meant his organs could only go to someone who'd either had the disease or had been vaccinated against it. That limited the pool. The vaccine began circulating in the 1980s but wasn't commonly given until the 1990s. Most people over 30 hadn't been vaccinated. I was among the exceptions. Because of Michelle. She was so vulnerable to catching anything while fighting leukemia that our family got all sorts of shots. Including hep B. Now Rhonda started becoming convinced.

But she still had one last piece to snap into place. It involved blood type.

I'm a B-positive. Less than 10 percent of all people are B-positive. However, I also could match with someone who was an O, which is the most common and can be donated to anyone. Konrad, indeed, was an O.

So it came down to this: if my organs came from someone who was B-positive, Konrad was not my donor.

During a routine visit by a nurse, Rhonda asked her to check the blood type of my donor.

The woman flipped through the chart and said, "O."

Rhonda laughed.

Oh my, she thought. *It must be true.*

———————

Rhonda and Mary agreed that being 99.999 percent sure wasn't enough. They needed confirmation from One Legacy.

Mary called Tracy Chang, an aftercare specialist who was her point of contact. Tracy was in the room during Mary's last moments with Konrad. She was the person Mary had told, "Whoever gets this heart better deserve it. Because Konrad had a good heart."

On this call, Mary detailed how she and Rhonda had connected every dot. She also explained that while neither family spoke about this possibility, rumors had been circulating from the start. They spread well beyond Orange County. Dave St. Peter with the Twins called us to ask about it after hearing it from a friend at Stanford, where Konrad and Warren had played football.

Mary said she wasn't asking Tracy to name the person who got Konrad's heart and left kidney. She only wanted verification of what she already believed to be true: that Konrad's organs went to me.

"Yes or no?" Mary asked.

"Yes," Tracy said.

Tracy said this was the first time she'd ever heard of an anonymous match between families that ended up knowing each other. It was even more improbable for organs to anonymously go from one professional athlete to another.

"It's magical," Tracy said.

"My word," Mary said, "is bittersweet."

During the few hours per day when I was lucid, I kept asking Rhonda about my donor. All she would say was that he'd been 29.

The fact I kept asking the same question, and kept being appeased by the same answer, showed my inability to retain information. Even once she and Mary connected and began investigating, Rhonda didn't tell me anything about it.

After 30 days at Cedars-Sinai, I transferred to Keck Medicine, the hospital at USC, for physical therapy. I was there when Mary got confirmation from One Legacy.

Rhonda knew she needed to ease into the subject.

"We think we know who the donor is," she said. "If we're right, he went to school with the kids."

I didn't respond, which she'd expected. But now it was a topic of conversation. It came up more often. Once I started asking questions, Rhonda knew it was time to walk me through it all.

This was a biggie to wrap my head around. *My donor was a kid I met when he was 11 and who went on to play in the NFL.*

Once it clicked, I wanted to meet the Reulands.

I wanted to hug them and thank them for raising such a selfless son, and to let them hear his heart beating in my chest.

———————

Konrad was a giant in every sense.

He was an enormous man—6-foot-6, 270 pounds—with an enormous appetite. He was the life of every party, the best friend that anyone could have. I know those things are often said after someone dies, but we've heard countless stories backing it up.

As a big, strong kid, he loved playing sports from a young age. Basketball was his favorite. His Orange County Piranhas AAU team held its own against the best in the country. After helping his high school basketball team win a state title as a freshman, Konrad played football for the first time as a sophomore. Two years later, he was the top tight end in the country.

He went to Notre Dame, didn't like it, and wound up at Stanford, catching passes from Andrew Luck and getting coached by Jim Harbaugh. Konrad wasn't drafted by an NFL team. But Harbaugh left Stanford for the 49ers that same year. He signed Konrad to San Francisco's practice squad. The next year, Konrad joined the Jets, catching passes from his former Piranhas teammate Mark Sanchez. Then Konrad hurt his knee. A free agent again, he signed with the Ravens. Jim Harbaugh put in a good word with Baltimore's coach, his brother John. The next season, Konrad went to training camp with the Colts, reuniting him with Luck. It didn't work out.

Konrad moved back to Orange County. Seeking one last shot at the NFL, he worked himself into the best shape of his life. Teams were keeping tabs on him; several reached out to his agent about a late-season tryout. Meanwhile, Konrad had begun preparing for life after football. To start a career in commercial real estate, he bought a four-unit apartment building. Many weekends, he went to church with Mary. In his free time, he drove to San Diego to visit Kimi, the 10-year-old niece of close family friends. Kimi was in a hospital fighting a fatal cancer. She called Konrad her best friend. He called her his inspiration. Mary usually knew when Konrad visited Kimi. Seeing him wearing makeup or with each of his fingernails painted a different color gave it away.

The night after Thanksgiving, Konrad was jogging on the treadmill at his apartment building when he felt a click behind his left eye, followed by a headache. He called Warren, a med school student who was home for the holiday. Warren handed the phone to their dad, Ralf, a physician. He told Konrad to get to the ER.

The click was an aneurysm manifesting inside his brain. Days later, Konrad was joking with a nurse in his hospital room when he made a strange face and screamed about an awful headache. The aneurysm had burst. He was rushed into surgery; 17 hours later, the bleeding stopped. But complications followed. Swelling, then pneumonia. The treatment for pneumonia triggered more swelling. Nothing more could be done. Hours later, Ravens coach John Harbaugh opened a postgame news conference by announcing Konrad's death.

Only seven months before, Konrad had been in his parents' kitchen filling out the paperwork to renew his driver's license. He asked Mary if she was an organ donor. She said she was; if she could no longer use her organs, maybe someone else could.

"I'm going to do it, too," he told her. She didn't realize he had until it was time for his selfless choice to be realized.

The night before meeting the Reulands, I hardly slept. ·

By now, Rhonda and Mary had talked on the phone many times. Although they'd yet to meet in person, each felt like she'd known the other forever. I hadn't talked to Mary or Ralf. Now we were going to their house.

What would I do? What would I say?

What *could* I do? What *could* I say?

How do you handle a debt you can never repay?

As a player, I could calm my nerves by looking over my notebooks and studying more about the pitcher I was going to face. This? There's no playbook for meeting the grieving parents of your heart donor.

I tried thinking about things from the Reulands' perspective. If my child's death had given someone else life, how would I want them to act? I took comfort in knowing this meeting was as much their doing as ours. I hoped they were as excited as we were.

I talked to God about how to handle this. Then, my mother's words came to me: "God is there for you. He's always going to be there. He's going to take care of you."

On a gorgeous spring afternoon 11 weeks after the transplant, Rhonda, Devon, his girlfriend, Mary, Frank, and I drove into a gated community in San Juan Capistrano.

A video crew hired by the American Heart Association was in place to capture everything. The Reulands had agreed to let us share the story to continue promoting Heart of 29 and to kick-start the work we'd be doing together to promote One Legacy and organ donation.

Rhonda held my hand as we walked down a pathway beside the house and into the backyard. When I stepped up onto the grass, Mary Reuland, Ralf, and their youngest son, Austin, walked toward us. Mary led the way. Her teary smile told me all I needed to know. This was going to be great.

"Welcome," she said, wrapping her arms around me.

I expected to cry. But the relief, joy, and excitement pumping through Konrad's heart kept me smiling wide.

"This is so good," I said to Ralf as we embraced.

Mary came back to check on me again. Her eyes redder than before, she said, "Remember, you're a part of our family now."

"Yes," I said. "Forever."

"You're part of our family, too," Rhonda said.

Rhonda thanked them for wanting to meet us, especially so soon.

"We are so grateful," Rhonda said. "There aren't words—there aren't adequate words."

"I'm glad we didn't have to wait a year," Mary said.

"I am, too!" I said, laughing.

The conversation flowed. Nothing was stiff or awkward. It was like old friends chatting.

"How are you feeling with that wonderful new heart you have?" Mary said.

"You know what's amazing?" I said. "The doctors come in and they say, 'Wow! You're breathing so deep and so smooth.' And I say, 'Yes!'"

"And they always say, 'Oh my gosh, that heart is so strong,'" Rhonda said.

"You got a good one," Mary said.

"Absolutely," Rhonda said.

"And it went into a good man," Mary said.

"I will take care of this heart," I said. "Because I've been given a second chance. God knows how I feel and what I'm going to do for Him."

───────────

We relocated inside. Passing through the kitchen, Mary pointed out the spot where Konrad sat when he filled out the paperwork that made him an organ donor.

As we settled into a sectional sofa in a family room, I noticed blown-up action pictures of Konrad leaning against the bar. On the wall above where the Reulands sat hung a recent family portrait, their last with Konrad. On the coffee table rested books titled *A Time to Grieve* and *Grief Therapy*.

Mary and Ralf told stories about Konrad's athletic career and about his appetite. That reminded me of something I wanted to know.

"Did Konrad like coffee?" I said.

"Yes," Mary said. "Our last few days with him in the hospital, I was giving him a lot of coffee. The nurses said it might help with his headaches. Why do you ask?"

The first 70-plus years of my life, I never liked coffee. Rhonda and I bought a Keurig machine strictly to serve guests. Neither of us ever used it. Until the transplant.

"It's the strangest thing," I said.

We were all baffled by this. How could a new heart and kidney cause a craving for coffee? There may not be an explanation in any medical books. But there was no denying that ever since Konrad became a part of me, I've enjoyed several cups a day, always with a little cream and no sugar.

Mary said that was how Konrad drank it, too.

———

Finally, it was time for the moment we were all waiting for.

Ralf brought home a stethoscope for this occasion. It was my pleasure to hand it to Mary.

"I'm going to ask Mom to listen to his heart and tell me how beautiful it sounds," I said.

She put the ear tips in, then realized she didn't know what to do next. She laughed and asked Ralf to handle the rest.

As he guided the bell end of the stethoscope across my chest, I didn't know what to do. I felt like I was intruding on this private, special moment between mother and son.

I sat still, trying not to even breathe too loud. I felt my pulse racing. Did that help?

"There it is," she said.

She smiled and melted onto my shoulder. I remained as still as I could.

"Does it sound the same?" Rhonda said.

Mary lifted her head and nodded. "I've got it memorized."

"Do you want to hear, sweetie?" Mary said to Ralf.

I resumed my stiff pose, focused on my breathing, as he again slid around the bell end in search of the sound. The moment he heard it, Ralf squeezed his eyes shut. He tried speaking but couldn't. He gathered himself.

In a strong voice, he said, "Welcome home, Konrad."

———————

A few weeks later, on the morning of April 4, I was sipping my morning cup of coffee—with a little cream, no sugar—when I realized we were days from the anniversary of Michelle's passing. The 22nd anniversary.

She would be 40 now.

Sometimes I think about the life she could've had, the woman she would have become. But it's all fantasy—a guessing game, really. Life is too hard to predict. There are too many moving parts. After all, had a bone marrow match been found for her—or, better yet, if I'd never had to learn the words acute nonlymphocytic leukemia—my life would have played out differently, too.

A lot of deep thoughts were on my mind this day. It would've been Konrad's 30th birthday. We were headed to Ascension Cemetery to pay our respects.

I went upstairs to get dressed and something snagged on my arm. A port left over from the transplant slipped out. Medically, this was insignificant. Doctors left it in just in case; if I was hospitalized, they could reuse it. The port was going to come out sooner or later. Symbolically, though, losing it was significant. I was unplugged. For the first time since I received the LVAD, everything inside my body belonged to me.

Well, now it did.

Rhonda and I wanted to commemorate Konrad's birthday in a special way, but we weren't sure how. We prayed for the wisdom to choose actions matching the tone we were seeking, a mix of mourning and gratitude. This included being respectful of the Reulands. While we wanted to visit Konrad's grave, we planned our visit around his family's schedule so they could have private time with him and with each other.

Mary said she and Austin were going early in the morning and again later in the afternoon with Ralf once he finished seeing patients. So Rhonda and I planned to be there in the middle of the day.

When we arrived around 1:00 PM, we were surprised to see Mary and Austin. A power outage in their neighborhood changed their schedule. Their smiles and hugs showed there was nothing awkward about us overlapping here.

"Remember," Mary said, "you're family."

We chatted for about half an hour, each sharing some exciting news. Mary told us that she and Ralf were going to become grandparents for the first time. Warren's girlfriend was pregnant. Rhonda and I laughed. We, too, would soon become first-time grandparents. Cheyenne was due in October, right around my birthday.

After Mary and Austin left, Rhonda found a nice, shady spot beside Konrad's grave to place the arrangement of white flowers we'd brought. On a card, we'd written the date and our wishes for a "Happy heavenly birthday."

I approached his grave and read his temporary tombstone.

Etched into gray marble were the words SON—BROTHER—FRIEND. Under a Catholic cross, the etching included the dates spanning his life, followed by TAKEN TOO SOON, FOREVER IN OUR HEARTS.

"Especially mine," I thought. "Especially mine."

I thanked him again for everything he'd done for my family and me. And I placed beside the tombstone a plastic cube holding a Heart of 29 pin and a signed baseball with these words:

HAPPY BIRTHDAY KONRAD. I PROMISE TO ALWAYS CARE FOR YOUR VERY PRICELESS GIFTS. TIL WE MEET AGAIN, I REMAIN FOREVER YOUR BROTHER IN CHRIST.

———————

Driving home, I recalled something Mary said.

"Konrad was going to die," she told me. "There was no way back. Once the aneurysm burst, his fate was sealed.

Because he signed up to donate his organs, someone was going to get his heart and kidney. I'm so glad it was you."

We're all going to die. Vicious medical conditions took Michelle and Konrad far too young, but something will catch each of us. It's cliché to say birth and death are the only things we're promised, but it's not so trite when you've faced it. You understand that life really is about what you do in between.

My dad left marks that penetrated my skin and scarred my soul. Tony and Harmon helped heal those wounds and showed me how a real man acts.

Over 19 summers in the prime of my life, I learned that a wave of my Louisville Slugger or a daring steal of home lifted thousands of people from their seats. I saw how something as simple as scribbling my name on a piece of paper made people happy.

Being forced out of baseball felt cruel and unfair, until I experienced real agony by losing a daughter and enduring the ripple effect that followed, destroying my marriage and my relationship with my other daughters. But without all that, I'd never have found Rhonda, Cheyenne, and Devon.

There's a balance to it all that I don't quite comprehend. I just know it's there. I appreciate that my life is richer for having had these experiences. All of them. They're all threads in my tapestry.

It took Michelle's demise for me to discover that people liked Rod Carew the person, not just the ballplayer. And I discovered that my success as a ballplayer gave me a platform to make a difference far more profound than anything that happens in baseball. Given the opportunity to do it again, I gladly seized it.

I've been blessed. Even when it may not have seemed like it, God has been there for me. He's taken care of me.

He's also shown me my purpose—why I was put here and why I was allowed to stay, why I've fought off every curveball life has thrown me.

My purpose is improving the lives of other people. Yet what I've come to learn is this: when your aim is helping others, the person you help most is yourself.

"The providence of God is like Hebrew words—it can only be read backward."

—John Flavel, 17th century minister

EPILOGUE

March 2020: Careulands

A SIGN IN OUR KITCHEN READS, THE CAREULAND FAMILY. ESTAB-
LISHED IN 2016. It was a gift from Mary and Ralf. There's
one in their house, too.

We began hanging out together after our story went public right around Easter in 2017. The story took off right away.
After all, a baseball Hall of Famer getting a new heart and a
second chance at life is pretty cool. A baseball Hall of Famer
getting a new heart and a second chance at life through the
tragic death of an NFL player he'd met when the donor was
a child...well, that's something they couldn't have scripted
over in Hollywood.

Days after the news went out, we held a news conference with the Reulands, Dr. Ajay, and Tom Mone, the CEO
of One Legacy. In the week and months that followed, we
sat for interviews with a steady stream of TV networks. In

the search for a different way to tell the story, one crew took us to the intersection of two railroad tracks. The ESPN version, by Gene Wojciechowski, earned a prestigious award for broadcast stories that impact communities.

As the Careulands, we threw out first pitches at Angel Stadium and Target Field. The Baltimore Ravens honored us on the field during a nationally broadcast game. When we met with their coach, John Harbaugh, Rhonda told him her tapestry analogy. He blankly stared at her for so long that she thought she'd said something wrong. Then he smiled and asked for permission to share it with his team.

On New Year's Day in 2018, the Careulands rode together in the Rose Parade atop Donate Life's "Gift of Time" float. It included a picture of Konrad recreated out of flowers; the same was done for 43 others who'd provided the ultimate gift. The float was honored as the most outstanding presentation of the parade's theme, which was "making a difference." Konrad, by the way, made quite a difference. His organs and tissue went to a total of 75 people. *Seventy-five!* Even in death, he left an enormous mark on the world.

In the summer of 2019, the four of us spoke at the annual conference for the American Association of Heart Failure Nurses.

Anytime someone wants to hear our story, we're glad to tell it. We recognize the exponential power we have to promote organ donation, heart health, and brain health. And, of course, I remain devoted to Be The Match and my golf tournament supporting the fight against pediatric cancer. This year will be our 25th event in Michelle's memory.

On my nightstand, I keep a framed picture of Michelle and another of Konrad. Every day, I wish them good morning and good night—just like I did as a kid with the baseball cards of Jackie Robinson and Ted Williams.

Some mornings, I'll drink a cup of coffee while working on a crossword puzzle from one of the gossip rags. I've been doing them ever since Michelle got me into it. Friends brought me so many magazines over all my times in the hospital that I still haven't reached the bottom of the pile.

I had 18 years with Michelle. She's now been gone far longer than we were together. Konrad and I had that one, brief interaction when he was 11. Yet they are both always with me. At times, I talk to each of them. Especially while I'm driving. It's as if they are along for the ride.

My best days, though, are spent with my granddaughter, Avalon.

She's two years old and sweet as can be. She also has a cute friend named Norah. That's Konrad's niece. Last summer, Norah and her parents moved to Orange County.

Seeing those two girls grow up is what it's all about. For all members of the Careuland clan.

Rhonda sums it up best with a piece of Scripture she paraphrases like this: "When God gives you mountains of challenges, once you overcome them, He blesses you with an abundance of joy."

Amen.

ACKNOWLEDGMENTS

NEVER HAVING PARTICIPATED in the crafting of a memoir, this was a fairly difficult subject on which to cut my teeth. I struggled with it from beginning to end. For me, though, the beginning was the massive heart attack and the journey that followed. Rod's childhood and baseball career were stories of which I was already well aware.

To say not realizing my über healthy husband was not über healthy is an understatement. As each day unfolded beginning September 20, 2015, I never knew there was so much to learn about heart health, LVADs, brain surgery and recovery, transplants—the list goes on.

I never could have survived this lengthy journey on my own. First and foremost, my gratitude begins with my Lord and Savior, Jesus Christ, who held my hand every moment of every day as I attempted to navigate the unknown path ahead of me. Every morning began with the same prayer, "*Help,*" after which

I turned my life back over to Him by asking Him to guide me according to His plan for that day and my life. Without His guidance, I'm fairly certain I would've melted into the ground like the Wicked Witch of the East from *The Wizard of Oz.*

To our pastor, Rick Warren, who lifted us up in prayer asking God to give Rod the breakthrough he needed and then learning that same week that Rod was officially listed for the transplants! Prayer is powerful, and prayer works!

I must also acknowledge several family and friends who stood by my side, lifted me up when I was ready to collapse, or cooked wonderful meals for us. Our son, Devon, and his fiancée, Mary, were there from day one and continue their support to this day. Our daughter, Cheyenne, who called daily to check on her Papi. By the transplant stage, we learned she was carrying our first grandchild, a beautiful baby girl, AviBleu, whom Rod would never have met. Our wonderful Lord certainly works in mysterious ways! Auntie Di, Uncle Wayne, Mom; I can't thank you enough. Thank you to Gordette and Tony Oliva, Dave St. Peter, and the entire Minnesota Twins organization; the Los Angeles Angels organization and Arte Moreno, Dennis Kuhl, and Tim Mead. Also to Jane Forbes Clark and Jeff Idelson of the Baseball Hall of Fame, who so graciously hosted a heart health evaluation during Induction Weekend for all members and spouses. Doug DeCinces, Manny Rodriguez, Frank Pace, Chili Davis, Noah McMahon, Pam and Joe Balla...there is no way I can list everyone. On the medical side, my heartfelt thanks to our various teams beginning with the referral by the president of St. Joseph Hospital, Deborah Proctor, who sent Rod to Mission Hospital's top cardiologist. It was that physician, Dr. Sanjay Bhojraj, who admitted Rod immediately after looking at his condition just three days following discharge from Riverside. Had this intervention not occurred, Rod would have passed at home. Dr. Bhojraj diagnosed heart failure and arranged Rod to be transferred to the Scripps network of hospitals in San Diego for advanced treatment. Which brings me to Scripps La Jolla's amazing LVAD team, including Dr. Ajay, Dr. Heywood, Jennifer, Lauren, and Rachel, and the Scripps Encinitas incredible brain surgery rehab team, especially speech therapist Paige LaRae McGill, who somehow convinced Rod he could trust her to take him for tests in the "dungeon."

A very special thank you to the Cedars Sinai heart and kidney transplant teams and Rod's world class team: Dr. Kobashigawa, Dr. Kittleson, Dr. Esmailian, Dr. Cohen, Dr. Jerry Marx, and so many more! I have so much to be grateful for!

And then there is Dr. Dan Meyer, one of Rod's Scripps LVAD surgeons, who, two weeks post–widowmaker heart attack looked me straight in the eye and said, "He will get a new heart," and remained within regular contact, guiding me along the way, until Rod received that new heart. This developed into a wonderful friendship between the Meyer and Carew families.

I also have to thank Jaime Aron, who took on the task of writing this book with Rod, and the American Heart Association, who supported both of them every step of the way.

I could go on and on. Instead, those friends who know they were there, I thank you from the bottom of my heart. To those who prayed for us and sent thoughtful cards and gifts, many of whom we didn't know, thank you!

I would be extremely remiss were I to not acknowledge my new sister, Mary Reuland, and the entire Reuland family. We are the Careulands. I cannot thank them enough for raising such a wonderful young man, Konrad, who checked the organ donor box on his driver's license and, in doing so, saved my husband's life. We are, and will forever be, extremely grateful.

And finally, I will forever hold endless gratitude to my husband for keeping his end of the promise and, since there was an option available to save his life, moving forward instead of throwing in the towel. For me, that's the definition of *One Tough Out*. I love you, honey.

—Rhonda Carew
Orange County, California
January 2020

A S A KID, I loved three things: playing baseball, watching baseball, and reading about baseball. I especially loved biographies and memoirs—books filled with colorful stories about how the greats of the game rose to the top and about the people they encountered along the way.

That's probably why I became a sports writer. I wanted to gather and tell those stories.

Strangely enough, it took *leaving* sports writing to wind up writing the kind of book I grew up reading. It's been my immense pleasure and a wonderful privilege to report and write this book.

One of my favorite moments during the reporting phase came at the end of a long day of intense conversations about Rod's difficult upbringing. Rod wandered over to the one, small display of his career hardware and looked at it wistfully.

I didn't break the moment by asking what he was thinking, as I felt pretty sure that I knew.

Another great moment came when talking about All-Star balloting. Rhonda and I laughed about how we each used to take stacks of ballots and try punching through them all at once. We also laughed at not knowing that the little squares that came out were known as chads until they became the focus of a presidential ballot. What made it great, however, was that Rod had no idea what we were talking about. Because he was *on* the ballot, he never filled one out.

I want to thank Rod and Rhonda, and Frank Pace, for their friendship and for their faith in me. Thanks also to Julia Lord for being the agent we needed, and to editor Michelle Bruton at Triumph Books.

Huge thanks go out to the folks at the American Heart Association who connected me to Heart of 29, and who helped sustain it, especially Nancy Brown, Laura Sol, John McFarland, Jason Dyer, and Amit Chitre. John also has my unending appreciation for being an invaluable editor and friend.

A wonderful byproduct of all this has been getting to know the folks at the Minnesota Twins. The organization is stocked with quality people, and it starts at the top with Dave St. Peter. Thanks to him and everyone I've worked with, especially Bryan Donaldson, Dustin Morse, and Brace Hemmelgarn.

Yet another wonderful byproduct has been dealing with the folks at the Baseball Hall of Fame. This book was made better thanks to Jeff Idelson, Tim Mead, Jon Shestakofsky, Craig Muder, and John Horne.

For a variety of reasons, thanks also go out to Alex Mensing at Be The Match, Adam Chodzko and Matt Birch of the Angels, Gina Besheer and Ian Catacutan from Cresta Verde, Mark Bonney and Neal Gabler of the Corona Fire Department, Dr. Dan Meyer, Dr. Gerald Marx, Talmage Boston, and Richard Williams. Huge kudos to Baseball-Reference. com, Baseball-Almanac.com, and other tremendous online repositories that aided with research.

Lastly, and mostly, thanks to my wife, Lori, and our sons Zac, Jake, and Josh for being so supportive of the time and effort that went into this book.

—Jaime Aron